*Dreams and the Invisible World*
*in Colonial New England*

# Dreams and the Invisible World in Colonial New England

Indians, Colonists, and the Seventeenth Century

## Ann Marie Plane

**PENN**

UNIVERSITY OF PENNSYLVANIA PRESS

Philadelphia

Published by
University of Pennsylvania Press
Philadelphia, Pennsylvania 19104-4112
www.upenn.edu/pennpress

Printed in the United States of America on acid-free paper
10  9  8  7  6  5  4  3  2  1

Library of Congress Cataloging-in-Publication Data
Plane, Ann Marie.
Dreams and the invisible world in colonial New England : Indians, colonists, and the seventeenth century / Ann Marie Plane. — 1st ed.
p. cm.
Includes bibliographical references and index.
ISBN 978-0-8122-4635-3 (hardcover : alk. paper)
1. Colonists—New England—Psychology—History—17th century. 2. Indians of North America—Colonization—Psychological aspects—New England—History—17th century. 3. Dreams—New England—History—17th century. 4. Visions—New England—History—17th century. 5. New England—Colonization—Psychological aspects—History—17th century. I. Title.
F7.P55 2014
974'.02—dc23                                                         2014009313

*For my parents,*
*Robert A. Plane and Mary Moore Plane,*
*who have always supported my dreams*

And I hope that in one thing, . . . I have performed the part of an *Historian*, viz. in endeavouring to relate things truly and impartially, and doing the best I could that I might not lead the *Reader* into a Mistake. *History* is indeed in it self a profitable Study. . . . And there is holy Scripture to encourage in a work of this nature, for what was the *Book of the Warrs of the Lord*, Num., 21. 14? And that Book of *Jasher* which we read of in *Joshuah* and in *Samuel?* Yea and the Book of the *Cronicles*, mentioned in the Book of Kings. . . . What were these Books, but the faithfull *Records* of the providentiall Dispensations of God, in the dayes of old? . . . And I earnestly wish that some effectual course may be taken (before it is too late) that a just *History of New-England,* be written and published to the world. That is a thing that hath been often spoken of, but was never done to this day; and yet the longer it is deferred, the more difficulty will there be in effecting of it.

—INCREASE MATHER, Preface to *A Brief History of the Warr with the Indians in New-England* (1676)

# Contents

*Chapter 6*
**Native Dream Reporting as Cultural Resistance**
*154*

**Conclusion**
*172*

**List of Abbreviations**
*179*

**Notes**
*183*

**Index**
*225*

**Acknowledgments**
*231*

# *Preface*

## ભ

Sometime in March or April 1629, an English silversmith cast "2 seales in silver" for the newly formed Massachusetts Bay Company. Shortly thereafter, Samuel Sharpe, a passenger on the *George*, carried one of the two official stamps to the rocky shores of Massachusetts Bay. The following year, Governor John Endecott brought the other—along with the official notice of his election, stamped in wax with the seal's imprint.[1]

On the seal, inside an oval field, stands a human figure bracketed by two pine trees, with copious foliage gathered strategically to hide the otherwise unclad midsection. The figure bears a bow in one hand, an arrow in the other. Much has been made of this stark image. Its deceptively simple design hides a world of meanings. As one scholar notes, the seal was intended "to define the colonizers and their mission," and it is undeniably true that the seal represents the Indians of Massachusetts Bay, or at least an English silversmith's version of them.[2] Generations of undergraduates have written indignant response papers about the plea that emanates—in a banner—from the central figure's mouth ("Come Over and Help Us"). The best of them rail at the condescension and arrogance of Europeans who would assume that the Algonquian-speaking indigenous peoples of Massachusetts would have either needed or wanted such help. Further, the absurdity of calling for it in English is highlighted only by the most perceptive.

But like so many seemingly transparent issues, the 1629 seal becomes more complicated on deeper acquaintance; and like most things involving the English colonists of Massachusetts, the most pressing references—even in the unstable present of the seventeenth-century—always referred back to the certainties of the past. This was a past known through scripture, a biblical past whose resurgence in the present was both eagerly sought and breathlessly

The 1629 Massachusetts Bay Colony Seal. Struck by Richard Trott, the seal represents Paul's vision of the so-called Macedonian Plea (Acts 16:9), which includes a central figure calling to the apostle to "Come Over and Help Us." Through this image, the Massachusetts Bay Company proprietors embedded New England colonization in the biblical example of Paul's wondrous vision. Image courtesy of the Office of the Secretary of the Commonwealth of Massachusetts.

awaited. For the legend emanating from this Algonquian Indian's mouth had been spoken before. Also known as the Macedonian Plea, it would have been instantly familiar both to puritan gentlemen and English silversmiths through Acts 16:9: "And a vision appeared to Paul in the night; There stood a man of Macedonia, and prayed him, saying, Come over into Macedonia, and help us." The passage continues: "And after he had seen the vision, immediately we endeavoured to go into Macedonia, assuredly gathering that the Lord had called us for to preach the gospel unto them."[3] Translators who put together the Genevan version of the Bible (preferred by most puritans) added a cautionary footnote: "The Saints did not easily believe every vision," implying that in this exceptional case, Paul's vision was both a true and a reliable communication from God.[4]

Paul is famous as a builder of the early church. In Acts 16, he goes into Greece with Silas and finds there a new disciple in Timothy. "As they went through the cities, they delivered them [the new believers] the decrees for to keep, that were ordained of the apostles and elders which were at Jerusalem. And so were the churches established in the faith, and increased in number daily."[5] But Paul and Timothy soon run afoul of the local authorities, who throw them in prison and beat them with rods, freeing them only after a providential earthquake had shaken the very foundations of the jail and converted the jailer himself.[6]

The men who designed, created, and used the first colony seal knew precisely the example it invoked. Massachusetts was designed to be a missionary enterprise, but it was also intended to build new churches—properly reformed and purified churches—"churches established in the faith, and increased in number daily." It was to bring order to the New World but always with one eye turned toward the Old World: "delivering the decrees for to keep, that were ordained of the apostles." Church builders, law givers, bringers of the Christian message; a generation of scholarship makes it plain that the aspirations of Massachusetts Bay were as much to create an ordered, lawful example for old England as they were to reach out to New England's indigenous peoples.

And yet, in all the discussion and analysis, it might be easy to miss one key fact: the fact that the Macedonian's message came to Paul in a vision, a vision which appeared in the night, sanctioned by God, and which directed him to preach Christ's message in the farthest corners, wherever those corners might be. In this way, then, the text of the seal leads us to say, with some accuracy, that the entire colonial enterprise in New England was based on a dream, and that its founders—rigorous puritans all—trumpeted these visionary origins in this first official image of their enterprise.

# Introduction

In the last months of his life, Samuel Sewall, a prominent merchant and chief justice of the Massachusetts Superior Court of Judicature, had a dream so remarkable that he recorded it in his diary in great detail:

> Last night I dreamed that a little boy had got away with my watch. I found him on the Common, and by giving him another Watch, persuaded him to give me that round which was engraven *Auris, mens, oculus, manus, os, pes; munere fungi Dum pergunt, praestat discere velle mori.*
>
> When I awaked I was much startled at it. The Lord help me to watch and pray that I may not enter into Temptation.[1]

Sewall had his dream in 1728, when he was already an elderly man, recently retired from the bench; he would die a little over a year later.[2] Sewall the diarist would never fully unravel the pun that Sewall the dreamer had constructed in the night. The little boy had stolen the old man's watch, given form in the dream as a timepiece "engraven" with some cautionary lines in Latin. Of course, the little thief also carried away a second type of "watch," whose meaning, as watchfulness or inner vigilance, is contained in Sewall's comments immediately following his dream report: "The Lord help me to watch and pray that I may not enter into Temptation." The type of punning in this dream is an example of a phenomenon that Sigmund Freud noted a century ago: that dreams often code abstract concepts through concrete imagery; a vigilant "watch" becomes, literally, a timepiece.[3] Of course, a thoughtful cross-cultural reading of this dream cannot stop with Freudian mechanics. In the modern era, as Mary

Baine Campbell notes, the rising influence of individualism associated with new medical, legal, and economic categories began to locate dreams as products of "the individual body"; an increasingly "isolated sense of subjectivity" would eventually undergird medicalized models of dreaming, including, centrally, Freud's own theory.[4] In contrast, in many early modern societies, there was not only belief in dreams but an "organized and communal nature [to] both dream and its interpretation."[5] Sewall's own society contained both—a nascent individualism and a communal engagement with reported dreams— and while these dual roles would be increasingly split between the colonizer and the colonized, or, in the darker terms of Freud's world, the "civilized" and the "primitive," the process of cleaving the individual from the communal was only just beginning, and such a split would ultimately be incomplete and partial at best. It is the beginning of this process in this period that makes the study of dream and vision in the colonialism of the seventeenth century so vital.

Sewall himself clearly took the dream's message to heart, enough so as to write it down in his voluminous diary. Viewing the night vision as a potentially divine message, he focused on the dream's "awakening" aspects. Just out of awareness, perhaps, were the ways in which the dream also spoke to the aging Sewall's anxieties about death, as foreshadowed by recent events in his life—his retirement from the Massachusetts Superior Court and his bouts with ill health. In the last lines of the diary's previous entry, made about a month before, Sewall noted: "[I] Pray that the Retirement and Leisure I am seeking for may be successfully improved in preparing for a better world."[6] Certainly the Latin lines on the watch in the dream speak about the struggle against death and decay: "While ear, mind, eye, hand, bone, foot continue to perform their functions, it is better to want to learn than to stagnate [fade, die]."[7] The central image itself— a mischievous boy, willfully taunting an old man—suggests perhaps Sewall's struggles with himself, as well as, more directly, his struggle as a justice of the superior court to maintain dominance over others (the "mischievous" lawbreakers) in his own society.

Dream reports such as Justice Sewall's have gone largely unanalyzed by historians of colonial America. Samuel Sewall wrote his dream down for himself, as he attempted to puzzle out the meanings and the messages associated with his mischievous and disobedient thief. Yet while the rest of Sewall's diary has been pawed over line by line, his dream reports have received relatively scant attention. Even a portrait as sensitive to the many influences on Sewall's consciousness as that provided by David D. Hall fails to do much more with Sewall's dreams than to note that he had them and that frequently they were of the nightmarish variety.[8] As Merle Curti noted many years ago, "The American interest in the nocturnal dream is for the most part an untold story."[9] That is nearly as true today as it was in 1966, when Curti wrote.

Curti's interests lay in historical theories about the origins and functions of dreaming. He used the occasional dream reports of the colonial period to set the stage for an intellectual history of dream theoreticians in the nineteenth and early twentieth centuries. Several decades later, historians of religion entered the scene. Hall folded dream narratives together with other "wonders" to elucidate his picture of providentialism in New England's popular piety. Scholars of nonconforming sects found reported dreams to be one avenue into the experience of religious enthusiasts in the colonial period. Quakers, Baptists, and Methodists saw dream experiences as particularly meaningful messages from the divine, and all included dream reports in spoken or printed narratives as a means of achieving various ends.[10] Dreams in this view are seen as an important means of coalescing self-experience and translating that experience into influential communications to others as part of various social movements.

Scholars of medieval and early modern Europe and England have done more with dreams, as well as with the history of the emotions generally. Scholars have explored the various theories and the copious religious thinking about dreams, and have also defined dreams (and related phenomena, like visions) in terms of their political and social import.[11] Medieval authors relied on the dream allegory in great works of fiction, and reports of actual dreams or visions also served as markers of divinity or authority in saints' lives and political propaganda.[12] These traditions continued into subsequent centuries, as shown, for example, in the dream allegory that structures one of the most enduring Protestant works of the seventeenth century, John Bunyan's *The Pilgrim's Progress*.[13] The early modern period saw religious struggle and persecution on both sides of the divide created by the Reformation. The Inquisition, with its extensive archives, has offered a rich body of evidence to historians through its investigations of visionaries—dreamers who sometimes managed to express and coalesce resistance to church or state power.[14]

But the power of dreams—the beauty, complexity, and richness of dream experience—and the full significance of dream narratives in unlocking the religious, social, cultural, and emotional history of colonial societies has yet to be explored. This book argues that for at least one early modern society, that of seventeenth-century New England, colonialist expansion encompassed the realm of wonders—the invisible world—just as it insinuated changes in areas more familiar to historians such as land tenure, political power, and trade.

New England's colonial society brought at least two distinctive cultural groups into contact and, often, into conflict. On the one hand, there were radical reformed English Protestants (Separatists, puritans, and a few other notable sectarians) who had arrived in the region in the 1620s and 1630s in a rapid and successful migration of families. Sharing common religious and political goals to a large extent, these people aimed to reproduce early modern English agrarian society, although the leadership was also influenced by utopian desires to make government consonant with radical Protestantism. On the other hand, New England remained home to Algonquian villagers, who, although devastated by successive waves of virgin soil epidemics, sought to continue their lifestyle of maize-based agriculture combined with seasonal hunting and gathering. In contrast to the patriarchal and hierarchical cosmos of the English—a cosmos dominated by a vengeful and paternal Jehovah—Natives lived in a realm of apparent wonders holding to an animist worldview in which animals, plants, stones, places, and even strangers were imbued with spiritual power, or manitou.

English Christians launched small though important missionary ventures among the Massachusett, Nauset, Wampanoag, and Nipmuck peoples in the 1640s. But little is known of the religious or symbolic systems of these people. Most historical scholarship has focused on explaining the material, military, and economic aspects of their rapid conquest, as well as the progress of Christian missionization.[15] Although these peoples were once thought to have disappeared in the press of European incursions, in the last decades a body of scholarship has emerged that explores their continued cultural vitality under English colonization.[16]

The study of dream belief can lead into a much larger exploration of the cosmology of early modern English colonists, including their representation of New England's Algonquian-speaking Natives. Indeed, as anthropologists agree, no study of dreams across cultures can be meaningful without exploring the entire indigenous theory of dreaming, including beliefs about and practices regarding dreams.[17] This book begins with the respective practices of dreaming or visioning that can be found in each society—those of both the English and the Indians. For each group, dream beliefs and practices played a central role in how individuals understood their world as well as in how they navigated colonialism's upheavals. Of course, much of what we know about Algonquian belief and practice comes to us only through the distorting lenses of colonial documents or as deduced from later anthropological characterizations, and certainly not in the language of the people themselves or, perhaps, of their descendants.

Sources allow us to grapple with the reported dreams of English colonists in greater depth than we can for those of Native peoples. Here too, though, discerning the effects of colonialism often demands a sensitive reading, one grounded in informed inference rather than direct evidence. Reported dreams display a variety of emotional and social preoccupations, only some of which are reasonably linked to colonialism's effects. Yet we know from certain examples—the Salem witchcraft outbreak, for instance—that colonial challenges could animate apparently internal conflicts, as when the trauma of Indian war on New England's northern frontier left the population of Salem ripe for demonic upheaval. The dreams and dreamlike experiences reported by individuals or recorded in colonial court records reflect these complex colonial contexts, revealing a multiply constituted dream repertoire, in which transplanted English dream beliefs and practices, including especially the tradition of the dream visitation, played out with new significance in the colonial context.

As the seventeenth century wore on, these societies struggled with each other not only in military, political, and economic realms but also in the realm of the sacred, the supernatural, and the cosmological—in something each might have recognized as otherwise "invisible" and, in fact, a realm the English did sometimes call the invisible world. From this vantage point, studies of colonialism that do not attend to the cosmological realm of dream belief and practice obscure a critical part of the participants' experience of these phenomena, rendering them literally invisible. While it might have heuristic value for modern thinkers to split off economic conquest from military conquest from religious conversion, the ways that colonial expansion was experienced, by both colonists and Native peoples, was inseparable from the world of psychic experience, imagination, and belief that dreams and visions both contain and transform. At many key junctures, this book argues, reported dreams and visions played an instrumental role in the interpretation of events and the organization of various responses by both groups.

Indeed, the rapid expansion of Anglo-Atlantic colonialism cannot be fully understood unless we take dream reports and their uses into account. Dreams give unique access to the lived experience of the seventeenth-century encounter for both colonizing and colonized peoples, sometimes serving as a medium for that encounter and other times as a reflection of it. Reported dreams stand as powerful texts that allow us to glimpse the emotional experience of colonization— its anxieties, traumas, dissociations, and self-protective defenses—and bring it to center stage in the understanding of this complex society. At the same time, as historians, anthropologists, philosophers, and cognitive scientists have argued, emotions do not exist a priori, outside of their shaping cultural contexts, and their experience and expression is, in all ways, part of culturally constructed learned behavior. As Monique Scheer argues, "Emotions are indeed something we do, not just have."[18] From this vantage point, we should view dreaming itself, along with the beliefs and practices surrounding it, as a deeply contextualized cultural experience that may at times also contain richly embodied "emotional practice." This book seeks to explore the varieties of dream experience in a rapidly colonizing society, even as it traces the emotional experiences that accompanied the wrenching changes and deadly challenges of that colonialism. As Scheer continues, to "[think] of emotion [or dreaming] in this way [makes] it like language, subject to conventions, learned from other members of a group, and deployed creatively."[19] Hence, to the extent that dreams and related phenomena can offer access into the emotional experience of life as lived by members of a colonizing society, their careful analysis offers historians a new perspective on familiar events.

For the English, a deep and pervasive ambivalence about dreams and visions remained a constant feature of understandings and interpretations of these phenomena. Unable to reject outright the possibility that dreams might be divine communications, most Christians—including many Catholics, but especially the radical Protestants who populated the New England colonies— retained a skeptical approach to dreams. While most early moderns thought dreams could be potent sources of knowledge about the dreamer's health, future, or present course, one could not rely securely on knowledge obtained in dreams. Such ambivalence set them up for conflict with the indigenous Algonquian peoples of the region, who often actively sought out dreams, trance, or vision as potent sources of insight or efficacious avenues of change. While Natives remained both subtle and sophisticated interpreters of dream knowledge, most European observers tarred them as gullible dupes of Satan, taken in by an indiscriminate trust in dreams. Despite sharp distinctions between European and Native dream practices and irrespective of the gulf between Native

American and English attitudes and cosmologies, some colonists were greatly interested in Indian dreaming, if only to recruit Native visioning to their own understanding of providence. The fact is, dream reports sometimes provoked conversations among members of the two groups, conversations that have previously gone unheard.

Over the course of the seventeenth century, dreaming became, at times, a source of potent conflict or contest. This occurred within English and English colonial society, when Quakers and other radicals embraced the dream as a true source of divine revelation, as well as between English and Native peoples, in moments when indigenous visionary experience played a role in frontier conflicts. Indigenous forms of dream practice—including the use of dreams by shamans and medicine men in healing and divination—came under almost immediate attack by Europeans eager to put an end to rituals they saw as satanic. Reported dreams might mobilize and justify Native resistance, undergirding in New England as elsewhere various "revitalization movements," sometimes leading to open resistance. And yet Indians were not the only ones who framed their politics in the idiom of dreams: English commentators like Increase Mather sometimes recorded purported dreams as a way of naturalizing all sorts of colonialist projects, including the persecution of Quakers and the use of violence against Indians. Even at century's end, dreams evoked wondrous fascination, while still eliciting the deep skepticism found in earlier eras. In short, just as the English would not fully colonize indigenous forms of dream belief, their ambivalent approach also made it impossible to colonize the dream, at least in the sense of controlling, managing, or banishing it.

In fact, as is argued here, dreams and dream reporting provided remarkable occasions in which the emotional experience of individual colonists might be acknowledged, albeit indirectly, and expressed in powerful ways. Analysis of recorded dream experience offers historians access to a seemingly "interior" experience of sensibility in colonial New England in a way few other sources can. In addition to revealing attempts to manage powerful longings or culturally troublesome emotions (covetousness or anger, for example), it should come as no surprise, among a people so consumed with the correct pursuit of reformed theology, that recorded dreams also encoded powerful examples of the "lived religion" of colonists of several confessions.

By the century's close, however, attacks on "enthusiasts" of all stripes—Quakers, Indians, even witches—meant that dreamt knowledge could be dangerous knowledge. Colonists discriminated among different types of wondrous experience, and context proved vitally important in determining between "real" apparitions and dreamt visitations, a discrimination that could have deadly results for an accused witch or a suspected criminal. Dream reporting might coalesce and organize resistance at the level of the individual or the group; it might also serve as an important medium through which disadvantaged others—Quakers, Indians—could express resistance that had no other outlet. Natives often asserted a continued communal vibrancy through their dream reporting, despite colonialism's daily challenges of poverty, racism, and disease. In response to literature that asserts modernizing theories of disenchantment, this book argues that the importance of dreams never disappeared, even for the English, as the resurgence of dream reporting during the spiritual awakenings of the mid-eighteenth century would suggest.[20]

Colonialism itself, which advanced through attention to elements both visible and invisible, did eventually deal a major blow to the indigenous Algonquian system of dreaming as well as to an entire way of experiencing and seeing the world. Indeed, the very texts by which we come to know of Native practices were the opening salvo in the process of appropriating and recasting Native experience.[21] By 1700, the European dominance of southern New England posed a very substantial challenge to New England Algonquians' intricate and long-established use of dreams and visions. That a distinctive culture of indigenous divination and the insightful use of dreamt thought still managed to survive the centuries is a testament to both the tenacity of and the insights inherent in indigenous understandings of the world. That Natives engaged Europeans about their different understandings and practices is indisputable; that these distinctive systems survived well into the eighteenth century, and that knowledge sent via dreams continued to be highly valued in the nineteenth and early twentieth centuries is attested by New England oral tradition. That some individuals report experience of insightful dreaming in their own families testifies to the centrality of dream practice in indigenous society long after the end of the colonial period.[22]

In their circulation as wonder texts, reported dreams provided a medium for communication to groups and individuals that might otherwise have remained voiceless. Reported dreams allowed for resistance when the hegemonic structures of colonialism squelched other forms of expression. As historical anthropologists John and Jean Comaroff note in regard to conjuring, the "refusal to answer to the voice of the dominant—or in the spoken voice at all—affirms that the argument between colonizer and subject often escapes the register of reasoned verbal debate."[23] Reported night dreams, visions, and shamanic trance states, like the wordless resistance of conjuring, reveal significant responses to colonization—including resistance, among other things. Resistance may also stem from what we might think of as "colonized" or subjugated parts of the self. Indeed, it is a truism of psychoanalytic technique that dream reports can be very useful in revealing aspects of self-experience that individuals might prefer to keep hidden. We need look no farther than Sewall's mischievous nighttime visitor to see that. Finally, in many cases, dreams speak about how colonizer and colonized grieved painful losses, mastered wrenching changes, and quelled the ever-present anxieties that accompanied European domination of Native Americans.

D ream reports recorded in diaries, witchcraft prosecutions, missionary writings, religious tracts, and compendia of various wonders constitute a body of evidence that has never before been treated as a coherent whole. The rapid colonization of New England stirred the night visions of individuals, both Native American and English. A variety of emotions—resentments, anxieties, joys—took form through the medium of the dream as well as its narration. Political programs—resistance, opposition, and aggressive assault—were also mobilized through the indirection of the dream report; such narratives might be attributed to supernatural forces, giving them greater power and authority.

There are many objections to the use of dream reports as historical evidence. Historians including Alan Macfarlane and Peter Burke observed as early as the 1970s that the historical dream narrative is "doubly censored," filtered as it is not only through the normal processes of transition from sleep to waking ("secondary revision"), and from private reflection to public narration, but also through its conversion into a fixed, written form.[24] Historians rightly fear an anachronistic caricature of the emotional lives of people of the past. The overenthusiastic application of a particular, often overly rigid, type of psychoanalytic scrutiny has mostly added to the burdens of those scholars who seek a fuller exploration of the role of emotion in various historical contexts.[25] In the psychohistory movement of the 1960s and 1970s it was all too easy to apply to historical figures a doctrinaire version of psychoanalytic theory, usually a rigid psychosexual theory framed in terms of Freudian, Kleinian, or Ego Psychology approaches and often lacking in the complexity and nuance that Freud's own writings possess. Historians and anthropologists have quite rightly objected to the Cartesian dualisms embedded in Freudian approaches and this discredited psychohistory, pushing it to the margins of historical discourse. Universalizing theories of human development, exploration of the role of repression, and approaches emphasizing inborn psychodynamic drives left little room for meaningful analysis of cultural content. The lack of a living partner in the analysis, the analysand, meant that there was little chance to check or corroborate the analyst's theories or to develop a rich context of patient associations. And the introduction of unfamiliar language and metaphors derived from psychoanalytic psychology made such works obscure or even inaccessible for historians not trained in these concepts.[26] Newer approaches have reinvented the history of the emotions, and these have deemphasized universalist approaches in favor of a new emphasis on the profound role of cultural context in shaping human emotion and bodily practice.[27]

It is fortunate that similar critiques of overly rigid interpretive schemes were launched inside psychoanalytic circles as well. Newer theories of dreaming replaced the older models. Freud's wonderfully nuanced use of dream materials was hampered by his conviction that dreams must always be the "disguised fulfillments of repressed [and unconscious] wishes."[28] Most second- and third-generation analysts remained wedded to this dictum, despite Erik Erikson's powerful argument for greater attention to the "manifest" content— the overt narrative and symbols in the dream—in his 1954 reappraisal of Freud's famous "Irma Dream."[29] Heinz Kohut, an adherent of Freud who gradually broke with his theories to build a model called Self Psychology, allowed that some dreams might simply reflect the "state of affairs" in the dreamer's emotional life at the time. This "self-state" dream has been generalized to allow for a variety of interpretive approaches, and the cross-fertilizing influence of other forms of depth psychology, including Jungian and Gestalt theorizing, has allowed for more hybrid and contingent approaches to dream interpretation than previously, some of which have been imported into intercultural situations.[30]

This book has been greatly influenced by modern and postmodern psychoanalytic theories as well as by theories of emotional practice, following a Bourdieuian emphasis on unconscious or procedural practices. These mostly function as a background sensibility, rather than as a foreground interpretive technique. However, I do argue that colonists' dreams in particular performed critical "selfobject" functions: soothing, repairing, reconciling, and allowing for the integration of painful or otherwise challenging emotion. This is most easily visible in the dreams of Samuel Sewall, which dominate Chapter 5, but the selfobject function of the recorded dream is apparent throughout the reports of this book, from the opening dream of John Winthrop in the 1630s through the angelic visitation experienced by Cotton Mather's wife in the early 1700s. Within Self Psychology and the so-called American Relational theoretical traditions, dreams are seen not as reflections of heroic, though primarily internal, individual struggles but as actually generative of new ways of being in the world; it is with some frequency that dream experiences are seen as helping in the process of integration of powerful emotion, both negative and positive. From this perspective, then, the dream of the stolen watch might indeed have spoken to Sewall's concern about his approach toward death, among many other things; but it could also have been a step along the way in reconciling himself to this impending event.[31] He certainly saw it as a potentially awakening providence—something to record and on which to reflect.

The early modern period did not make the neat distinctions between dreams and visions which we moderns insist upon. Contemporary clinical and cognitive theories support this early modern view as more accurate, positing that all sorts of dreamlike phenomena—whether they are true waking visions or the more common nighttime dreams—exist on a continuum of mental activity and therefore share many like features. The insight has more in common with early modern ideas than with some modern Western approaches that unduly segregate and dismiss waking and sleeping experience. As longtime dream researcher Ernest Hartmann recently summarized, dreaming is one form of mental functioning on a continuum "running from focused waking thought at one end, through fantasy, daydreaming and reverie, to dreaming at the other end."[32]

Of course any culturally oriented study of dreaming must take into account not only the work that dreams do for individuals but also the work reported dreams perform socially.[33] Dreams simply do not exist apart from the cultural and social frames that shape the dream event and its narration. Whether it is the sense that the dreamer makes of his or her nighttime visions, or whether it is in the ways that dreams are communicated to others, a dream told inevitably becomes a narrative and thence it can, like other social narratives, go on to influence various political, religious, or other circumstances. As Erikson observed, every dream is, of necessity, a social text: "One has never seen anybody else's dream nor has the slightest proof that it ever 'happened' the way one visualizes it. A dream is a verbal report of a series of remembered images, mostly visual, which are usually endowed with affect [i.e., emotion]. . . . The report of a dream, in turn, arouses in each listener and interpreter a different set of images, which are as incommunicable as is the dream itself."[34] Erikson underscores this fact with his observation that "patients learn to exploit our [the analyst's] interest in dreams by telling us in profuse nocturnal productions what they should struggle and learn to tell us in straight words."[35] Or, in other words, the analysand may at times veil criticisms or other communications by cloaking them under the protection of a seemingly incoherent dream. It is their very incoherence, their randomness, and their seeming separation from the concerns of everyday life that have misled historians into leaving dream reports to one side.

And yet where did people undergo more change, or have to integrate a more intense burst of new experience, than in a rapidly colonizing society like New England in the seventeenth century? Dream reporting helped to express on a social level the experiences of colonization—practical, emotional, and cultural. From the very first, Indians and missionaries found themselves conversing about dreams. Dreams were essential markers of cultural experience for both sides. Dream reports initiated conversations about the uses and meaning of dreams, about the supernatural, and about which path to choose at a variety of potent moments—regarding religious conversions, in rebellions, and in smaller accommodations of all kinds.

This book consists of six chapters often framed around a single dream text that embodies a central issue. Each chapter relies on a variety of sources, including diaries, letters, court testimony, missionaries' accounts, and conversion narratives. The argument moves from an explication of dream practice in both English colonial and New England Algonquian cultures (as much as one-sided historical sources allow) to a discussion of how Native dreams became part of the puritan world of wonders. Gendered roles and relations, along with other forms of identity, were also central to the experiencing of dreams. Within the English tradition dreams played a particularly problematic role for high-status men, who were burdened by powerful expectations of self-restraint, even as they may have used the dreams of their youth as "chartering" events, offering legible signs of their present or future course.

Dreams and dreamlike experiences (visions, waking dreams, trance, prayerful meditation, etc.) were central in both English and Algonquian cultures, undergirding shamanic practice among the Natives and demonic beliefs among the English. Because of a deep-seated ambivalence toward the dream—as both "deluding fancy" and potentially true revelation—the English could never completely dismiss the meaning of dreams, whether their own or those of the indigenous people they encountered. However, given their suspicion of dreaming, indigenous dream belief and practice was quickly cast as wholly diabolical. This makes the recuperation of Native dreaming—encapsulated in the reports of Indian dreams near the end of the century (Chapter 6)—so much the more remarkable as a subtle, yet effective, form of resistance to colonialism by Native peoples who had survived war, disease, and economic marginalization.

My focus remains on the seventeenth century, albeit a long seventeenth century. At the same time, certain practices of literacy, self-scrutiny, and religious introspection emergent in seventeenth-century New England would accompany the eventual development of new European folk conceptions of the self that imagined a more firmly bounded, less permeable individual. This new metaphor of the isolated, Cartesian self would provide crucial underpinnings for the development of Western psychological and psychoanalytic theory.[36] Yet, in contrast to arguments that dreams became less important as humanistic values emerged with the Enlightenment, the rise of evangelical religion and the frequent religious revivals of the early and mid-eighteenth century kept the conversations of both Indians and colonists focused on dreams.[37] Indeed, it was the inevitable failure of the English to completely colonize dreaming (to control, organize, and isolate the meanings or meaninglessness of dreams) that enabled the invisible world to retain its power. At the same time, English ambivalence and the existence of alternative approaches to the dream—in evangelicalism, or in the Native communities that embraced evangelical religion— allowed alternate practices to continue as vital forces and to occasionally emerge with syncretic forms of dream belief and dream practices.

Thus this book can be conceived as a journey into a colonial world of wonders—a world that was drenched in dreams and visions, that included both the visible and the invisible, and that was transformed both by conquest and by resistance.

# Chapter 1

## *English Dream Belief and Practice in the Tudor-Stuart World*

> And it shall come to pass in the last days, saith God, I will
> pour out of my Spirit upon all flesh: and your sons and your
> daughters shall prophesy, and your young men shall see
> visions, and your old men shall dream dreams. —Acts 2: 17

One night in March 1633/4, John Winthrop, governor of Massachusetts Bay, started up in bed, still in the grips of a remarkable dream. For some months, the Winthrop family had been convulsed by the conversion crisis of young Stephen, the governor's fourteen-year-old son. The lad had been held "under suche Affliction of minde, as he could not be brought to apprehende any comfort in God . . . Satan buffeting him: so . . . he went mourninge & languishinge daylye."[1] But "at lengthe," Stephen was "freed from his temptations & [began] to finde comfort in Godes promises."[2] At the same time, a younger brother, probably the thirteen-year-old Adam, began to experience God's grace as well. This lad was, in his father's words, "no whit shorte of [Stephen] in the knowledge of Godes will," but while Stephen asked for—and was granted—church membership, Adam's "youth" kept the younger boy "from daringe to offer himselfe to the Congregation."[3] It was in this context, then, that Winthrop had an amazing dream, a dream so startling that he woke up, and, transported by astonishment, shook his wife awake to tell her too. Because it followed on the heels of these dramatic stirrings, Winthrop thought it "not impertinent" to record the dream in his diary as well.[4]

The dream had presented Winthrop with an amazing scene, "viz., that comminge into his Chamber he fo[u]nde his wife (she was a verye gratious woman) in bedd & 3: or 4: of hir Children lyinge by her with moste sweet & smylinge co[u]ntenances, with Crownes upon their heades & blue ribandes about their necks." What to make of this tableau? The dream seemed to point in one direction, especially when combined with the recent turmoil regarding their boys' conversions: "When he awaked he tould his wife his dreame: & made this interpretation of it, that God would take of her Children to make them fellowe heires with Christ in his kingdom."[5]

A "gracious woman" (as in "filled with grace"—not necessarily the real Margaret Winthrop) had sat in bed, surrounded by her children. The young-sters had splendid crowns on their heads, with ribbons of blue (a biblical sym-bol of faithful observance) trailing around their necks.[6] Winthrop felt or knew that this was a vision of heaven and a sign of assurance that his wife and chil-dren were among the "elect," those chosen by God to go to a heavenly reward. The couple thought it over together, there in the darkness. What should they make of this night vision? Was it a visitation from God, or just a vain fancy that had ruffled Winthrop's sleep?

The dream had clearly been quite striking—emotionally gripping, even. Radical reformed Protestants of the type known as puritans cultivated insecu-rity throughout their lifetimes; to feel assured of one's salvation was generally considered a sign of error. The Radical Reformation teachings were quite clear: one could never be sure that God's mercy would extend to oneself or one's loved ones; indeed, signs of assurance might be satanic tricks, designed to lull the faithful into error. Thus piety required the cultivation of a constant state of uncertainty. Yet, emotionally speaking, this constant uncertainty was difficult to sustain. Every puritan hoped against hope for some sign of assurance that he was saved. For a puritan father to know that his wife and children were among the elect, as this dream seemed to suggest, would have been almost too good to be true. Hence Winthrop was wise, in the view of his contemporaries, to regard this dream with only a very cautious optimism; indeed, he noted that he re-corded it because of its exceptional nature, even "(thoughe no Credite nor re-gard [be] to be had of dremes in these dayes)."[7] Still, in order to be sure, he wrote it down.

A whole world is revealed in the ambivalence of this journal entry. In addi-tion to a traditional puritan anxiety of mind over one's salvation or depravity, the dream also speaks to two other important issues, separate but related.

First, what exactly did Winthrop mean when he spoke of dreams being of little credit in "these latter days"? puritans lived in the early modern "world of wonders," constantly searching out signs of God's pleasure or displeasure in the events of everyday life.[8] But supposedly the only true authority for these rigorous Protestants was scripture—the Bible. Thus, dreams themselves were controversial phenomena. While all agreed that the patriarchs of old had bene-fited from dreams, visions, and portents that had revealed God's will, perhaps such means of communication were no longer needed; it was certain that they could not be relied upon as truth. The scriptural literalist could not expect new and direct revelations of God's will.[9] The use of vulgar dream dictionaries, "keys" into the meanings of dream images, or any white magic based on dreams—all part of contemporary English and European practice—was es-chewed along with any other attempt to use trickery to discern the mind of God.

Still, although dreams might usually consist of nothing but vain and idle fancies, the potential existed for the rare dream to be something more than what the colonists deemed just a "common Dream."[10] Thus, a dream—although an ambiguous, curious, and ultimately untrustworthy thing—could not simply be thrown out as altogether insignificant. There was always a small chance that a dream, especially one such as this, might be an authentic communication of God's will.

In addition, this dream, and certainly others like it, may have reflected spe-cial anxieties linked to the colonial project. Winthrop played a unique role as the governor of the Massachusetts Bay Colony. Yet he reported his dream, like much personal experience, in the third person, describing Stephen only as "the sonne of one of the magistrates" and himself in a roundabout way as "the father of these Children."[11] Indeed, only knowledge of the diary's style reveals that this was his own dream and not that of some unnamed New England father. Given his role as father to the civil polity, the potential of this dream to be a portent not only of personal circumstances but also of the whole New England errand hovers throughout the report.

The crowns that Winthrop saw—his sense of God's special favor toward his wife and children—may thus also be read metaphorically as a providential message regarding New England and its mission. Indeed, the puritan sense of self allowed little separation between the circumstances of individuals and those of the community. Individual experiences might merge with those of the colony as a whole, as any reader of an execution sermon or a captivity narrative immediately learns. In New England, evildoers were pressured to confess—not to save their own souls, which were most likely already lost—but to preserve the community from God's retribution. Rainbows and comets, hailstorms and providential rains were carefully observed as indicators of God's temper.[12] In this context, Winthrop's dream carried a second, potentially public message about the fate of the colony: Would God smile upon it? Was its mission just and right? Could it survive the threats that surrounded it? These came from both external forces, like the Indians, and internal threats such as the all-too-human vanities and divisiveness that Winthrop worried about in his famous sermon from the *Arbella*.[13]

Despite his disclaimer about giving "no credit nor regard" to dreams in "these days," John Winthrop and his contemporaries valued dreams, at least some dreams, and found meaning within them. This chapter traces the rich historical and cultural contexts in which seventeenth-century English men and women understood and interpreted their dreams and argues that their deep ambivalence about the dream left them unable to reject dreamt knowledge out of hand. While it is difficult to periodize change over time in the *longue durée* of dream belief, New England colonists inherited a broadly European tradition of dreaming mediated heavily by the Protestant Reformation and its continuing controversies throughout the period from the 1570s to the mid-seventeenth century. English dream beliefs and practices drew on a wealth of imagery and example—from the Bible, from classical antiquity, and from their own more recent history of religious strife during the Reformation—to create a rich tapestry of meanings. While we do not know exactly which dream practices colonists pursued, we do know that many if not most colonists approached dreams with a deep ambivalence, which seems to have discouraged most public sharing of specific, individual dream visions in favor of either more private communication (with intimate friends or through emergent practices of journal writing) or the public transmission of depersonalized, unindividuated wonder tales.

Taught to regard dreams as mere froth or, worse, as diabolical delusion, individuals seem to have perceived dreams as potentially meaningful, occasionally bringing useful communications about both one's physical condition and one's spiritual estate. Colonists were particularly drawn to predictive dreams, such as Winthrop's dream about his family's spiritual estate. Dreams were not supposed to be trustworthy, but, for colonists recently uprooted from their homeland and facing an uncertain future in this colonial context, the predictive power of dreams—and their potential to serve as portents, warning, or guides—took on a special importance. At the same time, this chapter contends that dream reporting served critical emotional functions, alternately soothing or awakening the dreamer spiritually and, sometimes, doing both at once.

Despite the controversy about the reliability of dreams and a reportedly thoroughgoing disavowal of dreams by puritan reformers, early colonists' practices of dreaming seem mainly to have mirrored and reproduced larger English and (framed more broadly) European practices of dreaming, including the long-standing ambivalence toward dreams and dreamt knowledge common to European Christian culture, perhaps intensified by puritan rigor. Dreams were seen as divine, diabolical, or natural in origin. Dreams might reveal one's health, one's humoral temper, or one's future. Sometimes they revealed God's mind. But dreams might also mislead, ensnaring otherwise good Christians in Satan's plots. Dreams might be personal, intended for the individual, but they could also have larger meanings, even commenting on the entire colonial enterprise. New England's early colonists shared in a potent Reformation culture of dreaming, and their practices of dreaming thus included both caution and self-scrutiny, even as they promised the occasional glimpse of wondrous providence.

Dreams and dreaming had long played a major role in European cultures. Although Protestants often cast aspersions on Catholics, whom they accused of accepting dreams too uncritically, both Catholic and Protestant thinkers regarded dreams with cautious skepticism.[14] Early in its history, the Catholic Church had addressed a variety of classical, Semitic, and folk traditions of dream use, rejecting some and Christianizing others. In these earlier traditions, dreams had been used for divination, healing, and conjuring. But, as described by historian Maria V. Jordán, "The Church's official position since the Council of Ancira (314 [CE]) had condemned all prediction and prognostication based on dreams, classifying such attempts as a pagan stain on Christian culture."[15] Despite the best efforts of the church to rein in folk traditions, the use of dreams never entirely followed church teachings. Ancient dream dictionaries were reprinted and various folk practices regarding dreams continued in use throughout the medieval era; even medieval scholars took night visions to be "filled with ambiguous possibility."[16] By the fifteenth and sixteenth centuries, dreamers and visionaries came under particular scrutiny because their prophecies, now disseminated through a burgeoning print culture, often challenged either church leadership or temporal authority, or both.[17]

Educated New England colonists like Winthrop would have been familiar with their own nation's pre-Reformation Catholic traditions, which were frequently invoked as part of somber warnings about the dangers inherent in trusting dreams. Stories of Catholic visionaries included that of the Elizabeth Barton, the "Maid of Kent," whose dreams and visions had openly criticized King Henry VIII. Her life was recorded in an anthology popular with New England readers, Thomas Beard's *Theatre of God's Judgments*, and both Barton and her visions served an important role in Beard. An examination of her story helps in understanding the sixteenth-century dream beliefs and controversies that shaped Winthop's understandings of his own night vision.

Beard's Barton was a powerful critic of crown authority, a theme that would have resonated with the religious radicals who had quit Old England for New. Yet at the same time, she offered a prototypical example of the "credulous" Catholic belief in visions that radical Protestants rejected. Since Winthrop and the early New England colonists were intimately familiar with this English Reformation history—the roots of Winthrop's dream in some sense—our story stretches back to the dreams and visions that punctuated the turbulent religious strife of Henry, the Marian martyrs, and the reform movements of the 1560s and 1570s, at least as these dream events saturated the historical imaginary of New England readers.

Elizabeth Barton's life as a prophet began in an illness later cured by miraculous intervention, and she came to model herself after visionaries such as Saint Catherine of Siena and Saint Bridget of Sweden.[18] Barton's visions gripped the imagination of the English public, awash as it was in the turmoil of Henry VIII's reign. As with many such prophets, two male churchmen—Richard Master, the pastor at Aldington, and Edward Bocking, a monk at Canterbury—played a critical role in publicizing her prophecies. Like many other visionaries, including the famous Lucrecia de León of Spain, Barton was able to achieve influence beyond the purely local sphere because of the new culture of pious reading: these patrons ("divers great men") arranged that "a book was put in print, touching her fained miracles and revelations."[19] While Barton herself ultimately entered a convent and became a nun, her visions continued. In Beard's report, she "counterfeited such manner of trances and distortions in her body" as to win "great credit amongst the people."[20] However, Barton and her promoters soon ran afoul of the authorities: "Not content to delude the people, she began also to meddle with the King himself, Henry the eight; saying, That if he proceeded to be divorced from his wife Queene Katherine, he should not remaine King one month after, and in the reputation of God not one day."[21] It is not surprising that these pronouncements led her to be arrested and arraigned for treason, whence she and her accomplices confessed and were hanged at Tyburne in April 1534, Barton's head being cut off and "set upon London bridge, and the other[s] on certaine gates of the City."[22] As Henry and other monarchs discovered, visionary prophets like Barton could coalesce diffuse political discontent into a very real and threatening challenge.

Dreams could be, as the Barton narrative would continue to convey, a very serious business. Throughout the sixteenth century, Protestant authors expressed scorn for the miracles that had dominated Catholic hagiography even as they developed their own compendium of Protestant wonders. These views would have been familiar reading for Winthrop and his contemporaries. Indeed, the contributions of Winthrop's uncle William to the compendium of the Protestant martyrologist John Foxe were a source of pride for the family, who were very familiar with its contents.[23] Writing in the 1570s, Foxe reported a dream about the holy Ethelwold, a medieval friar, writing dismissively: "Of such prodigious fantasies our monkish histories be full; and not only our histories of England, but also the heathen stories of the Gentiles, be stuffed with such kind of dreams of much like effect."[24] Reported dreams and visions had played a role in Catholic accounts by confirming the individual's holiness, but in the Reformation period, scholars on both sides of the religious divide, Catholic and Protestant alike, rethought the status of dreams as sources of divine revelation, and theologians on both sides exhibited a new skepticism about whether one could ever trust night dreams or visions.[25] In speaking of the many predictive dreams reported "in the books of the monks and of the ethnic [i.e., non-Christian] writers," Foxe complained: "For what cannot either the idle vanity of man's head or the deception of the lying spirit work by man, in fore-showing such earthly events as happen commonly in this present world?" Still, he never dismissed them altogether, leaving the door open for truly revelatory divine dreams: "[There] is a difference to be understood between these earthly dreams, speaking of earthly things and matters of human superstition; and between other spiritual revelations sent by God touching spiritual matters of the church, pertaining to man's salvation."[26]

S tereotypes about puritans would have them categorically reject dreams as sources of knowledge. Indeed, Gervase Holles, a staunch Royalist during England's Civil War years, reported that he had once had a predictive dream of his wife's death, but that "hir father and mother . . . being rigid puritanes, made slight of it."[27] (As Holles was quick to note, the prediction was correct—his wife died just a few days later.)

But radicals were a good deal less certain than Holles or other critics would have us believe. John Foxe's cautious presentation of one 1557 vision attests to similar concerns in the late sixteenth century. Foxe notes that he was uncertain as to whether to include the story, because some would doubtless "be offended with [the] setting forth things of that sort uncertain," and others would want to know of the wondrous occurrence. He worried that even if readers believed that the vision had occurred, his inclusion of it would only encourage "the common error of believing rash miracles, fantasies, visions, dreams, and apparitions."[28] Indeed, were not dreams and similar phenomena just the sort of untrustworthy sources that Protestants eschewed, with their emphasis on the primacy of scripture? As Foxe averred, "neither am I ignorant that the papists, in their books and legends of saints, have their prodigious visions and apparitions of angels, of our Lady, of Christ, and other saints," nor did he think that these should "be believed for true."[29]

Nevertheless, Foxe defended his inclusion of the vision in question, "granting first, and admitting with the words of Basil . . . 'Not every dream is straightway a prophecy,'" but noting that as the vision was had from reliable individuals who had heard it "out of the man's own mouth," he would leave it up to the reader's own hearing, "for him to judge thereof as God shall rule his mind."[30]

As historian Keith Thomas noted in his classic work *Religion and the Decline of Magic*, "Although most orthodox members of the Church of England assumed that the Reformation had brought an end to miracles, they were less certain about the status of religious prophecy. Some took the view that Christians now had all the revelation they needed, but others felt that the possibility of further messages from God could not be entirely ruled out."[31] Thomas also offers many instances in which the puritan ministry and laity alike paid careful attention to their dreams.[32]

Thus, during the half-century before and after Winthrop's dream of grace, dreams remained important for Protestants of several stripes and Catholic alike. There seems to have been a generalized European culture of dream belief and practice, albeit one that had a few distinctive variants.[33] As A. Roger Ekirch argues in a study of nighttime during the early modern era, "dreams played a profound role in early modern life, every bit as revealing, according to popular sentiment, of prospects ahead as of times past." Dreams were thought to reveal a man's inner temperament or to reflect ordinary or unpleasant feelings; dreams could bring visitations with the dead and sometimes predicted one's own death; and dreams could guide action or provide spiritual inspiration.[34]

Following long-standing Christian practice, early modern thinkers divided dreams into three major categories: "natural" or "merely carnal" (indicative of the state of the body, its humoral temperament, position during sleep, etc.); "diabolical" (inspired by Satan—at best an "idle fancy" and at worse a misleading source of sin); or "divine" (inspired by God). The mainstream English clergyman Thomas Cooper, writing in 1617, described them this way: "Such as proceed immediately from the Lord . . . therefore called Divine"; "Divellish Dreames framed in the braine by Satan"; and "Naturall dreames, proceeding from naturall causes." He further divided natural dreams into three groups: "1. As thoughts of the minde: 2. Affections of the heart; 3. Or constitution of the bodie."[35] These last followed humoral theory: "To cholericke persons[,] dreames of Warres, to Phelegmaticke of Waters, Fearefull dreames to Melancholicke persons, &c."[36] The humoral origin of some dreams was echoed in contemporary dream dictionaries, which drew more or less directly from sources in antiquity.[37] As Cooper noted, "The Maistery [mystery] will bee how wee shall discerne and distinguish betweene these Dreames."[38]

Part of the problem with dreams, then, was that they could be hard to categorize clearly. Some dreams that seemed meaningless might, in fact, be messages of a sort, whereas dreams that appeared to contain divine communications might, in a terrible twist, turn out to have been satanic delusions. In noting that moderns should no longer expect divine dreams, Cooper wrote: "And heere wee are wisely also to distinguish of the Times[;] For seeing now we have the Gospell sufficient to reveale the will of God, therefore we are not in these daies to build upon Dreames." Even if "they were ordinary before and under the Law, yet now if any shall . . . expect resolution heereby, wee are to conclude that it is rather a Satanicall illusion then any warning from the Lord, and therefore at no hand to be heeded of us." Cooper or his printer highlighted his point with a blunt marginal note: "No divine dreames now to be expected 2. *Tim* 3. 17."[39]

It seems most likely that New England's first generations of colonists shared in this promiscuous mix of assumptions about the derivation and meaning of dreams. All inherited the generations-old tradition of the church's struggle to control pre-Christian European practices of divination and conjuring; all had been saturated in the Elizabethan generation's struggle over scriptural literalism, with its concomitant (and contradictory) creation of the new Protestant martyrology purveyed by Foxe and Beard, which itself often wove tales of dreams and visions into its message. Most would have been aware of the commonly accepted theories of Galenic medicine (as recycled by commentators like Cooper, above) about the intimate linkages between humoral temperament and the specific content of dream imagery. Some, perhaps those less scrupulous or less devout, might have seen or used dream keys or dictionaries at some point in time. Certainly some conventional interpretations of dream symbols would have been part of the mental universe colonists brought as an Old World inheritance of folk wisdom. However, specific evidence of the use of dream books or dream keys does not exist. A check of extant New England book lists turns up no known dream dictionaries or guides in the libraries of Elder Brewster in Plymouth, John Winthrop II in Connecticut, or in any of the carefully reconstructed lists of books available to the first generations.[40]

Periodization of dream belief and changes to dream practice are also elusive. The middle seventeenth century saw a rise in public discussion of dreams on both sides of the Atlantic, as competing groups on the religious far left, notably the Quakers, widely embraced them as a channel for divine revelation. This embrace formed a central charge in the arguments against Quakerism, but Baptists and various pietist sects had made claims of direct and immediate revelation even before. Midcentury millennialism thus highlighted the dream anew, forcing even mainstream puritans to retreat from their supposed dismissal of the dream and come to terms with the value of dream interpretation for even the most pious.[41] As Alan Macfarlane discovered in his study of the nonconformist minister Ralph Josselin, most of the dreams in Josselin's diary were recorded between 1650 and 1659, a fact that Macfarlane correlates with the "particular political and religious upheaval" of this decade; an upheaval, one presumes, that upped the ante on knowing what dreams meant at the same time as it gave dreams a new prominence as revelation in the eyes of many.[42]

Nonconforming members of the Church of England seem to have sat in an uneasy position with regard to this upsurge of enthusiasm. Having given up any strict rejection of dreams, but wary of Satan's wiles, they had to grapple anew with how far to accept dreams as meaningful. Most appear still to have regarded dreams as worthy of examination. Philip Goodwin was a puritan minister and author whose *Mystery of Dreams* appeared in 1658. Though Goodwin's book is not known to have been available to New England readers, there are some reasons to take it as a statement perhaps representative of a generalized view among the New England orthodoxy on dreams. While younger than Winthrop's generation, Goodwin had been educated at Cambridge from 1623 to 1627 and thus was contemporary with many of the younger ministers in New England's first generation of migrants. His book remains the only known full-length midcentury tract about dreams by someone with puritan sympathies, and it stressed a moderate regard for dreams despite the frenzy of interregnum religious heterodoxy in which narration of dreams and visions played a prominent part.[43] Goodwin echoed Cooper's and Foxe's earlier cautions to discriminate between true and false revelation, reporting a common objection to dream study: "God we grant in former times spoke by visions and Dreames, but in these last dayes he speaks by his Sonne, Heb. 1."[44] Yet Goodwin defended the importance of dreams despite this, noting that while dreams were the predominant conduit for revelation before Christ's arrival, they might still be meaningful to seventeenth-century Christians, even if the most reliable teachings now came from scripture: "So in these last dayes when God speaks by his Sonne, he may also speak by visions and Dreams, though not so frequently." Goodwin continued that "the preaching of the Gospel is Gods usuall speech and ordinary course, requiring mens chiefest care;" yet dreams might still be important. Goodwin cited scripture to support his notion: "'Tis a Promise first reported by the Prophet *Joel*, 2. 28. And after repeated in the *Acts of the Apostles*, Chap. 2 ver. 17. *That in the last dayes young men should see visions, and old men should dreame Dreames.*[45] Goodwin further noted that while some may "imagine useless" the exploration of dreams, nevertheless "be not discouraged (dear Christian) from a diligent endeavour to get a due understanding in the state of Dreames," suggesting that *"this may be still very profitable."*[46]

Goodwin's view was reinforced a decade or so later by a puritan divine highly regarded by New England's ministry, Richard Baxter. As Baxter wrote, "'It is possible that God may make new revelations to particular persons about their particular duties, events, or matters of fact, in subordination to the Scripture, either by inspiration, vision, or apparition, or voice; for he hath not told us that he will never do such a thing.'"[47] He continued, however, that to expect or to pray for such a revelation "'is but a presumptuous tempting of God. And all sober Christians should be the more cautious of being deceived by their own imaginations, because certain experience telleth us, that most in our age that have pretended to prophecy, or to inspirations, or revelations, have been melancholy, crack-brained persons, near to madness, who have proved deluded in the end.'"[48] Thus, the prescriptive literature agreed that although dreams were never completely reliable sources for new revelation, they could not be wholly ruled out, a position that would have been as familiar to medieval or even early Christian thinkers as it was to New England men such as John Winthrop.[49] We must imagine that within this overarching consensus lay many gradations of actual practice, but dreams seem to have fallen within a more general European fascination with wonders and wonder lore. While the radical reformed Protestants who dominated New England colonization may have tended toward the conservative edge of this spectrum, work in popular religion and popular magical belief has shown that a great variety of folk practices were broadly shared among New England colonists from a variety of backgrounds.[50]

If anyone in New England should have rejected a dream, therefore, it would have been John Winthrop. Thus, the governor's cautious embrace of his reassuring nighttime vision suggests that few colonists would reject dreaming (or the knowledge it promised) out of hand. Viewed within long-standing Christian traditions and categorizations, albeit tempered by the Radical Reformation's emphasis on the primacy of the written scripture, knowledge gained in dreams was still something to be pondered, and few would have thrown out the interpretation of dream material altogether. Goodwin later made an impassioned case for the potential communications in dreams: "A Dream is a close covered Dish brought in by night for the Soul to feed on; And is it not meet for a man, after to uncover the Dish, to see and know upon what Meat he hath eaten?"[51] Citing another example, from the life history of B. Cowper, "who . . . reports a Dream he had from God, guiding him to the place of his publick Ministry most remarkeably," Goodwin made his point yet more plainly, quoting Cowper: "*And that the ever living Lord, who sleepeth not, may thus in these latter times, warn the Souls of his Servants, when their Bodies be a sleep, none I trust (saies he) will deny the same.*"[52]

The most important store of dream knowledge that English men and women brought with them across the Atlantic was the centuries-old lore of dreams, both those found in the Bible and others recounted in popular books (Foxe and Beard) including a mix of folktales and historical examples. Early modern authors usually cited a predictable chain of famous dreamers, commonly mentioning familiar Bible stories, including Joseph's interpretations of Pharaoh's dreams and Daniel's interpretation of Nebuchadnezzar's. Authors also mentioned a host of classical examples as well. For example, Thomas Beard noted the story of Balthazar (he meant Belshazzar) as told in Daniel, chapter 5. This king, the son and successor of Nebuchadnezzar, defiled sacred cups taken from the temple in Jerusalem by using them for "prophane" feasting. Beard reported with a hint of satisfaction, "God being stirred up to wrath against him, appointed his destruction even whilest he thus dranke and made merry in the midst of his jollity," so that in the night the astonished king saw a "strange and fearerfull [*sic*] signe" namely "a bodilesse hand writing upon the wall over against the candlesticke; the words of which writing portended the destruction of his kingdome, which presently ensued; for the very same night hee was murthered, and the Scepter seised upon by Darius King of the Medes."[53] It was just this sort of story of a heedless sinner, a prophetic vision, and an inexorable doom that helped to prepare many a youth for conversion—indeed, this sort of story may have been read in the Winthrop house during Stephen's conversion crisis—helping to break open a hardened heart, afflicting his spirit, and inspiring the "mourninge & languishing" that preceded his successful conversion experience.

Scripture study also underscored the historical example of those gifted with special insight in interpreting dreams. Goodwin cites Daniel 1:17 ("also he gave Daniel understanding of all visions & dreams;")[54] he also termed Joseph, the interpreter of Pharaoh's dreams in Genesis, chapters 40–41, "a Captain-Dreamer; for he had not only an admirable Transact in imagining Dreames, but a marvelous insight for the interpreting of Dreames."[55] Goodwin's argument was clear: the insights of these patriarchs could only have come as a gift from God, and therefore there could be nothing wrong with studying dreams oneself; to do so was simply to search the world for God's intentions, something every religious person ought to do out of habit.[56]

Examples from the classical world were also acceptable models for Christian readers seeking more information about their dreams.[57] In one breathtaking passage, Goodwin cited Aristotle, Cicero, Galen, Hippocrates, Aquinas, Luther, and Polanus, thereby developing a chain of continuity from ancient times to his day. Like the authors of popular dream dictionaries in the period, Goodwin recounted famous predictive dreams, including that of Calpurnia, the wife of Julius Caesar, which had foretold her husband's death, as well as the dream of Augustus's physician, which saved the emperor's life.[58]

To those who might reject this pre-Christian tradition, those interested in dreams mounted a spirited defense, offering revisionist Christian reasons to regard dreams closely. Goodwin noted of the ancient physicians, "And if it were laudable in them, to look into Dreames to learn out the state of mens bodies, may it not be commendable in others, thereby to discover the case of mens souls?"[59] He cited examples of dreams being sent by the gods either to inform or to deceive, noting the ancient tradition that dreams flew to men as winged creatures.[60] He also reported that "Heathen Writers" thought dreams were sent via two doors—truthful ones through a door of horn, and fallacious ones through a door of ivory: "For Horn say they may be looked through, and Truth is easie to be looked into; but Yvory is thick and dark: so deceit and falshood is hardly descried [discerned with difficulty]." Goodwin gave even this well-known tradition a Christian spin: "Dreames of Truth that proceed from God are sooner seen; but Dreames of falsehood that fall in from Satan, are not so discoverable, though to be discovered [is] desireable."[61]

While they might affect disinterest or eschew the vulgar dream keys, New England colonists lapped up literature saturated in dream lore. These were what Beard called "our home-bred English stories," and it was these stories, along with Protestant martyrology, that formed the cultural backdrop for many if not most of New England's religious refugees.[62] John Foxe's compendium, though created in the wake of the Marian persecution of the mid-sixteenth century, remained staple literature for those of Winthrop's generation, and thus it should be regarded as an index of contemporary knowledge.[63] So it is import-ant that dreams and visions play a prominent role in many, if not most, of Foxe's stories. Foxe included the memorable tale of John Bradford, who was supposed to have forecast in a dream his arrest, trial, and execution by fire, as well as a lengthy section on John Philpot, who reported in a 1555 letter from prison his dream vision of "a great beautiful city, all of the colour of azure, and white, four square, in a marvelous beautiful composition in the midst of the sky."[64]

New Englanders also absorbed Foxe's wondrous stories of predictive dreams in the household of Master John Rough, the pastor of a nonconformist congregation in London. Rough experienced a series of dreams shortly before being arrested and executed by fire in 1557. In a dream, Rough beheld his con-gregation's deacon, Cutbert Symson, being led away by guards. Awakening, he called his wife, "saying, 'Kate, strike a light, for I am much troubled with my brother Cutbert this night.'" Rough tried to read, eventually falling back asleep, whereupon "he dreamed the like dream again; and, awakening therewith, he said, 'Oh! Kate, my brother Cutbert is gone.'" So they lighted a candle again, and rose." Just then, Symson came to the house, carrying a book with a list of the "names and accounts" of everyone in the congregation. "When master Rough had seen [him], he said, 'Brother Cutbert, ye are welcome; for I have been sore troubled with you this night;' and so told him his dream." Rough asked Symson to take a few notes from the book and then put it away, "and to carry it no more about him," presumably for fear that it would fall into the hands of the authorities if Symson were indeed arrested. At first, Symson protested that "he would not so do: for dreams, he said, were but fantasies, and not to be credited." But then "master Rough straitly charged him, in the name of the Lord, to do it." Symson eventually left the book in safekeeping with Rough's wife. Soon after, Symson would be arrested as the dream had foretold, but by this miraculous providence the list of names would be saved.[65]

Rough's predictive dreams continued to toll a warning to the faithful, creating an emotionally saturated spiritual narrative. Foxe's stories taught readers how to cast their own dream experiences as spiritually potent experiences, frequently centered on the dream's prophetic capacity. Rough's dreams continued: "He thought in his dream, that he was carried himself forcibly to the bishop, and that the bishop plucked off his beard, and cast it into the fire, saying these words, 'Now I may say I have had a piece of a heretic burned in my house.'" This curious image is reminiscent of folk practices to protect against the ill effects of witches, and, in fact, at least one sixteenth-century English dream dictionary indicated that to dream of a beard "betokeneth harme." Since, however, the same text said that having a long beard in a dream also connoted strength, the condensed image of the beard might have signaled to his contemporaries both the harm that would befall him shortly, as well as, perhaps, his strength in resisting Catholic authorities.[66]

The narrative doubles its power by crediting Rough's two-year-old daughter and his wife with predictive dreams as well: the little girl, Rachel, who was "in his bed with him at that time[,] . . . awoke . . . and cried: 'Alas, alas, my father is gone, my father is gone;' and, for all that they could do or speak, long it was or [ere] she could be persuaded that he was there. A candle being lighted, and she, coming better to herself, saw him, and took him about the neck, and said, 'Father, now I will hold you, that you go not away:' and so twice or thrice repeated the same." When they fell asleep again, in "the same night," Mistress Rough, "being troubled in like case, dreamed that she saw one James Mearing's wife [Margaret Mearing, an excommunicated member of Rough's congregation] . . . going down the street with a bloody banner in her hand, and a fire-pan on her head. Then suddenly she arising to go see her, she thought she stumbled on a great hog, and had a mighty fall thereby; through the sudden fear whereof she awoke, and said, 'I am never able to rise again.' "[67]

These strange and prophetic warnings pointed out how dreams might predict spiritually potent events with accuracy. Rough's, Symson's, and Mearing's arrests and executions all followed shortly on this memorable night of troubled dreams. Even jail could not stop the visions. During his imprisonment and after being tortured at Newgate, Symson had "a certain vision or apparition very strange," which he reported to several friends and associates. While in the stocks, his room having been secured for the night by locks, someone entered the room, who had "no candle or torch that he could see, but giving a brightness and light most comfortable and joyful to his heart, saying 'Hah!' unto him, and departed again. Who it was he could not tell." Symson "declared" the story of this visitation to several persons, remaining consistent in his account. In both the event itself and the recounting of it, "he received such joyful comfort, that he also expressed no little solace in telling and declaring the same."[68]

K eith Thomas noted of John Foxe's *Actes and Monuments*, "Through Foxe's great book the tradition that a godly man might have supernatural knowledge of the future was widely disseminated among English Protestants."[69] Like most men and women of the sixteenth and seventeenth centuries, John Winthrop and his contemporaries would have seen dreams, even their own dreams, as a potent though perhaps unreliable source of prediction. What types of dreams were recorded and what record of interpretation or other dream practices do we find in the first generation of colonial New England's existence?

It is fortunate that one did not have to be one of Foxe's martyrs, doomed to death by fire, to have dreams worthy of record. Instead, dreams recorded by English men and women of the Tudor-Stuart period fell into a number of easily recognizable categories that seem to have been universally recognized, despite confessional differences.

The most-recorded English dreams of this period were predictive. While many authors dismissed dreams as the results of food and drink, humoral temperament, or other natural causes, people rarely wrote down such ordinary dream events.[70] Of the second type of dreams, those inspired by Satan, only a very few reported dreams were chalked up to the workings of that Old Serpent. Many recorded horrific nightmares or other terrifying encounters, and the compilers of various compendia of wonders happily included such "deluded dreams" when it suited their sectarian purposes.[71] But few attributed their own dreams to demonic influence. Indeed, most reported dreams were written down because the dreamer thought they were divinely inspired, whether predictive in nature or not. These were usually divided into two further categories, either "hopeful" or "awakening."

Thus, the recorded dreams that appear in written sources, both in England and New England, consist of remarkable dreams—dreams that were so puzzling, so emotionally powerful, or so apparently predictive that they were recounted and recorded. As with other historical records, recorded dreams constitute an uneven and unbalanced sample. The usual effects of gender, wealth, age, and education shape the historic record: more men than women recorded their dreams; dream recorders tended to come from the ranks of educated, wealthier, and more leisured people who had better access to literacy and private writing. Until the advent of daily journals or dream diaries—which, in New England, began to appear in the 1670s but did not flower until the next century—recorded dreams tended to be those that seemed especially puzzling or memorable, including those that appeared to be predictive or spiritually significant.[72] Like Winthrop's, some dreams were first communicated to spouses or other family members, often just upon awakening and in the middle of the night. Others were written down for personal reflection. Some became part of regional or national folklore, circulating through oral gossip networks before finding their way into written compendia.[73] Predictive dreams were frequently recorded after events had proven the prediction correct. (Those that did not come true were, apparently, soon forgotten, a general feature of prophetic dreaming throughout the ages.) But sometimes, a dream had such emotional power that the dreamer recorded it, perhaps as a way of dissipating some of its sting. John Winthrop's own father was troubled in 1621 with a dream that his nephew Carew Mildmay "was dead," and duly recorded it in his diary.[74]

Both wonder lore and the print culture that codified and disseminated such stories across Europe played a large role in shaping expectations of the predictive dream. We have already seen how Foxe's compendium included the predictive dreams of John Bradford, John Rough, and Rough's wife and daughter.[75] As scholars have noted, dreams in the early modern period were seen as sources of knowledge not available by other means, and they were often conceived as a special form of seeing, albeit an inward sight, rather than as a form of thought.[76] Dreams might bring news—about illnesses cured, about events going on in the lives of distant relatives, or even about crimes committed.

For example, in the late sixteenth century, Mistress Hall, a pious woman under the care of the noted nonconformist minister Anthony Gilby, had a predictive dream about an illness both spiritual and physical, later published in the 1660 autobiography of her son: "For on a time being in great distress of Conscience, she thought in her Dream, there stood by her a grave Personage, in the Gown, and other Habits of a Physitian, who enquiring of her estate, and receiving a sad and querulous answer from her, took her by the hand, and bad[e] her be of good Comfort, for this should be the last Fit that ever she should feel of this kinde."[77] She remarked "that upon that condition, she could well be content for the time, with that, or any other torment: [and] reply was made to her, as she thought, with a redoubled assurance of that happy issue of this her last tryal; whereat she began to conceive an unspeakable joy." Yet, when she awoke, the dream "left her more disconsolate, as then conceiting [believing] her happiness imaginary, her misery real.[78] At this juncture, the invalid was comforted by Gilby, "who, upon the Relation of this her pleasing Vision, . . . began to perswade her, that [the] Dream was no other than Divine, and that she had good reason to think that gracious premonition was sent her from God himself," who, because of her suffering, left "the common road of his proceedings" to offer her "relief."[79] And, indeed, buoyed by this comforter, the lady began to feel better, and "found that happy prediction verified to her."[80]

Another common type of predictive dream was that which foretold the deaths of close relatives. Thus, Fynes Moryson made a lengthy record of his presumed predictive powers in dreams, regarding the death of each of his parents.[81] Forty years later, Ralph Josselin wondered at a dream in which he predicted (correctly as it happened), the death and subsequent "replacement" of three of his children.[82] Sometimes individuals may even have hoped for a predictive dream. Near the end of his life, Josselin himself hoped that he "'might even foreseeingly dream.'"[83]

In a world filled with death and uncertainty, predictive dreams perhaps offered a measure of control, even as they sometimes repeated earlier traumatic situations; individuals anticipating a loss could grieve it in advance through the images they saw in dreams. Gervase Holles, as we saw above, was troubled in 1634 with a dream foretelling the death of his wife and newborn child, "a dream . . . which tolde me every circumstance of what was immediately to befall me."[84] The impending birth with its attendant dangers had apparently reawakened a much earlier loss, the death of his own mother when he was a very young child. In a moving example of the emotional power of dreamt experience, Holles wrote: "I dreamt my wife was brought to bed of a daughter and that shee and the childe were both dead, and that I (in a great deale of affliction) walking under the north wall of the close in the Friers Minorites at Grimesby (the place where I was borne) my owne mother walked on the other side hir hand continually touching mine on the top of the wall; and so (my heart beating violently within me) I awakened."[85]

Despite (or perhaps because of) his fears for his wife, Holles writes, "This dreame I concealed from hir." When his in-laws saw him "sad," they begged him to know the reason, but quickly rejected the prophetic warning, because it came from his dream. Holles writes, "But the day after made it too true in every sillable. For the Sunday morning following shee was delivered of a daughter, and both were dead within a hower after."[86] Later in his narrative, Holles offered his own theory on how predictive dreams might work: "When there is between two an harmony in their affections, there is likewise betweene their soules an acquaintance and sometimes an intelligence." It was this, he thought, that could account for these unlikely warnings.[87]

Reports of predictive dreams offered plenty of fodder for wonder tales. Repeated as oral tales and eventually collected in writing, this type of reported dream was presented as a goad to the faithful rather than as entertainment, though they surely served both purposes. Thus, Edward Burghall's collection of providences related to the Civil War included the story of Master George Mainwaring, of Bunbury, who continued to keep a maidservant despite a string of four illegitimate pregnancies. In 1631, Mainwaring's daughter, "a hopefull yong Gentlewoman," was taken suddenly with "a Plurisy." On the night before his daughter died, Mainwaring had "a very strange Dream," later thought to have predicted her death, in which "Hee thought he saw a dead Corps, laide on a Bier, carried out of a little Chamber adjoining to his own, & passing thro' it, he saw a round Circle all red like the Breadth of a Sheet, hovering to & fro." Burghall commented, "Such Dreams as these are not to be slighted. Its like he was waked by it to enquire further concerning his Servant."[88] Clearly, Burghall thought the dream foretold the daughter's death, which in its turn was conceived as punishment for Mainwaring's impiety with regard to his maid.

Although supposedly dismissive of dreams, some pious New Englanders actually extolled dreams as a guide to action. John Dane, an early colonist on Boston's north shore, remembered that his mother, "when she lived in starford [in England], one nyte, in her slepe, she fell into a dream, and waking she was mutch taken with it. She told my father, and could not cepe [keep] it out of hur mind." The dream was "that sutch a minester, I haue forget his name, should preach sutch a weke and sutch a day at elsuam, [Elsenham] on sutch a text. The thouts of it did so take with hur [these thoughts, represented as having origins outside the self, lodged themselves within her] that she inquiered, and as she dreamed, so it was; the same man, the same day, the same text. She and my brother How herd him." Dane recalls, "I, then being so young, cannot Remember euery thing; but I doubt not but that she made good improuement of that sarmon."[89] It makes sense that this family story of a predictive dream would be carefully guarded, analyzed, and transmitted to later generations, given its theme of spiritual improvement and divine sanction of a particular, presumably puritan, minister as messenger.

English folk belief taught that it was particularly wise to heed the predictive dreams of pregnant women, who were thought to be frequent recipients of powerful visions.[90] Many such dreams achieved a legendary status: "Of such a like dream we read of the mother of Athelstan;" reports Foxe, "how the moon did spring out of her womb, and gave light to all England!"; or, a bit later, "The mother of . . . Ethelwold, who being great with him, did see a golden eagle fly out of her mouth, &c."[91] English Catholics treasured the story of Sir Thomas More, whose mother had a vision the night after her marriage, "in which she sawe in her sleepe, as it were ingraven in her wedding ring the number and favour of all her children she was to have." Of these, "the face of one was so darke and obscure that she could not well discerne it, and indeede afterwards she suffered of one of her children an untimelie deliverie [miscarriage]; but the face of one of her other[s], she beheld shining most gloriously, whereby no doubt Sir Thomas his fame and sanctitite was foresh[i]ned and presignifyed."[92]

Predictive dreams were not limited to Catholics. However, as the reaction of Holles's in-laws suggests, by the mid-seventeenth-century, nonconformists sometimes treated them with disdain. The puritan memoirist Lucy Hutchinson reported a dream that had become family legend, from the time of her birth in 1620: "My mother, while she was with child of me, dreamt that she was walking in the garden with my father, and that a starre came downe into her hand, with other circumstances which, though I have often heard, I minded not enough to remember perfectly." Hutchinson's father and mother discussed the dream, and "my father told her, her dreame signified she should have a daughter of some extraordinary eminency." Hutchinson goes on to argue that the uncritical acceptance of "such vaine prophecies" assured their fulfillment. Her parents' belief in the dream "wrought as farre as it could its own accomplishment; for my father and mother fancying me then beautifull, and more than ordinarily apprehensive, applied all their cares and spar'd no cast to emproove me in my education," which turned the young Lucy into a veritable showpiece of accomplishments, truly a shining star of sorts.[93]

Despite Hutchinson's dismissive tone, New England colonists negotiating the rigors of emigration sometimes took great comfort in their dreams. While the sources are never tremendously abundant, it is clear from reports in diaries and elsewhere that New Englanders did attend to dreams, along with other practices of prediction, to discern God's intentions in what must have been one of the biggest choices of their lives. Dreams led some to embark on the frightening and unknown colonial venture, while dreams kept emigrants connected to distant family members, perhaps helping them to grieve the loss of friends, relations, and familiar surroundings.[94]

John Wilson, one of the most respected ministers of Boston, told John Winthrop "that before he was resolued to come into this Countrye, he dreamed he was [already] here, & that he sawe a Churche arise out of the earthe, which grew vp & became a merveylous goodly churche."[95] Presumably this dream had been prayed about, and had helped to determine his decision to join the New England colonists. Winthrop also tells the story of "one Marisfield, a poore Godly man of Exeter, beinge verye desirous to come to vs, but not able to transport his famylye." One Master Marshall, a "riche merchante" who could not emigrate himself, "beinge troubled in his dreams about the said poore man could not be quiett till he had sent for him & given him the 50. li & lent him 100. li willinge him withall, that if he wanted he should send to him for more." The story had a sober moral, however, as "this marisfield grewe suddainly riche, & then lost his godlinesse, & his wealth soon after,"[96] suggesting the corrupting influence of easy riches in Winthrop's eyes.

Examples from the post-Restoration diary of Edward Taylor suggest the ways in which dreams might express both the rigors of emigration and the almost messianic journey that emigrants believed they were undertaking. Taylor, who arrived from England in the 1660s, reported one unusual dream in a diary he kept while aboard ship. "After dinner, I reading the fourth chapter of John in Greek, was so sleepy that when I had done I lay down." Then "dropping into a sleep, and dreaming of my brethren, [I] was so oppressed with sorrow that I had much to do to forbear weeping out." The dream's powerful feelings continued, and Taylor thought he awakened because of them: "Being over-pressed with this passion I awaked, and was almost downright sick."[97] While Taylor's real brothers appear a few times in his diary, the context for "brethren" here would seem to be the larger Christian and, specifically, radical reformed Protestant brethren.

In this case, the dream seems to speak directly to the colonial setting. The fourth chapter of the book of John opens with Jesus fleeing the wrath of the Pharisees, entering into Samaria alone, without his disciples. The chapter is dominated by the story of the Samaritan woman who draws water from Jacob's well for Jesus, an encounter that eventually results in the conversion of the Samaritans. How similar was Taylor's own flight from the angry Pharisees of Restoration England into the wilderness of Samaritan New England? As the woman says in the parable, "How is it, that thou being a Jewe, askest drinke of me, which am a woman of Samaria? For the Jewes medle not with the Samaritans."[98] This story of exile, traveling, thirst in the desert, and the eventual conversion of Samaria perhaps resonated powerfully with Taylor the emigrant, helping to produce the powerful "passion" with which he awaked.

Just a few days later, Taylor reported a second dream, this one involving a real brother. For several days, the ship had seemed to be near land, and Taylor assiduously recorded the telltale signs in his diary. But that very day, June 26, despite sounding for land, they still "found no ground." Of that night, Taylor wrote, "At night I was much troubled in a dream of my brother Joseph, for I dreamed that he was dead."[99] This predictive dream underscores the separation that emigrants experienced as they undertook the journey across the Atlantic. It is doubtless no accident that Taylor's sleeping mind fixed on "Joseph," whose Biblical namesake was one of the most famous involuntary exiles—and an exiled younger brother at that—as well as one of the foremost dreamers in the good book.

Taylor's story brings us back to the puritan mission into the wilderness. This mission constitutes a second, very important context in which to read Winthrop's dream of conversion with which this chapter began. Of course, a very real and immediate conversion crisis had played out in the Winthrop household just before he dreamed of his wife and "Children lyinge by her with moste sweet & smylinge co[u]ntenances, with Crownes upon their heades & blue ribandes about their necks."[100] The crown was a particularly potent and revealing symbol with links to the temporal king (such an ambivalent figure for the religious reformers who made up New England's first colonists) as well as to the heavenly kingdom presided over by Christ and God the Father. In a society saturated in hierarchy, where everyone's relationships were constantly evaluated in term of social order, inferior or superior, and in a society busily creating new hierarchies in relationship to indigenous peoples, it is a short step from Winthrop's hopes for heavenly glory in his own family to his hopes for the triumph of the New England errand.

Let us linger for a moment with these crowns. We think of them today as associated mostly with temporal rule, and the image certainly had this meaning in the early modern world. But a second, period-specific meaning to the crown was its common association with martyrdom and salvation. As one sixteenth-century dream dictionary reported rather vaguely, "To be crowned, betokeneth worshyppe."[101] Many a deathbed scene was marked by this imagery, as when the dying mother of the Royalist Alice Thornton invoked the words of Christ from her deathbed: "According to His speech to St. John, 'Be thou faithfull, and I will give thee a crowne of life.' [Rev. ii. 10]."[102] Thornton consoled herself in her grief, expressing the hope that when her mother closed her eyes and "laid downe her head and her hands, . . . [and] sweetely fell asleepe in the Lord," this would be "the day of her coronation, I hope, in heaven, with her Father."[103]

Philip Goodwin offered a typically puritan caution regarding the hope of a heavenly crown. In his discussion of those who deluded themselves with fantasies of spiritual assurance, he wrote: "Upon their grants of Grace they expect Crowns of Glory, having high hopes of Heavenly happiness." But, Goodwin warns, "*These are false Dreames.* [And] These Dreames of waking men be doors to sleeping Dreames; and how soon may men fall from one false Dreame to another."[104] From this perspective, Winthrop's dream was leading him remarkably close to serious sin—an overconfident assurance—revealing the dangerous trickery that could be perpetrated through dreams.

But what was such caution when a great errand had been embarked upon? A goodly church, children enfolded in the arms of Grace herself—these were promising signs of future success in the New England wilderness, and puritan colonists, like other early modern English men and women, looked to dreams to indicate the prospects for their colonial venture. In this world of wonders, almost anything seemed to convey God's plan; when the people of Watertown watched a snake attempt to kill a mouse, they were shocked to see the mouse best the snake, killing it after "a longe fight." When John Wilson, the minister at Boston and "a verye sincere holy man" heard of it, he "gave this Interpretation, that, the snake was the devil, the mouse was a pore contemptible people which God had brought hether, which should overcome Sathan heere & disposesse him of his kingdome."[105] The crowns that Winthrop saw in his dream—his sense of God's special election of his wife and children—were almost assuredly read metaphorically as a providential message not just about their particular estate but as regarding New England and its mission as a whole.

Of course, given the skepticism of radical reformers regarding the divine dreams in these "latter days," dreams ought never be a sole cause for action. In fact, when the townsmen of Dorchester petitioned the colony in 1636 for permission to form a new church after most of the original congregation left for Connecticut, their request was rejected because of concerns about the orthodoxy of their conversion narratives: "Most of them . . . had builded their Comfort of salvation upon unsound groundes, viz: some upon dreams & ravishments of spirit by fittes."[106] If this were not enough of a caution, those embroiled along with Anne Hutchinson in the Free Grace controversy just a year later were suspected of having relied upon direct revelation, including scriptural verse and direct communications from God via the holy spirit. As Winthrop reported in his journal about Hutchinson's examination in court, "after many speeches to and fro, at last she was so full as she could not contain, but vented her revelations; amongst which this was one, that she had it revealed to her, that she should come into New England, and should here be persecuted, and that God would ruin us and our posterity. . . . So the court proceeded and banished her."[107]

Error lurked at every turn. Disguised by sleep, otherwise hidden truths might be revealed in dreams. But the individual could also be led astray. Even sin could begin with the dream. Later in the century, dreams might be viewed as "the Entertainments of our Souls . . . when they having shaken off for a time the Fetters of the Senses, are upon the Wing, in the Suburbs of Eternity."[108] But most authors of the earlier seventeenth century would have eschewed such fanciful language, for dreams represented far more serious business. As the century wore on, dreams would find a place in Enlightenment thought, becoming one point of entry for philosophers—Francis Bacon, Thomas Hobbes, Henry More, and others—into a number of key questions about the relationship between body and soul, the experience of the soul after death, the workings of Satan, the role of environment in creating psychic experience, and a host of other issues.[109]

Many of the core concerns of the sixteenth century continued to dominate

seventeenth-century thought. The three categories of dream—as natural, diabolical, or divinely inspired—remained unchanged. Dreams were potentially
important intermediaries between the "visible" (quotidian) and "invisible" (supernatural) worlds. Individuals were supposed to regard dreams with great
suspicion, but both educated and lay people alike paid attention to their "remarkable" dreams and believed they might be predictive. Drawing on a great
store of folk belief about dreams, New England's early colonists brought with
them a body of dream belief steeped in centuries of European tradition and
decades of Reformation controversy.

As the later seventeenth-century English commentator Thomas Tryon
summed it up, some might "think . . . the whole subject of Dreams is altogether Vanity, or perhaps, as some may conceive Superstitious, and unlawful to
be taken notice of." But, he argued in defense of further exploration, the "natural temperament or complexion" (the humors) were, along with many "secret
Diseases," sooner "found out by their Dreams, than by any outward signs."[110] In
addition, "since the Heart of man is deceitful above all things," he "that would
truly know himself" might take note of "his usual Dreams, there being scarce
any thing that more discovers the secret bent of our minds and inclinations to
Vertue or Vice, or this or that particular Evil, as Pride, Covetousness, Sensuality, or the like, then these nocturnal sallies and reaches of the Soul." Dreams,
Tryon thought, were "more free & undisguis'd, & with less reserve than such as
are manifested when we are awake."[111] And finally he referred, albeit obliquely,
to the possibility of divine revelation through dreams: "Dreams are one of the
clearest natural Arguments of the Immortality of our Souls," and "one of the
usual wayes, whereby God vouchsafed of old to Reveal his commands and se-
crets to the Prophets and holy men."[112] Indeed, although "abundance of ignorant People (foolish Women, and Men as weak) have in all Times and do
frequently at this day make many ridiculous & superstitious Observations from
their Dreams," still, it was one of God's "gracious promises, touching the Glory
and fuller manifestations of the Gospel dispensation, *that then their young men
should see Visions and their old men Dream Dreams.*"[113]

John Winthrop and Thomas Tryon would have disagreed on many things.
But the two men shared in a common storehouse of lore and legend about the
power of dreams to reveal truth, as well as their potential to be misread. The
cultural habits that English colonists brought with them to New England did

not entirely rule out the importance of dreams, even as both their cultural heritage and their theology taught them to treat dreams, as other wonders, with great caution. Dreams could authorize great undertakings. They might reassure the unsteady and suggest new paths to those who had lost their way. They were thought in some cases to provide accurate predictions or helpful advice, while in others they represented dangerous delusion. Above all, believers were to approach dreams with a cautious restraint. But, as these English colonists embarked on the greatest venture of their lives, they brought with them a sense that events in the invisible world were just as significant to their future success as those of the visible world. Dreams—those winged messengers of the invisible realm—carried potent meanings for the early colonists, meanings that even their deep ambivalence and suspicion of dreams could not altogether destroy.

# Chapter 2

*Representation of Indigenous Dreaming at Contact and Beyond*

Roger Williams could not understand most of what the Natives were trying
to tell him. He was far from familiar territory and the only English man,
having "travailed to an Iland of the wildest in our parts." He had left his small
boat along the shore, "the wind being contrary." Only "little could I speake to
them to their understandings, especially because of the change of their Dialect,
or manner of Speech, from our neighbours [i.e., the Natives who lived closer to
Providence]."[1] And yet, it would have been nice to be able to communicate
more freely, as Williams had apparently arrived in a village where a special ritual was already under way. As he was told, a man, probably the sachem (leader)
or a member of the sachem's lineage, had had a vision or a dream "in the night."
This night vision was of "the Sun (whom they worship for a God) darting a
Beame into his Breast, which he [the dreamer] conceived to be the Messenger
of his Death." As Williams observed, "this poore Native call'd his Friends and
neighbours, and prepared some little refreshing for them, but himself was kept
waking and Fasting in great Humiliations and Invocations for 10. dayes and
nights."[2] Williams ended his story by saying that he tried, as best he could,
given the language barrier, and "through the help of God," to speak "of the *True*
and *living only Wise God*, of the Creation: of Man, and his *fall* from God, &c."
He felt he had some success, so much so, "that at parting many burst forth, *Oh
when will you come againe, to bring us some more newes of this God?*"[3]

Roger Williams—nemesis and later friend and faithful correspondent of
John Winthrop—leaves a valuable record in this story. On the one hand, his
observation of this ceremony suggests something that other sources support:
that the Native peoples of New England had a highly developed understanding

of dreams, one that would inform their interaction with Europeans from the very beginning. On the other hand, the gaps and elisions in the account make clear that this is not a description of Native practices as Natives themselves might have told it. Rather, like virtually all the documents on which this study is based, Williams's account represents Native practices as understood by the English, and, later, as reinterpreted by historical ethnographers. Thus, what we see when we look at period sources about indigenous dream belief is highly limited, the more so when we realize that most English observers, however interested in Native cultures, believed these people were almost universally misled "by "Diabolicall Dreams."[4]

With these limits in mind, and reading the sources within the context of widely distributed Native American practices, we can at least note that New England's Native peoples, like members of other Northeastern Woodland cultures, took dreams very seriously, trusting the insight that came from dreams and their interpretation. Dreams might signal important events, including social changes like the coming of Europeans or the challenges of Christianity. Shamans (*powwaws*, "medicine men") used dreams and related states (including trance and visioning) to tap into spiritual power and steer it towards various aims, both good and evil. Despite some differences between the hunter-gatherer cultures of northern New England and the agriculturalists of the southern parts of the region, there seem to have been some general similarities among Algonquian dream practices across the area that now comprises New Brunswick, Nova Scotia, and the New England states. Much as Christian Europe drew on a common fund of knowledge despite differences of confession or ethnicity, so too did Native New Englanders share similar practices with regard to dreams.

Dreams, and the spirit guides sometimes revealed within them, were vastly important for Algonquian peoples as indeed they were for peoples across Native North America. Individuals cultivated and treasured dreams of such spiritual power, and communities most likely treated those who were known to be powerful dreamers with some care. According to the early twentieth-century anthropologist Frank Speck, the Penobscot called such an individual *ki•ugwaʾsowi•ʾno*, or "a man who searches about in dreams."[5] Dreams were used in divination, especially among northern New England Algonquians, as a regular part of setting out on the hunt, when a dreamer would be asked to "go to sleep, and 'look around' (*gwi•laʾwabo*)," with the intention of locating game.[6] Sometimes dreams begged, as Williams' encounter suggests, for some sort of public recognition, or for a public "performance." As the seventeenth-century French Recollect missionary, Chrestien Le Clercq, reported of the Mi'kmaq, dream experience was fundamentally social: "Parents dream for their children, captains for villages. They have also men who interpret and explain their dreams."[7]

But above all else, dreams and visions represented a means through which individuals in the quotidian realm of the everyday might enter into contact with manitou, emanations of spiritual power that pervaded places, animal spirits, spiritually potent individuals, and natural features, such as the sun. Kathleen J. Bragdon, an ethnographer and ethnolinguist who has worked extensively with the languages of southern New England, writes, "The dreamed was real, and the beings encountered in dreams were a living presence. They were part of the Native social world, and they were understood to work together with human beings."[8] Certainly the evidence bears out the observation that Natives told and retold their dreams, discussed them both privately and publicly, sought to engage European colonists in conversation about them and, as we shall see, sometimes acted on their dreams and the knowledge brought to them in dream states.

Despite what must have been the considerable contrast between European and Native American cosmologies, European sources suggest that the dream theory of Algonquians and Europeans began to form enough of an overlap to allow for creative misunderstandings, perhaps from both sides. Because of their own uncertainty about the status and power of dreams, their fears of the active presence of the Devil and his helpers, and their attention to the various wonders of the invisible world, colonists took a special interest in Indian dream reports, dream beliefs, and spiritual practices. While obviously this produces a historical record based almost entirely on European perceptions, these materials, when combined with other materials drawn from later ethnographic research, allow historians to trace at least the outlines of Algonquian dream practices at and just after European contact, as well as a considerably richer picture of European perceptions of those practices. Any study of indigenous dream practice immediately demands attention to the relationship between dreaming and the larger context of *powwawing* (shamanic ritual) in which the dream was often embedded.

Study of Native American dreaming leads us immediately into a cosmology and ontology quite distinct from that of early modern Europeans. As colonists attempted to fit Algonquian practices into their established notions of the world, they invariably cast Indian dream belief, especially the use of dreams in shamanism, in the frames familiar to them. Some reported that Algonquian dreams appeared to be divinely inspired "providences," and these were treated by colonial authors as "wonders," coming to function eventually like other sorts of wonder tales. But most often Europeans cast Algonquian dream practices as diabolical. The Algonquian dream system was deeply interwoven with pow-wowing. And here, Europeans—especially the Protestant missionaries of the 1650s—did not hesitate in trying to stamp out Native American practices by outlawing such practices wherever they could and by requiring those Natives who chose to convert to Christianity to renounce such practices altogether. Thus, reports of Native dreaming throughout the historical period were never neutral texts; instead, they were often salvos in a contest between Europeans and Natives. This chapter addresses the beliefs and practices of indigenous dreamers, making the case that although dreaming was an essential and widely distributed Algonquian cultural practice, for the English, Algonquian dreaming practices verged on witchcraft and their dream experience therefore was taken to be diabolically inspired. Among Indians, however, continual resort to dreaming and attempts to engage the English in conversation centered on these practices suggested a continuum of responses from genuine spiritual conversion to outright resistance, as well as a desire to engage the English in a dialogue about things located in the invisible world, as much as in the more quotidian concerns of everyday life.

A wide variety of sources help to outline Native American dream beliefs and practices in seventeenth-century New England as the indigenous people might themselves have understood them. From the tales of first contact preserved in folklore, to the descriptions of dream practices reported to early anthropologists in the region, to the reported dreams and descriptions of their uses in shamanism as recorded in narratives and missionary tracts, the Algonquian use of dreams was tied to a cosmology that valued manitou, or spiritual power, which was found throughout daily life. When English colonists came into contact with New England's indigenous peoples, their gaze settled on the uses of dreams and trance in various ritual contexts, including shamanism. Because these fairly public practices were different from the more cautious European approaches to the dream, Native dream practices were compared to the most likely analogy in the colonists' experience: witchcraft. English missionaries thought they risked God's displeasure if they left these obvious dealings with Satan unchallenged. As the century advanced, Christian Indians would face pressure to renounce dreaming altogether. Nevertheless, Native dream practices remained remarkably vibrant throughout the colonial period. This chapter contends that, over time, the entire indigenous dream complex came to be represented in English narratives as diabolical activity. This characterization of Native dream practices and beliefs can be taken as symbolic of the larger European struggle to colonize New England's Native cultures. In this context then, continued trust in dreams stood as a central vehicle for Natives' struggles to resist colonization.

The first encounter with colonization may have been foretold in dreams. Indians later claimed to have known of the arrival of Europeans before they actually disembarked on New England shores and to have obtained that knowledge in predictive visions.[9] Such dream reports sometimes became powerful stories that might advance or undercut established groups within Native societies. Oral traditions such as these are hard to work with, as we now know how extensively the nineteenth-century contexts in which they were told affected the shape and wording of the tale. But such are the limits of the evidence. One example of the genre was recorded by the folklorist Silas Rand in 1869 but describes events as much as three centuries earlier. A young Mi'kmaq woman had a dream "that a small island came floating in towards the land, with tall trees on it, and living beings, among whom was a man dressed in rabbit-skin garments."[10] The next morning "she related her dream, and sought for an interpretation." The storyteller explains, "It was the custom in those days, when any one had a remarkable dream, to consult the wise men, and especially the magicians and soothsayers." The elders "pondered over the girl's dream, but could make nothing of it."[11] Remarkably,

> The next day, an event occurred that explained it all. Getting up in the morning, what should they see but a singular little island, as they supposed, which had drifted near to the land and become stationary there! There were trees on it, and branches to the trees, on which a number of bears, as they supposed, were crawling about. They all seized their bows, arrows, and spears, and rushed down to the shore, intending to shoot the bears; what was their surprise to find that these supposed bears were men, and that some of them were lowering down into the water a very singularly constructed canoe, into which several of them

jumped and paddled ashore. Among them was a man dressed
in white—a priest with his white stole on—who came towards
them making signs of friendship, raising his hand towards
heaven, and addressing them in an earnest manner, but in a
language which they could not understand.[12]

Now everyone asked the girl: "Was it such an island as this that she had seen?"
When she said yes, it was, "Some of them, especially the necromancers, were
displeased, they did not like it that the coming of these foreigners should have
been intimated to this young girl, and not to them."[13] The storyteller gave a religious explanation, suggesting that if any Indian enemy had been about to attack, the usual dream specialists "could have foreseen and foretold it by the
power of their magic." But "of the coming of this teacher of a new religion they
could know nothing."[14] Clearly implied in this story are the ways in which having a powerful dream could convey status in the ordinary world. The dream
was delivered to this girl, rather than to an established medicine man, which
shook the authority of the dream specialists (at least if we are to believe the
story), in much the same way as later adoptions of Christianity would provide
various people, some of low status, with new avenues through which to attain
and exercise spiritual power.[15]

Oral traditions can have a remarkable stability. Indeed, although some aspects of this nineteenth-century version seem hard to believe, they are echoed
in the tales recounted by Joseph Nicolar (Penobscot) at the end of the nineteenth century. Nicolar, who was fluent in Penobscot and able to consult with
others who also knew oral tradition well, "link[ed] the arrival of Europeans
with portentous natural phenomena"—earthquakes and "dense fog"—signaling
that "long before recorded contact, Native peoples told stories about intermit-
tent sightings of strangers."[16] In one story, a loon that transforms into an "aged
woman" points to the people "floating there . . . toward the mid-ocean," and
identifies them as the cause of a strange famine: "The[se] people," she explains,
who are described as being carried along on a white swan (a ship under sail
might have looked like a migratory swan), "have brought upon you this trouble
and hunger, you cannot find the animals because the days have been so dark,
you cannot find fish because there is a covering over all the fish which the
power of these people have placed there, it is the spiritual power that is in
them." She added, "If the power that is in you has not the force to overcome it,
woe unto you."[17]

Some glimpses of a similar prophecy about the arrival of European colonists are visible in a dream reported as early as 1647, in a dramatic encounter on Cape Cod. As the missionary John Eliot and his fellow ministers John Wilson and Thomas Shepard made an exploratory visit to the people there, a man—possibly a powwaw—interrupted their meal, announcing that he had already dreamed of their arrival years before. As he told it, during the "great sickness" about two years before the English arrived (thus 1618), he had fallen into a restless sleep. He thought "he saw a great many men come to those parts in cloths, just as the English now are appareled, and among them there arose up a man all in black, with a thing in his hand which he now sees was all one English mans book." This "black man" stood "upon a higher place than all the rest," (reminiscent of a preacher's pulpit). The men in clothes stood on one side, and the Indians on the other. The man told the Indians "that God was *moosquantum* or angry with them, and that he would kill them for their sinnes." But at this moment the dreamer leaped to his feet and asked, "What God will do with him[self] and his Squaw and Papooses[?]" He asked two times, but did not get an answer. After the third query, the black man turned to him "and then he smil'd upon him, and told him that he and his Papooses should be safe, and that God would give unto them Mitchen, [that is,] victuals and other good things."[18] As Shepard noted, "this dream made us think [that] surely this Indian will regard the black man [Eliot] now come among them rather then [as greater than] any others of them."[19] But, to the surprise of the Englishmen, "whether Satan, or fear, and guilt, or [the] world prevailed, we can not say, but this is certaine, that he withdrew from the Sermon, and although hee came [back] at the latter end of it, as hoping it had been done, yet we could not perswade him then to stay and hear, but away he flung, and we saw him no more till next day."[20]

By the time of this incident, Indians in the region had had decades of contact with Europeans, but only about a generation of direct experience with European settler colonies, and formal missionary efforts had just begun.[21] The first sustained colonial settlements had been established in the early decades of the seventeenth century with the French in Acadia (Nova Scotia) and the English, first in Maine, and then in what is now coastal Massachusetts. To the north, the impact of settlement initially appeared to be relatively slight; French missionaries sought to learn about Native systems of belief so as to best advance the cause of Christian conversion. In the process, they created some of the richest records of Algonquian beliefs, including dream belief. But since

French fur trading relied upon keeping indigenous hunters in the forest and developing enough collaboration to encourage the trade, the overall impact of the French on Native societies was less than elsewhere in the region.

The English experimented with fur trade entrepôts as well, opening trade centers along the Maine coast. But these were intended as adjuncts to the major thrust of English activity, which was the creation of so-called settler colonies, where English men and women might sustain themselves with agriculture and the production of marketable commodities with which to repay colonial investors. Beginning with Plymouth Colony in 1620 and rapidly expanding with the founding of other English colonies, including Massachusetts Bay in 1629 and Connecticut shortly thereafter, Native American society, particularly in southern New England, came under intense pressure in the decades from the first virgin soil epidemics of the 1610s to the convulsion of King Philip's (Metacom's) War in 1675 and 1676. Following on the first colonial war (with the Pequots) in the 1630s, the English began a more serious missionary campaign in the regions to the north, south and west of Boston.[22]

In response to English preaching, many Indian listeners reaffirmed the power and authority of indigenous systems of knowledge, albeit couched with somewhat more circumspection than in the foregoing story. Many Natives claimed that their forefathers had long known of God, even expressing this knowledge in the familiar and pregnant metaphors of sleeping sinners in need of true "awakenings." One "aged Indian" told the English " 'that these very things which Mr. Eliot taught them as the Commandements of god . . . they had heard [from] some old men who were now dead."[23] The same was confirmed by another "godly and able Christian who hath much converse with them; . . . *viz*. 'That their forefathers did know God, but that after this, they fell into a great sleep, and when they did awaken they quite forgot him,['] (for under such metaphoricall language they usually express what eminent things they meane)."[24]

While it came as a shock to Reverend Eliot and the others, it is not a surprise that such dream reports were used somewhat tactically as a means to gain advantage in the colonial encounter between two very different types of sacred specialists, ministers and *powwaws* (shamans). Nor should it be a surprise that such stories quickly formed a genre of their own. The Mi'kmaq told Catholic missionaries similar tales. As described by Chrestien Le Clercq, these "Gaspesians" reported a dream that had revealed the symbol of the cross. During a period of "a very dangerous and deadly malady" (perhaps a contact-era virgin soil epidemic), "certain old men . . . whom they considered the best, the wisest, and the most influential, fell asleep, all overwhelmed with weariness and despair at seeing a desolation so general."[25] That these men may well have set out on a vision quest is revealed later in the document, when Le Clercq notes that, after the dream occurred, "consequently these good old men returned to the wigwams whence they had set out the previous day."[26] "It was, say they, in this sleep filled with bitterness that a man, beautiful as could be, appeared to them with a Cross in his hand. He told them to take heart, to go back to their homes, to make Crosses like that which were shown them, and to present these to the heads of families with the assurance that if they would receive the Crosses with respect they would find these without question the remedy for all their ills."[27] Le Clercq explained that after this dream revelation, the Indians met and "all together resolved, by common consent, that all would receive with honour the sacred sign of the Cross, which was presented to them from heaven for making an end of their misery and a beginning of their happiness."[28] In their telling, the decision to wear the sign of a cross did, indeed, end the epidemic.

Working within the frame of European beliefs about dreams, Le Clercq considered the story as a potentially providential vision, perhaps a sign from God about the preparation of these Indians for conversion to Christianity. Nevertheless, he expressed skepticism about the wisdom of trusting in messages revealed through dreams, cautioning at the outset of his story, "I do not know what judgment you will pass upon the manner in which our Indians say they have received the Cross, according to the tradition of their ancestors."[29] Elsewhere, he reserved especially harsh words for what he saw as a gullible Native reliance on the dream: "Dreams take the place of prophecy, inspiration, laws, commandment, and govern their enterprises in war and peace, in trade, fishing, and hunting. It is, indeed, a kind of oracle."[30] Le Clercq argued that the Gaspesians, "believing that it is a universal spirit that commands them, so far even that if it orders them to kill a man or commit any other bad action they execute it at once."[31] Of the vision of the cross in particular, he noted, "As the Indians believe in dreams, even to the extent of superstition, they did not neglect this one in their extreme need."[32]

Another reading of this same material suggests a different message altogether: the Natives were careful to distinguish their adoption of the cross from an acceptance of Christian teachings. The cross functions in a totemic manner—as a talisman or a badge linking them to the received vision. Since this vision occurred before European contact, the underlying message of the story for the

Natives may have been to reaffirm the efficacy of their own practices of vision questing. If the European colonists believed that dreams must be treated with caution, Natives, in contrast, actively sought powerful or helpful dreams. In this process, they reasserted the power of their "old men" to dream dreams. This legend affirmed with renewed vigor the power of dreaming and dream interpretation as an activity with considerable community support and credibility.[33]

Early interactions with Europeans also reveal the ways in which Natives kept dreamt knowledge at the center of intercultural discussion, and how their insistence on dreams may even have sometimes impacted individual Europeans, perhaps even altering their own dreams. In a 1613 account of his interactions with the Montagnais, Samuel de Champlain, the founder of Quebec, noted that the Montagnais he encountered in 1608 lived in "such constant dread of their enemies, that they often took fright at night in their dreams, and would send their wives and children to our fort."[34] Champlain sent out extra sentries and admonished the Indians "that they should not take dreams as truth upon which to rely, since most of them are only fables," but to little effect.[35] In the campaign against the Iroquois the next year, the Montagnais and their allies tried to enlist Champlain's own manitou in their struggle: relying upon shamanic divination each day as they got closer to their enemies' homeland, he reported that the Indians "often would come and ask me whether I had had dreams and had seen their enemies."[36] Each day Champlain told them no, until one day, Champlain reported: "I went to take a rest [after securing the camp] and while asleep I dreamed that I saw in the lake near a mountain our enemies, the Iroquois, drowning before our eyes. I wanted to succour them, but our Indian allies said to me that we should let them all perish; for they were bad men. When I awoke they did not fail to ask me as usual whether I had dreamed anything. I told them what I had seen in my dream. This gave them such confidence that they no longer had any doubt as to the good fortune awaiting them."[37] Despite earlier protestations that the Montagnais ought not to believe all their dreams, it is possible that Champlain himself was reassured by this predictive dream, a dream that, happily for them, preceded a decisive victory against the Iroquois. At the least, this recollection reveals how Native allies often succeeded in moving reported dreams to the center of colonial interactions.[38]

*    *    *

How did European accounts present Algonquian dreams? How might we describe the dream beliefs and practices New England Algonquians espoused, and how have ethnographers described the larger indigenous cosmology in which dream practice was embedded?

Crucial information was recorded by the English missionaries of the 1650s, who wrote down the questions posed by Indian listeners, questions that reveal a struggle over belief systems. Indians wrestled with Christian teachings that asked them to renounce deeply embedded practices of visioning and trance possession. As they struggled to accommodate these new approaches, they asked missionaries about European theories of dreaming and whether they should "believe in" their dreams. Their questions were posed in a spoken English arrived at through fairly complex processes of translation. It should be no surprise, then, that the "Indian" questions perhaps tell us more about the European missionaries than they do about indigenous societies. Indeed, the questions mirrored the very points that were at issue in Reformation Europe, as the faithful struggled over whether or not to "credit" dreams "in these latter days."

Indian converts asked things like, "In wicked dreames doth the soule sin?"[39] And, "doth God make bad men dream good Dreames?"[40] One minister noted the importance of this type of questioning, especially "those that concern the evill of thoughts and dreames, &c.," both as being "of great and weighty concernment," and "such as indeed evince a more then common working of the spirit [in them] by the word."[41] Of course, it is unfortunate for historians that the missionary authors did not write down how they answered these questions.

Despite their limitations, these queries, when combined with ethnolinguistic evidence teased from period writings in the Massachusett language, lead us into New England Algonquian cosmology. Ethnographers assert that New England Algonquians conceptualized the self as containing a "dream soul" that traveled outside the sleeping body during dreams. Whether this was a "thing-like" soul, or simply a state of consciousness, is hard to tell at this remove as English concepts permeate the early descriptions of Native cultures.[42] As Roger Williams noted of the Narragansett, the word "*Cowwéwonck*," which he translated as "The Soule," derived from "*Cowwene* to sleep, because, say they, it workes and operates when the body sleepes."[43] Thus, potential Indian converts wondered, "Seeing [that] we see not God with our eyes, if a man dream that he seeth God, doth his soule then see him?"[44]

The "dual soul" has been identified as a common concept across

Algonquian-speaking communities. Bragdon summarizes: "The dream soul, or *Cowwéwonck*, which traveled in dreams and left the body during illness, was said to roam at night, appearing as a light, while the body slept. The other, *Míchachunck*, or the 'clear' soul, thought to be located in the heart, was the animating force of every individual."[45] The dream soul and its quest for contact with spiritually powerful others could secure aid and protection that the waking person might invoke at times of need: "As the dream soul sought enlightenment, guardian spirits were entreated for their aid in all manner of human enterprises, and the stronger one's spirit helper(s), the greater one's well-being."[46] Indeed, when a young man named Penowanyanquis was murdered with a rapier thrust, Roger Williams, who sat beside him as he died, reported that he frequently invoked a spirit helper in the throes of his suffering: the man "call'd much upon *Muckquachuckquand* [the Children's God], which of other Natives I understood (as they believed) had appeared to the dying young man, many yeares before, and bid him when ever he was in distresse [to] call upon him."[47]

The dream soul could interact with dream souls of other persons as well as with the spirits of other-than-human beings in the spirit world. Like other Eastern Woodland peoples, the Native New England peoples divided the cosmos into three parts, "the sky, or upper world, the earth, or middle world, and the under(water) domains."[48] As Bragdon notes, "The thresholds of the three realms were regularly crossed by humans in dream-soul form, powwaws in nonhuman form, the souls of the dead, and beings-other-than-human seeking entry into the (real) social world. . . . The boundaries between the world of humans and beings other than human were fluid, just as the boundaries between physical states were illusory."[49]

New England Natives courted visions in a variety of settings, most formally in puberty rituals, but also throughout life. Many sorts of creatures or things served as "manifestations of Manitou, the impersonal force that permeated the world, observable in anything marvelous, beautiful, or dangerous." Native dreamers encountered manitous or found spirit guides "through vision quests, the seeking out of sacred spaces, dreams, and induced trance, and through soul travel, accomplished while asleep."[50] Sometimes—as with the sachem's dream that opened the chapter—the things expressed in dreams demanded expression in waking life, in order to channel these powerful forces away from harmful outcomes.[51] Roger Williams listed "*Ntunnaquomen*" as "I have had a good dream" and "*Nummattaquomen*" as "I have had a bad dream," and notes:

"When they have a bad Dreame, which they conceive to be a threatning from God, they fall to prayer at all times of the night, especially early before day,"[52] a practice which, drawing on the many examples found in the psalms, suggested to him a great capacity for piety.

Early students of Algonquian religious systems were careful to distinguish dreaming from the shamanic trances of religious specialists, even though the two were often linked. As with the young Mi'kmaq girl who saw the floating island, it was possible for ordinary people to dream a powerful or useful dream. It is likely that there were particular conditions governing which dreams were seen as significant. Such culturally agreed norms may have also governed which dreams ought to be shared with the wider community and by what means that sharing occurred.[53] An individual might gain authority or even renown for his or her powerful dreaming. For example, the Penobscot distinguished the dreamer's power from other types of spiritual authority.[54]

Both the historical record and later evidence from ethnography, folklore, and oral tradition suggest that there were at least two distinct types of spiritual specialists in Native New England societies. One type specialized in herbal medicines, which required the mastery of a vast body of traditional wisdom about the conditions and appropriate ritual manner in which one gathered and used these medications.[55] A second type, the powwaws, were powerful figures in their own right, both respected and feared, specialists in crossing thresholds into otherworldly realms where they would effect cures and (it is thought) send misfortune to their enemies. The powwaw was a liminal figure who had special abilities that gave him (or her) access to great power, but could do so in socially constructive or destructive ways. The powwaw could use that power, which was at once both potentially helpful and harmful, to effect either great good or great ill. Bragdon suggests multiple spiritual specialists based on her review of primary sources both in English and in New England Algonquian languages: "In spite of the tendency in the literature . . . to refer to all religious practitioners as members of a homogeneous category, there appear to have been distinctions in their function and status. Roger Williams recorded several terms for religious practitioners, including *powwaw*, 'their priest,' *maunêtu*, 'a conjurer,' *nanouwétea*, 'an over-seer and orderer of their worship,' and the *mockuttásuit*, 'who winds up and buries the dead.'"[56] The Narragansett of southern New England made a distinction between "overseers of worship" and "a learned body of ritual leaders, whose roles complemented one another."[57]

Many ethnographers note that the visions experienced by powwaws had an extraordinary power, separating them from those of "ordinary visions seekers." Bragdon notes, "the extreme power of their visions and the fact that their Manitou was unsought."[58] Speck observes that among his early twentieth-century Penobscot informants, the shaman's power was described as both innate and unsought: "No one professes to know just how any shaman first obtained his power or even how he operated it. In the minds of the most of these Indians, I think, the shaman is thought to have acquired power involuntarily, presumably to have been born with it or to have had it grow on him."[59] Key links connected shamans to special sources of power—such that powwaws often bore the same names as the manitou with which they were associated. "Transformation, and human/animal metamorphoses" were central to the sorts of spiritual practices engaged by New England Algonquians.[60] Perhaps such metamorphoses "occurred during sleep or trance when the dream soul left the body."[61] Writing at the end of the nineteenth century, Joseph Nicolar (Penobscot) described spiritual specialists: "In the daytime, they examined the land and water, nights they arose in the air."[62] As Bragdon explains from her reading of the records, "Encounters with and instruction from tutelary spirits . . . occurred when soul flight took place." To achieve such transformation, shamans may have engaged in "trance, vision, dreams and the use of hallucinatory drugs such as tobacco."[63]

A s Europeans learned about manitou, powwaws, and dream beliefs, they inquired further about Native American cosmology. It would be a short and fateful step from inquiry into Native American beliefs to condemnation of those beliefs, mainly because European listeners immediately attempted to assimilate Native belief into the more familiar concepts of their own culture. To them, Natives appeared to be living under Satan's power. The dreams that Natives experienced thus seemed to be diabolical, when not predictive wonders. Because they actively sought out dream experience, Native peoples appeared to Europeans to be at best tempting fate, and at worst to be already in collusion with Satan. As Champlain noted in his account of the Montagnais, the Indians "believe that all their dreams are true, and indeed there are many of them who say they have had visions and dreamed things which came to pass, or will come to pass."[64] But Champlain quickly dismissed these as "brutish beliefs"; "to tell the truth about these things, they are visions from the devil who deceives them and leads them astray."[65]

Europeans found support for their view of diabolical intervention in their understanding of the structure of the Algonquian cosmos, which they thought mirrored familiar European concepts. A pair of powerful antagonists was reported to dominate the Native cosmology. By the early seventeenth century, "these powerful antagonists of the upper and under(water) world" (the Thunderbird of the upper or sky world, and the underwater serpent of the lower or water world) "were . . . symbolically linked to, an analogous pair of other-than-human beings: Cautantowwit (or Kiehtan) and Abbomocho (or Hobbamok)."[66] In southern New England Cautantowwit was associated with sending the first kernels of corn to the people and was also described as a creator as well as the overseer of the home of the dead. Hobbamok was associated with "death, night, the northeast wind, the dark, and the color black," and was linked to the underworld. He appeared in several forms, "but most often as an eel or a snake,"[67] and is frequently referred to by powwaws and former powwaws. For Europeans, it seemed obvious that these were representations of God the father and his antagonist, Satan. In his 1634 account, William Wood noted the Indians had two main "gods," Kiehtan, a force for good, and Hobbamock, which "as far as we can conceive, is the devil."[68]

But Europeans had it wrong. Contact-period Algonquians espoused an animist belief commonly found among small-scale hunting and agrarian cultures. Manitous (other-than-human powers) inhabited the everyday landscape and had multiple forms. Roger Williams noted that "they branch their Godhead into many Gods" and that "they attribute it [God] to Creatures."[69] In fact, Williams counted at least thirty-seven distinct "gods," "all which in their solemne Worships they invocate," and that, "there is a generall Custome amongst them, at the apprehension of any Excellency in Men, Women, Birds, Beasts, Fish, &c. to cry out Manittóo, that is, [']it is a God[']."[70] Thus, when Hiacoomes, the first Christian Indian convert on Martha's Vineyard, was invited to speak about Christianity before the sachem and some of the principal men of the east end of the island in the year 1646, he was queried closely by one of them, Miohqsoo, as to "How many Gods the English worshipped?" Answering, "ONE, and no more," Miohqsoo "reckoned up about 37 principal Gods which he had," and asked, "Shall I . . . throw away all these 37 for the sake of one only?"[71]

Scholars point out the great differences between European and Indian cosmological approaches. Folklorist William S. Simmons notes, "Typically the English glossed over native concepts, such as *powwows* (or shamans) and

guardian spirits, as if they were identical with English witches and devils . . .
[and] assumed that Indian *powwows* were witches and that Indian culture suffered from a kind of diabolical enchantment."[72] As Bragdon writes, "English
settlers, and especially missionaries, seized quickly on this pairing [of Cautantowwit and Hobbamok] as evidence of rudimentary recognition of the duality
of good and evil."[73] But there was only a partial similarity at best. The English
(and all Christians, Catholic and Protestant) bifurcated the invisible world into
the divine and the diabolical, the first part inspired by God the father and the
second , ruled by Satan. Such a clear division into "good" and "evil" is radically
different from what seems to have been an Algonquian acceptance of the ambivalent nature of all spiritual power. Of course, if not channeled with appropriate care, power that was potentially good could quickly cause great evil. This
care is evident in the many cultural proscriptions about how best to approach
and interact with various forms, manifestations, and locations of great manitou. Manitou could even reside within the ordinary body. Thus Roger Williams
remarked, "They conceive that there are many Gods or divine Powers within
the body of a man: In his pulse, his heart, his Lungs, &c."[74] The dual nature of
spiritual power was manifest in the caution with which people approached
powwaws, who could effect great cures, but might also cause great harm with
their "sorcery." As Bragdon puts it, "Cautantowwit's distant benignity was less
significant than the more local and powerful, if more ambivalent forces of good
and evil embodied in Abbomocho."[75]

In the attempt to recuperate Native American beliefs from European prejudice, it is easy to miss the ways that European and Native American beliefs
could and sometimes did overlap. As noted by historian James P. Ronda, the
encounter between the Jesuit Paul Le Jeune and the Montagnais (Algonquian)
holy man Carigonan revealed that the two "shared more than they realized.
Each embraced a religious system that emphasized the supernatural and its
interaction with man. The Jesuit believed that human beings could be affected
for good or ill by the actions of spirits and demons; Carigonan acknowledged
the existence of equally influential beings called *khichikouai*. Both . . . accepted
the dichotomy of soul and body as well."[76] The chief disagreements occurred
regarding "the realm of religious practice—the manipulation of the sacred." As
Ronda notes, "Le Jeune did not claim to have any personal supernatural powers, but Carigonan claimed direct communication with and control over supernatural forces. He believed himself capable of healing the sick, insuring good
hunts, and killing distant enemies. He told Le Jeune that his soul could leave

his body at will. Claims such as these reinforced Le Jeune's conviction that Carigonan was indeed a sorcerer and a formidable enemy of the faith."[77]

Just as with the Montagnais to the north, there were some rough analogies between the New England Algonquian and English ways of looking at the world. Indeed, it was these analogies that abetted English misperceptions of Native belief systems. But to see the full effect of these, we must first turn the analogy completely around. In the case of witchcraft, for example, the English perhaps had something akin to a "dual soul" category in their cosmology. If we accept the real power of the invisible world for the English, we can recognize that they had their own concept of a spiritual specialist (the witch) who regularly entered a realm of dangerous power and who, while there, interacted with many individuals from the quotidian world. As we shall see (Chapter 5), in many witchcraft cases, "specters" appeared, both to those "afflicted" by witches and to drowsy neighbors late at night, who were sure they saw the "shape" of a neighbor woman in the bedchamber, even though it was well past dark and all the doors and shutters were bolted tightly. These specters interacted with the shapes of others, as well as with living, embodied individuals, and sometimes both the embodied person and his or her specter were present in the same moment, as when afflicted girls at the Salem trials complained of being tormented by the shape of a witch even as she stood quietly at the bar.

It was a short but understandable step from these witch beliefs to the assertion that Native powwaws were "simply" witches by another name. Indeed, Roger Williams was so convinced of the involvement of Satan that he relied only on hearsay for his descriptions of powwowing: "For after once being in their Houses and beholding what their Worship was, I durst never bee an eye witnesse, Spectatour, or looker on, least I should have been partaker of Sathans Inventions and Worships, contrary to *Ephes.* 5.11" (which offers a prohibition against "fellowship with the unfruiteful workes of darkenes").[78] William Wood expressed similar caution, noting of his description of Passaconaway, a powerful sachem and powwaw, "This I write but [only] on the report of the Indians, who constantly affirm stranger things."[79] John Eliot listened to the testimony of two converts who renounced powwowing. They said that "the principall imployment is to cure the sick by certaine odd gestures and beatings of themselves, and then they pull out the sicknesse by applying their hands to the sick person and so blow it away."[80] But Eliot's comment on this was "so that their Pawwows are great witches having fellowship with the old Serpent, to whom they pray."[81] Daniel Gookin complained, "These powwows are reputed, and I conceive justly, to hold familiarity with the devil. . . . Satan doth strongly endeavour to keep up this practice among the Indians: and these powwows are . . . great hinderers of the Indians embracing the gospel."[82]

The English took the invisible world seriously, and therefore they could not simply dismiss the power of dreaming unequivocally. Indeed, it was because they took dreaming seriously that they condemned both the Indians' embrace of dream experience and the work of Native powwaws. For the English, the dream itself was a tricky entity that could carry divine or diabolical intent, that could be meaningful or utterly meaningless, and that therefore should not be actively sought. The English could not describe the work of powwaws outside of these powerful—and distorting—European frames. Cultural prejudice, abetted by difficulties with the language, invariably shaped their view. Shamans and powwowing were also often identified as the chief obstacles to Christian conversion.[83] Clearly, our evidence about powwowing (almost all of which comes from the pens of English observers) is thus tremendously skewed. But it is also indisputable that individuals in both societies believed that the powwaw was dealing in real power with potentially serious or even life-threatening consequences.

A long with the condemnation of powwawing as diabolical came a parallel condemnation of the dream practices that had long been central to the work of medicine men and women. Indeed, dreams sat at the center of a powwaw's power. Having a significant dream vision was an essential step to becoming a spiritual practitioner, and this fact was confirmed in a conversion narrative. In renouncing powwowing, two young Christian Indians reported, "if any of the Indians fall into any strange dreame wherein Chepian ["the devil"] appears unto them as a serpent, then the next day they tell the other Indians of it."[84] The quote continues: "[and for] two dayes after the rest of the Indians dance and rejoyce for what they tell them about this Serpent, and so they become their Pawwaws."[85]

In addition, great duels that sometimes emerged between powwaws were carried out as contests between their dream souls. As Speck argued, the New England shaman was indeed "a wonder worker whose magic power was derived from the spiritual and animal world. His chief activity was to overcome rivals and demonstrate wherever he could the superiority of his own strength." He had the ability to cause "sickness or misfortune, of removing the same, and [to contest] his power with that of rivals, while occasionally we learn of more altruistic services rendered in warfare and in ridding the world of monsters."[86] As Speck's contacts reported, supernatural dueling between spiritual specialists had often been common, even in living memory.

Dream soul capture was an essential weapon in the shaman's arsenal. Simmons concludes that the powwaw conducted his attacks on enemies or rivals by employing both "magical intrusion" (the implantation of a physical object by the spirit helper in the intended victim's body) and dream soul capture (in which the shaman captured the victim's dream soul and kept it " 'in this Form of a Fly, closely imprisoned; and according as they dealt with this, so it Fared with the Body it belonged to.' "[87] Speck also recorded many instances where a person "encountered in dreams the spirit helper (*baohi•'-gan*) of malevolent persons," and in some of these cases, the dreamer inflicted injuries on this spirit helper that, on awakening, affected that person in the ordinary social world as well.[88]

English observers described the powwaws' trancelike states, akin to waking dreams using animalistic imagery. Roger Williams reported that powwaws would join with the people, "in a laborious bodily service, unto sweating, especially of the Priest, who spends himself in strange Antick Gestures, and Actions even unto fainting."[89] Daniel Gookin noted, "by their diabolicall spells, mutterings, exorcisms, they seem to do wonders. They use extraordinary strange motions of their bodies, insomuch that they will sweat until they foam; and thus continue for some hours together, stroking and hovering over the sick."[90] William Wood reported that the powwaw uses "the violent expression of many a hideous bellowing and groaning," and then "proceeds in his invocations, sometimes roaring like a bear, other times groaning like a dying horse, foaming at the mouth like a chased boar, smiting on his naked breast and thighs with such violence as if he were mad. Thus will he continue sometimes half a day, spending his lungs, sweating out his fat, and tormenting his body in diabolical worship. Sometimes the Devil for requital of their worship recovers the [sick] party, to nuzzle them up in their devilish religion."[91]

In addition to the individual powwaw's actions while conducting a cure, some powwaws carried on divination through "trance mediumship" in larger community rituals, especially around the conduct of King Philip's War.[92] Simmons summarized several reported divination rituals: "a male . . . enters a trance, the trance state being associated with insensitivity to fire; the person in the trance communicates with otherwise inaccessible spirit powers and then regains consciousness to report on the experience. ... this ritual may have caused the temporary absence of the dream soul, which left the body forever at death."[93]

Specialists also obtained *pawwanomas* (guardian spirits—the English called them "imps") through dreams or visions received during a vision quest. Missionary Thomas Mayhew reported that on Martha's Vineyard, these sometimes had "residence" in the powwaw's body.[94] As Bragdon notes, "in some cases, a remarkable fusion of guardian spirits and dream soul resulted in a being known as a 'guardian soul.' Sometimes shamans identified so strongly with these guardian souls that they became their alter-egos."[95] Tequanonim, a powwaw on Martha's Vineyard who converted in the 1640s, testified that "he had been possessed from the crown of the head to the soals of the foot with Pawwawnomas, not only in the shape of living Creatures, as Fowls, Fishes and creeping things, but Brasse, Iron, and Stone."[96] These "helpers" were integral to curing. Winslow's account also described this, as in his discussion of Hobbamok: "This Hobbamock appears in sundry forms unto them, as in the shape of a man, a deer, a fawn, an eagle, &c. but most ordinarily a snake. He appears not to all, but [to] the chiefest and most judicious amongst them; though all of them strive to attain to that hellish height of honor."[97]

The *pawwanomas* made it especially dangerous to give up powwowing. In 1651, a Martha's Vineyard shaman confessed his sin before Thomas Mayhew and renounced his powwowing. The shaman did

> discover the bottome of his witchcraft, confessing that at first he came to be a Pawwaw by Diabolicall Dreams, wherein he saw the Devill in the likenesse of four living Creatures; one was like a man which he saw in the Aire, and this told him that he did know all things upon the Island, and what was to be done; and this he said had its residence over his whole body. Another was like a crow, and did look out sharply to discover mischiefs coming towards him, and had its residence in his head. The third was like to a Pidgeon, and had its place in his breast, and was very cunning about any businesse. The fourth was like a Serpent, very subtile to do mischief, and also to do great cures, and these he said were meere Devils [the English might have understood them as animal familiars], and such as he had trusted to for safetie, and did labour to raise up for the accomplishment of

any thing in his diabolicall craft, but now he saith, that he did desire that the Lord would free him from them, and that he did repent in his heart, because of his sinne.[98]

Former powwaws who had converted complained that their pawwanomas frequently troubled them, physically and psychically, after being renounced. One converted powwaw from Martha's Vineyard testified that since his conversion, "for seven Years, the said Snake [his pawwanomas] gave him great Disturbance, but that he never after his praying to God in Christ, employed that said Snake in any thing, about which time the said Snake ceased to appear to him."[99] As Frank Speck reported of the supernatural events discussed in several Penobscot stories, those powwaws who renounced their powers could experience "great physical disturbance and even danger of death," and one informant remembered that when a powwaw converted to Christianity and gave up his powers, "it cost him such pangs that he shook and trembled all over and nearly died before his power left him."[100]

Both powwowing, with its workings in the realm of dream souls, and the active pursuit of dreams and visions by ordinary men and women came under sustained attack from missionaries and other English observers. While there may have been common ground in beliefs that dreams could contain spiritually powerful messages, these similarities melted away in the horror with which English observers detailed the "diabolical conjuring" of the powwaws.

Thus, the English missionaries began to encourage changes that would attempt to strike at the very heart of Native practices, including the use of dreams and trance states. One of the first laws made among the praying Indians at Concord in 1646 ordered, "That there shall be no more Pawwowing amongst the Indians, and if any shall hereafter Pawwow, both he that shall Powwow & he that shall procure him to Powwaw, shall pay 20 s. apiece."[101] In 1647, the missionary John Eliot bragged that the praying Indians "have utterly forsaken all their Powwaws, and given over that diabolicall exercise, being convinced that it is quite contrary to praying until God," and he noted that "sundry of their Powwaws have renounced their wicked imployment, have condemned it as evill, and resolved never to use it any more."[102]

Eliot observed that some spiritual specialists, "seeing their imployment and gaines were utterly gone [from] here, have fled to other places, where they are still entertained, and have raised lies, slanders, and an evill report upon those that heare the Word."[103] Perhaps here Eliot referred to Passaconaway, an Indian sachem at Merrimack River, who refused to receive Eliot when he visited. Instead, "together with both his sons, [he] fled the presence of the light, and durst not stand their ground, not be at home when he [Eliot] came [to preach], pretending feare of being killed by a man forsooth that came only with a book in his hand."[104] Others reportedly attempted to disrupt the progress of conversion. When Hiacoomes, a man of "mean" descent and not much regarded by the Indians, began to attend the English church meeting as well as to receive religious instruction from Thomas Mayhew, "the News of it coming to the Sachims, and Pawwaws of the Island, they were [still] . . . much alarmed at it: and some of them endeavoured with all their Might, to discourage him from holding Communication with the English, and from receiving an Instructions from them." But all their efforts prove to be in vain, as Hiacoomes, "having now had a Taste of that Knowledge of God and Christ which is Life eternal," refused to step away from the Christian path.[105]

Powwaws themselves struggled to maintain the advantage over the English, although these newcomers were endowed with considerable manitou and possessed of a special relationship to the Christian God, who was regarded as a powerful manitou in his own right. Matthew Mayhew tells the story of Martha's Vineyard powwaws who were sought out by a woman from the mainland who had not been cured by local shamans. When one powwaw caught a "troublesome spirit" in a deerskin, it was determined that this spirit had belonged to "'an Englishman drowned in the Adjacent Sound.'" The powwaw who had effected the cure "warned her that 'unless she removed to Martha's Vineyard, she would again be Sick, for being an English Spirit he could not long confine it.'"[106] Roger Williams, himself likely regarded as something of a wonder-worker by the Native people who interacted with him, was credited with interrupting the shamans' powers in a story, probably from the 1660s, in which "two of their witches weere assured by the Devill [that] they had noe power" to harm the "Sagemores sonne whome Mr. Williams educated" for "as long as hee was in [Williams's] custodie."[107] Of course, the effects of virgin soil epidemics, rampant in areas of first contact like Martha's Vineyard, might also have explained the new inefficacy of the powwaw's arts.

Powwaws often figured prominently in missionary stories as antagonists to Christians. One gets a repeated sense of contest—Eliot vs. Passaconaway, the powwaws vs. Hiacoomes, and so forth—which, as Simmons explains, fits in both with puritan notions of contesting with the Devil and with indigenous practices of contests, rivalries, or duels between powwaws.[108] The rejection of powwowing was a prominent motif in stories of individual conversion and in accounts of the building of the Indian "praying towns." Still, despite their triumphal tone, these stories give us a sense of the magnitude of the missionaries' errand. When believers were not caught in fear of reprisals from angry powwaws, they struggled against the difficult task of giving up their sources of curing and help just at a moment of tremendous upheaval, including terrible epidemics and other crises. Such practices were deeply woven into the indigenous cosmology. To give them up was to alter one's basic sense of how the universe worked, the place of human beings within it, and a crucial sense of efficacy in enlisting the manitous to one's aid. As Gookin noted on the eve of King Philip's War, this left potential converts in a quandary about how to heal the sick without powwowing, which was an especially pressing question in the context of virgin soil epidemics. As he wrote, "It is no small discouragement unto the Indians in yielding obedience unto the gospel, for then, say they, if we once pray to God, we must abandon our powwows; and then, when we are sick and wounded, who shall heal our maladies?"[109]

Christian converts had to risk the loss of one form of supernatural help in order to gain another. One story about the renunciation of powwowing following a powerful spiritual communication has echoes of the English tradition that a new mother might have visions about her child, as well as of the Native tradition of dreams that foretold the coming of Christianity. As Experience Mayhew explains, "A few years before the English first settled on . . . [Martha's] Vineyard," a woman named Wuttununohkomkooh had a son.[110] Having "buried [her] first five Children successively, every one of them within ten Days of their Birth, notwithstanding all their Use of the Pawwaws and Medicines to preserve them," the mother was "then greatly distressed with fear that she should lose this Child as she had done the former."[111] Overcome with a sense that the earlier interventions of powwaws and medicines would be useless, "she with a sorrowful Heart took him up and went out into the Field, that she might there weep out her Sorrow." As she sat, "Musing on the Insufficiency of human Help, she found it powerfully suggested to her Mind, that there is one Almighty God who is to be prayed to; that this God hath created all things that we see; and that the God who had given her Child to her, was able to preserve and continue his Life."[112] The child eventually grew up to become an important Christian minister. But as soon as his mother heard of the first English

Christians, who settled in 1642 at the east end of the island, she "alledged that they were Worshippers of the same God to whom she had prayed."[113] The story contrasts the inefficacy of the powwaw with the power of the Christian God, even as it dramatized once again the occurrence of miraculous prediction in forecasting the coming of Christian teachings. It was a wonder tale that could be accepted by English and Indian Christians alike as authorizing the rejection of traditional practices; and it underscores the ways that renunciation of the powwaw—with his dreams and his ambivalent power—took a prominent place in narratives of conversion.

D reaming opened the door to other worlds. Dreams could foretell European arrival; they provided access to spiritual power, both for ordinary folk and for spiritual specialists; one might even hope to injure enemies or to remove hurts by actions in dreams. It is also true that fears about shamanism, which was closely linked to Native dream belief, led English colonists to try to stamp out indigenous dream practices. While the English protested that dreams had no meaning, they were apparently not entirely sure. It was the Natives' use of "diabolical dreams" that led English ministers to insist that Indian converts to Christianity renounce centuries-old dream beliefs. In this way, English encounters with Natives ultimately led to colonialist attempts to eradicate these traditional practices.

As in many other parts of North America, New England's Native peoples would eventually mobilize resistance against colonialism with the help of reported dreams; resistance movements were often inspired by a visionary dreamer.[114] Later evidence is convincing on this point. But one early event—an attack on Plymouth Colony forces—appears as well to have been inspired by a dream. This report must be treated with extreme caution, however, since it comes from the famously fanciful book, *New English Canaan*, written by Thomas Morton. To say that Morton had an axe to grind against the Plymouth colonists can only be an understatement. Though the report certainly bears the marks of Morton's flowery prose and may indeed be entirely fabricated, the details of the conflict are borne out in sources friendlier to Plymouth, including Edward Winslow's *Good News from New England* (1624). Since some of the Wessagusset colonists had very intimate relationships with the Native peoples, it is conceivable that he had this story from an indigenous witness and simply embellished and Europeanized the tale.[115]

As Morton's story goes, the Plymouth colonists opened some graves at "Pasonayessit" and took away a "herse Cloath," made of "two greate Beares skinnes sowed together at full lenth," that had been "propped up over the grave" of the mother of the sachem Chuatawback (most likely a corruption of Chickataubut).[116] In a dream, which he recounted to his countrymen, his mother's ghost appeared to the sachem, and demanded that he avenge this desecration: "Before mine eies were fast closed, mee thought I saw a vision, (at which my) spirit was much troubled & trembling at that dolefull sight." When his mother's ghost appeared, "[She] cried aloude [']behold my sonne whom I have cherisht, see the papps that gave thee suck, the hands that lappd thee warme and fed thee oft, canst thou forget to take revenge of those uild [wild] people, that hath my monument defaced in despitefull manner, disdaining our ancient antiquities, and honourable Customes[?]: See now the Sachems grave lies like unto the common people, of ignoble race defaced: thy mother doth complaine, implores thy aide against this thievish people new [newly] come hether[;] if this be suffered, I shall not rest in quiet within my everlasting habitation.[']"[117] The sachem continued, "This said, the spirit vanished, and I[,] all in a sweat, not able scarce to speake, began to gett some strength, and recollect my spirits that were ded, all which I thought to let you understand, to have our Councell, and your aide likewise."[118] After the sachem was done speaking, "straight way arose the grand Captaine, and cried aloud [']come, let us to Armes, it doth concerne us all, let us bid them Battaile.[']"[119] The Indians went forth and met the Plymouth scouting party. Forcing them to abandon one landing spot and put to sea, the Indians met them again at another, but were, after the Indian's "Captaine" was shot in the elbow, routed, "and straight way fled, . . . and yealded up the honor of the day, to the English party, who were such a terror to them after, that the Salvages durst never make to a head against them any more."[120]

Morton's purpose in telling this story was undoubtedly to emphasize the barbarities of his rivals—the "wild" and "thievish" Plymouth men, who would desecrate a grave site—and to contrast that with the innate civility of an Indian people now doomed to defeat. At best, Morton's report represents extensive refashioning of an Indian dream report for the author's own purposes. But in fact, this dream report may well have been a complete fabrication that Morton inserted for his own purposes: none of the other early primary sources recounts a dream vision, and the story appears to conflate some real events in Plymouth's early history.[121] The vengeful spirit returning to ask the living to perform some action, the dreamer caught in sleep paralysis—these were established

European folk motifs. In murder cases, for example, a victim's ghost might appear to relatives or friends in a dream, and there is little evidence that these were also common Native motifs.[122] Whether Morton's report is a Europeanized gloss of a Native dream type or a complete fabrication wrapped in Native clothing, one should not read too much into this chancy source. The one thing that it points up is that European colonizers at least found it plausible that Indian visions might inspire violent retaliation against them, and if the evidence from the 1620s is thin, there is irrefutable evidence from later in the century that they were right.

Despite colonists' attempts—direct and indirect, conscious and unwitting—to stamp out objectionable Native dream practices, surviving sources suggest the vibrancy and longevity of Algonquian beliefs and practices around dreaming, visioning, and even indigenous curing. While open powwowing might have disappeared from the praying towns around Boston and on Martha's Vineyard, reports of continued use occur throughout the seventeenth and into the eighteenth century throughout New England.[123] The exploits of late nineteenth-century Gay Head (Martha's Vineyard) "witches" were told and retold well into the twentieth century: one witch "could transform herself into a bear at will; another took the form of a bird or a white feather when she wished to pry into the affairs of others."[124] Scholars agree that, in the words of one, "Motifs in these legends could be either Anglo-American or Indian in origin. . . . English folk belief [in witches] was friendly to the survival of such beliefs among the Indians."[125]

Practice of insightful and predictive dreaming among New England Indians was documented in the early twentieth century. As Speck reported for the northern parts of the region, dreams and the messages contained within them remained critically important. Speck's early twentieth-century Penobscot informants reported many active instances of dream soul contests: one woman dreamed that a dog came into her camp and bit her on the elbow. "When she hit the dog it fell over dead. It then presented the appearance of a certain person whom she knew. When she awoke she found that her elbow was sore and it remained so for the rest of her life. The person whose likeness she saw in the dead dog in her dream died shortly after."[126] Gladys Tantaquidgeon (Mohegan) reported that among the Mohegan of eastern Connecticut, "There is a belief that dreams are messages from their ancestors who are in the spirit world. These spiritual advisors appear in dreams to guide and instruct the dreamer."[127] Tantaquidgeon's niece Melissa Jayne Fawcett (also known as Melissa Tantaquidgeon Zobel) reports that the elder Tantaquidgeon believed "that dream messages from ancestors yield magic strong enough to revive the lifeblood of a people." Fawcett reports as well that the word "pauwau" in Algonquian languages "refers to one who dreams as well as to a medicine person, for the two are synonymous. The power to dream dreams and make them come true is central to Indian medicine."[128]

R oger Williams could not have guessed either the importance of the ritual he observed that day, long ago, on "an Iland of the wildest in our parts," or the ways in which his observations would become part of a challenge to an indigenous system of dream experience, practices, and beliefs.[129] Later, Williams would argue that the work of Indian conversion would have to wait until Christ's second coming, when he would appoint new apostles.[130] At the end of his life, Williams would explain further: "When we deal with Indians about Religion, our work is to prove unto them by Reason, that the Bible is Gods Word." While, in his view, they were "by Nature . . . much affected with a kind of Deity [manitou]," the task would be to convince them "that all their Revelations, and Visions, and Dreams (in which the Devil wonderfully abuseth them) are False and Cheating."[131]

For the modern student, the truth is not so plain. Each of these systems of dream belief—that of the English colonists (detailed in Chapter 1) and that of New England's Algonquian peoples—shaped individuals' understandings of their dream experiences. But in the encounter between them beginning with the sustained colonization of the early seventeenth century, understandings of the other would remain flawed and incomplete. After 1620, Natives and English colonists began to create a common social world, albeit unequal and segmented, and for members of both groups, dreams were things of power and importance. Despite English protestations that dreams should not be "regarded," both peoples were accustomed to some sort of public sharing of dreams and visions, albeit with different practices about the nature and purpose of reporting dreams. The English could not exclude the possibility of some divinely inspired dream messages, but they thought these rare; the occasional predictive dream was also a possibility. But in their view, Native use of divination, dream soul capture, and the active seeking of vision experience could only represent a risky flirtation with the Devil. For their part, Indians recruited English manitou and English dream belief into their own spiritual worlds, or, when converted to Christianity, purportedly renounced traditional dream practices in favor of the greater spiritual protection they believed lay in Jehovah.

Because people on both sides of the colonial divide believed in the power of something the English glossed as an "invisible world," they often sought to act in accord with the events that played out on that stage. English and Native versions of this world beyond the quotidian were quite different. But as they attempted to make sense of each other's meanings, rough equivalencies began to emerge—indeed, the English view of Native dream practices and shamanic activity began to colonize such practices, deeming them diabolical in origins, and therefore creating them as objects of reform. The invisible realm could never be completely comprehended—that was part of its nature. The English assault on Native dream practices would never be fully successful, and Native responses to colonialism would continue to be influenced by events occurring in the invisible realm of the dream soul. Processes of conversion would never be complete.

Precisely because the English never completely dismissed dreams or the knowledge derived from them, they were unable to ignore Native powwowing and divination. For both the English and the Indians, the world of dreams contained the possibility of real harm—whether through powwaws' dueling or the practice of witchcraft. There are no "pure" texts—no descriptions of Native practices separate from the pervasive influence of English dream belief. Nevertheless, we can see that as Indian dreams became firmly identified as "diabolicall," and as that view became enshrined in conversion narratives, the invisible worlds of English and Indian were forced into closer contact with each other, and colonialism's effects—already visible in terms of disease, trade, and conflicts over land—would extend into the invisible world. It is fitting, then, that resistance would eventually emanate from there as well.

# Chapter 3

## *Lived Religion and Embedded Emotion in Midcentury Dream Reporting*

To the English, dreams could never be completely trusted. The Indians' reliance on dreaming as a source of insight seemed solid proof that colonists had entered the Devil's own country. Each encounter with native peoples heightened alarm about the manifestly diabolical nature of Native dream belief, especially the resort to visionary states, soul flight, and soul capture that were the special province of the powwaw. To Native peoples, in contrast, dreams and visions were reliable sources of knowledge and action. For them, dreaming, including traditional practices of shamanism and divination, offered key sources of support and inspiration in resisting the advancing predations of English colonization, as will be developed more fully later on.

While seventeenth-century New England was often a place of shifting alliances or multiple allegiances, colonial relations of power meant that over time a growing dichotomy emerged between "civilized" approaches to dreaming (those of the English, the Christian, the colonist) and "diabolical" uses for them (those of the powwaw, and, increasingly, the Indian in general). At home, the "other" had usually been Catholic; in the turbulence of midcentury political and social crisis, other scapegoats would come to share this demonized role. In New England as in Old, Anabaptists and Quakers would prove useful targets. Witches too, and, perhaps, women more generally, were thought to be especially vulnerable to being "deluded by dreams." The invisible world, headed by Christ, was dominated by constant tension in the age-old struggle with the Devil; although some dreams might be literally heaven-sent, many were meant to beguile the dreamer. In 1658 Philip Goodwin wrote of vain dreams, "As some entice away children in the day, by bringing them idle ba[u]bles and toys to play with; so Satan subtilly draws away mens mindes in the night, by sending in foolish fancies and vain Dreames to please them. . . . Satan makes men vain, by bereaving them of their right mindes and rich endowments, by representing such forms and foolish fictions, as abut which their hearts dance, their thoughts take delight."

This rejection of the dream was saturated with ambivalence, however. Try as they might to project the worst excesses of deluded dreaming onto various others—Papists, Indians, women, or Quakers—dreams were not rejected altogether. Night visions were still thought to have their uses, in diagnosing ailments, as predictions, or as spiritual warnings, and dreams could sometimes convey tantalizing glimpses of things to come.[12] To reject all dreams as mere fancy would be to reject the divine. Goodwin was therefore quick to note that, "Good Dreames, whereof God is the Authour, ought to be known: For 1. *Such have been, & 2. Such may yet be.* . . . Calvin in his Commentaries upon [the book of] Daniel, though he grants divers Dreames have been so salacious and frivolous, as did evidence much of the Devil; yet some Dreames have been so ponderous and serious, as might signifie something of God: . . . In such Dreames, we may imagine some moving hand of Almighty God. . . . From God may come (yea shall come) good Dreams in these latter times."[3]

In what ways, then, did colonists pay attention to their dreams? How, at times, did they accord them special power or status? This chapter explores the meaning of dreams as experienced by the colonists in the middle decades of the seventeenth century. As English colonial society matured, reported dreams played an often-important role in the colonists' emotional, spiritual, and public lives. Dream beliefs and practices would therefore help to guide English colonists despite their protestations of caution, in a variety of ways. Thus dreams and dream reporting played a role for both English and Algonquian peoples in helping each group to negotiate the demands of New England's emergent colonial society.

And the demands were great. In the 1620s, Plymouth Colony struggled to establish itself, coexisting uneasily with Thomas Weston's colony at Wessagusset. By the 1630s, large numbers of new colonists arrived to populate the Massachusetts Bay venture, centered at Boston, with its large and expansive harbor and extensive rivers giving access to the interior. Other settlements sprang up to the west and south at New Haven and Saybrook, while Thomas Hooker and his followers set out from Massachusetts in this decade as well, founding a settlement that would become Connecticut Colony at Hartford. All too soon, the expansion of English settlements and competition with Dutch traders from New Netherlands had provoked conflict with neighboring Indians in a short-lived but bloody war with the Pequots during 1636 and 1637. Internal schisms had rocked the colonists in the 1630s as well, and dissenters such as Roger Williams, Anne Hutchinson, John Wheelwright, and a variety of free grace proponents either were expelled or chose to leave Massachusetts Bay Colony. Moving to the fringes, these religious radicals founded settlements in New Hampshire, at Piscataqua, and in what later became the colony of Rhode Island, at Providence, Portsmouth, and Newport. By the 1640s, England herself was engulfed in civil war between a puritan Parliament and those who supported the crown. In the 1650s and 1660s, New Englanders followed the events of the Interregnum closely. These included Oliver Cromwell's Protectorate and the eventual restoration of King Charles II in 1660. It was in this context of religious struggle during the 1640s that Massachusetts ministers had begun their missions to the Indians, and colonists would prove inflexible in their demand that Indian converts renounce all dealings with powwaws—not just as healers but also as agents who might use divination or dream soul capture to advance strategic goals. By midcentury, civil war in England had caused many English people to embrace enthusiastic religious practices, including the use of wondrous dreams or prophetic visions. Scapegoating and demonization of the other may have been especially tempting tactics for all sides in a time of such tumultuous change. Many moderates feared that enthusiasms were running rampant.

Given this dramatic backdrop, just how did colonists use dreams at midcentury? How and when did dreams become important to record, and what role did dream reporting play in pious self-reflection, prophetic visioning, or developing practices of self-representation?

While the total number of reported dreams from midcentury New England remains small, these texts show an enduring fascination with wondrous, possibly divine dreams, as well as a resort to dreams at critical moments of life transition. Reported dreams of this period are notable in reflecting the pressing concerns of the day, especially a central preoccupation of this hierarchically organized society: the submission before or rebellion against authority, including its corollary, neglect of duty to spouse, children, or faith. Dream reports often brought an individual's most closely guarded emotional and spiritual proccupations to the fore, highlighting religious struggles, or enabling the historian to glimpse emotional experience that otherwise would be hidden from view. Some found in their dreams the vile lusts that were hidden away during the day; many found awe-inspiring wonders, and at least a few seem to have experienced dreams as bringing both soothing reassurances and startling warnings—sometimes within the very same dream. Dreams may have been more important at certain moments of the life course. Winthrop's dream (above, Chapter 1) occurred at the center of a conversion crisis in his household. The materials explored in the present chapter hint that dreams might serve a chartering purpose for those on the brink of adulthood—marking them out for greatness or, worse, for condemnation.

Along with wonder came a desire to contain and make sense of the dream. Dream reports show a strong concern with exercising due restraint, both in personal struggles over the manifest content of the dreams and, for all but one, in the interpretation of the dreams' meaning as well. English dream reporting was usually a private affair, with journals or letters serving as key outlets. Dream reports sometimes entered the oral culture to become wonder tales, although it is hard to track the process by which this transition took place. Unlike later eras, when conversion narratives form a crucial archive for dream reporting, records of reported dreams in seventeenth-century New England are not found in the recorded statements of those seeking church membership, and instead come primarily from just a handful of individuals, virtually all male.[4] Because the dream could, by its very nature, lead the dreamer into impossible flights of fancy, dream reporting also had the function of restoring balance, order, and control over a night-vision that, by its very nature was imbalanced, disordered, and uncontrolled. Dream reporting, then, had both a rather masculine and a somewhat colonizing function as well. The dreamer's reflections tamed the feminine (wild, savage, uncontrolled, passionate), reining in or restraining the dream through sober, reflective, and ordering functions of narration, whether spoken or written. From this vantage point, the Indians were the least of the colonists' worries. More troublesome were the unruly lusts, heretical enthusiasms, or erotic indulgence of the passions found in, respectively, the sinful individual dreamer, the Quaker convert, or the vengeful witch.

Despite all these caveats, throughout the middle decades of the seventeenth century English men and women still looked to powerful dreams for inspiration, warning, and guidance with some of their most pressing concerns. Dreaming constituted an important part of lived religious experience, in particular as a means of searching for one's own spiritual estate. At particular moments of life crisis, dreamt knowledge could provide critical guidance, even among those firm believers in the New England Way who unequivocally rejected the direct revelation experienced by Quaker adherents. It perhaps should not be surprising that theological concerns made their way fairly often into these night visions. A dreamt climb to heaven allowed the young Samuel Sewall to ponder the dangers of reliance on a covenant of works, while the Quaker convert Peter Easton, like many men of this period, struggled with covetousness, sensuality, and rebellious thoughts in his night visions. In addition, while the study of dreams provides unusually rich access to lived religious experience, this chapter also contends that dream reporting provided a critical form of embedded emotional experience and self regulation in this culture. Through a close examination of some of the reports, we see the dreamers' struggles to contain and manage powerful emotions even as we also see the ways these posed particular problems for the dreamer. Masculine restraint—idealized in this society—could fall prey to the depredations of unrestrained emotion. As Anne Lombard described puritan masculinity, "The ideal of responsible, rational manhood was formulated as part of a conscious attempt to suppress the rowdy, disorderly, sometimes violent behavior endemic to the popular culture of early modern England."[5] Dreams presented a nightly feast of unruly, ungovernable impulses, temptations, and delusions that individuals pondered, contained, and redirected in waking life. Reported dream images often centered on aspirations to power or status, the maintenance or loss of control over self or others, and themes of loss and mourning.

This nascent gendering of dream practices in which the dream might be coded feminine while the dream report served a containing and ordering, and, for according to the gender norms of this society, a masculine function, may have helped eventually to deepen the dichotomies of colonial society. Over time the split deepened between English colonists (coded as male) and Native Americans, who, in colonizing rhetoric, were either increasingly feminized or presented, in an apparent contradiction, as unusually hypermasculine. Whether strangely feminine or overly masculine, neither stereotype accorded Natives the sober, restrained manliness so idealized by the colonists. By the 1680s Increase Mather would condemn witches, Indians, and Quakers as pliable, gullible, and therefore all among the corruptible, vulnerable to Satan's wiles. The rhetoric used to talk about reported dreams reveals the troubling tensions of New England's maturing colonial society.

Despite the deep confessional divide between Sewall and Easton, both shared in a common culture that saw dreams as potential messages of divine will, while nevertheless requiring very different approaches to dream experience. At midcentury, the dreamed was still both real and revealing. The dreamer's relationship to his or her dream was beginning to be scripted as a struggle for control—a struggle that would mirror the struggle against disorders, and disordered dreamers, of all kinds.

D reams often present the dreamer with unbridled and unruly feelings, which various societies then understand and channel in culturally specific ways. The early modern individual did not conceptualize a dream, as would Freud two centuries later, as a compromise, the result of a collision between emotional impulses and culturally inspired repression. Instead, seventeenth-century men and women understood dreams as the result of imbalances in body and mind provoked either by outside forces (God, Satan) or by causes located in the dreamer's person: sinful desires, perhaps, or the result of a particular humoral temperament. Assaulted from without or disturbed from within, the proper response was one that attempted to restore balance and repel temptation. Thus, on waking, the dreamer often attempted to scrutinize the dream for any cautionary message in an effort to restore an idealized restraint over these unruly and often confusing night visions. Samuel Sewall noted feeling both "much troubled" and "much wondring" after one dream; on another occasion he described "a sad Dream that held me a great while," and after a third he wrote, "I was much affected with it when I waked."[6] English men and women seem mainly to have shared their dream experiences, if they shared them, with intimates, and the dream report only rarely made its way beyond the household, except for those dreams that eventually circulated as wonder tales. We catch only glimpses of such reporting, as when John and Margaret Winthrop discussed his dream of Grace (Chapter 1), or nonreporting, as when Samuel Sewall noted that his mother-in-law, who had been very ill, "slept without so much as dreaming," the "best night" in a long time.[7]

Given widely accepted belief in the deluding nature of dreams and the duty of Christians to guard against them, many dreamers embraced a cautious approach. As Philip Goodwin noted in his midcentury guide to dreams, "the safest course to secure our souls from Satans Deceits in delusive Dreames, is to fear God, and with the utmost care we can, to keep unto Gods whole commanding-word, for the want of which divers have been deceived by Satan in deluding Dreames."[8] He likened the dream to the Bible story of Laban tricking Jacob, "bringing to his bed blear-eyed Leah for beautifull Rachel; [and] so in the night the Devil hath deceived divers, bringing to them in sleep ugly lies for lovely Truths."[9] Or again, "A good Christian indeed sets his soul to watch while his body sleeps. Like the Prophet, Isa 21. 8. *Who cried, a Lion my Lord, I stand continually upon the watch-tower in the day time, and I am set in my ward whole nights*."[10]

As a threatening contrast sharpened between the idealized restraint of a good Christian and the "disordered" use of dreams by various "others" in colonial society, the English men who reported their dreams sat at one critical point of mediation through which the disruption and potential chaos of colonial violence might be contained. The rhetoric unleashed against "credulous" Indian shamans was also applied to witches and religious enthusiasts. The dreams that men chose to record showcase themes of control, mastery, and hierarchy. But, perhaps predictably, the themes of these reported dreams—and of their representation in writing the next day—betrayed especially intense strivings, along with wonder, shame, and anxiety.

Reflection on dreams was a way to counteract any evil that might come from them. Goodwin wrote, "Our duty is, To find the true sence of them, & To make the right use of them. That we may learn their lesson, care is required, In making Praier to God, & In asking Counsell of Men."[11] So, first, he recommended heartfelt prayer to God regarding the reason for the dream, after which the dreamer might "Consult with Men," citing, "so did Nebuchadnezer when a Dreame had made him afraid, and thoughts upon his bed had troubled him: He entreats Daniel to tell him the interpretation thereof . . . Dan 4. 9, 19."[12]

This struggle to contain, reflect, and restrain was constantly kept in motion by an eager acceptance of the wondrous itself. New England diarists usually recorded only those dreams (as would Samuel Sewall) that left them "much startled."[13] The first dream reports, those of John Winthrop and John Wilson (see Chapter 1), certainly fitted into this category; each in its own way offered a vision of future success and glory. While it was clearly possible to receive an awakening vision at any point in life, several of the most vivid dreams occurred to young men in their early twenties (Michael Wigglesworth, Samuel Sewall, and Cotton Mather) suggesting that this liminal moment, just before marriage and entry into full adulthood, might have been a time when a chartering dream event—a wonder or sign—was especially desirable. Themes of aspiration, achievement, and anxiety dominate these dream reports, suggesting the possibility that a powerful dream had a special role for European men coming of age, just as it did for the region's Native Americans.

A young tutor at Harvard, Michael Wigglesworth, offers a good example of the struggle to control and contain—often without success—and the way that private dream reporting thus meshed with reformed religious practice. Wigglesworth struggled mightily with dreams and the desires they contained; famously, he would eventually elaborate a dream image into a narrative poem that would make him one of the most widely read authors of the seventeenth century.[14] Edmund Morgan, who edited Wigglesworth's diary, notes that his life neatly confirms "the unhappy popular conception" of the puritans. Morgan says of the miserable man: "If worrying would have saved New England, Wigglesworth would have saved it."[15] More recently, Richard Godbeer has contextualized Wigglesworth's agonized reflections on his "filthy lusts," including intense affection for Harvard students which some have interpreted as an explicitly homosexual desire.[16] Regardless, the diary makes for somewhat painful reading because of Wigglesworth's relentless self-blame.

Goodwin's discussion of "filthy dreams," however, makes clear that Wigglesworth's torment was not misplaced. The midcentury author places the blame for "that particular sinne of uncleanness strictly so called," squarely on the dreamer: "This is a deep ditch or puddle pit, into which a man may be miserably plunged by the meer imaginations of his minde." Citing Matthew 5:28, Goodwin noted the famous dictum that a man might commit adultery in his heart, and just so, "A man that hath no body with him in his bed, may in the sleeping time of the night, be adulterously naught by the filthy Dreames of his minde."[17] Goodwin is clear that the Devil did not create the sin: Satan "need not bring any thing with him, onely improve the evil that is already, unto the forming of most filthy Dreames," and Goodwin also noted that, like a cunning fisherman, "When he [the Devil] would fain so . . . catch these choice peeces the precious Saints of God, he subtilly sets upon them in the night, as his fittest time wherein to tempt and take them."[18] And thus, though "they sleep in sinne, but sinne does not sleep in them; yea, though in sinne they certainly sleep, yet to sinne their souls are always awake."[19]

In his early twenties and unmarried, Wigglesworth was beset by frequent wet dreams, which he recorded in intentionally cryptic shorthand, asking God for better self-control. The entry for February 17, 1652/3, is typical: "The last night [I had] a filthy dream and so pollution escaped me in my sleep for which

I desire to hang down my head with shame and beseech the Lord not to make me possess the sin of my youth and give me into the hands of my abomination." After listing his faults, he noted, "I loathe my self, and could even take vengeance of my self for these abominations. Yet I feel, a stone in my heart that knows not how to melt."[20] Wigglesworth noted these sinful dream events throughout the rest of this year, and the entries suggest that his masturbatory urges and involuntary ejaculations were followed by intense feelings of shame and self-hatred, violent enough to bring, as he said, wishes to "take vengeance of my self."[21] To make matters worse, the diary reveals that he was convinced he had a venereal disease, something which he was advised to cure through marriage, presumably to a virgin (a common folk belief).[22] In one additional entry two and a half years later, after he was married but during a period of abstinence due to his "grievous disease," Wigglesworth again despaired: "Some night pollution escaped me notwithstanding my earnest prayer to the contrary."[23] This series of entries—a record of private, secret shame—describes for us something that perhaps was also experienced by many of Wigglesworth's age-mates, but which he alone recorded.[24]

Even as the young man struggled with his sinful body, he had to wrestle with his sinful heart as well, and eventually, he would dream of divine punishment: "being at a private meeting" on October 14, 1653, Wigglesworth noted, "God brought to my mind in special my want of love and dutifulness to my parents, which I beg'd pardon of. And the very next morning news is brought me of my father's death."[25] Wigglesworth's father had not been a kind man. On one visit home, the older man had castigated the younger for the folly and expense of making the journey at all, and then the younger man noted, "in sundry other respects god makes my father an instrument of . . . discovering my weak and silly management of every business, that he makes my savour to stink in my owne nosethrils."[26] The young man described feeling raw afterward, for rather than a love which would "covers a multitude of infirmitys," his father's criticism "rakes them open to the bottom."[27] But at news of his death, the younger man immediately began "to confess before the Lord my sins against him in want of naturall affection to, and sympathy with my afflicted parents, in my not prizing them and their life which god hath graciously continued so long."[28] On the eighteenth, he noted another wet dream and attributed it to Satan's influence: "Oh Lord deliver me from the power of that evil one."[29] Buffeted by his feelings about a father who had badgered and scolded him without mercy and, at the same time, feverishly preparing to preach a sermon at

Charlestown that he must have hoped would result in a calling to ministry there, Wigglesworth spent three days struggling with his lecture.

Then, on October 24, 1653, Wigglesworth had a frightening and awe-inspiring dream. He described it thus: "At night in my sleep I dream'd of the approach of the great and dreadful day of judgment; and was thereby exceedingly awakened in spirit (as I thought) to follow god with teares and crys until he gave me some hopes of his gracious good wil toward me." Yet, disappointment inevitably ensued: "The next day I found my self unable to make any work of it at my studys," and he chalked the whole up to a failing that many nonconformists bemoaned: "Pride prevailing."[30] In puritan thought, individual believers oscillated between "hardness" and the "breaking open" of their hearts in relation to conversion (again, a pairing of grandiosity and shame).[31] Wigglesworth was no exception. By winter, he had made a "catalogue" of his whole life, and, he wrote, the Lord chose to "break my heart" because of his many sins, showing him that he deserved "to be kickt out of this world because I have not had naturall affections to my natural father, but requited [returned, offered] him and all my governours evil for good."[32] What was worse, he was as well "to be shut out of the world to come, because I have rebell'd against and dishonour'd and disregarded my heavenly father, been a viper in his bosom where he has nourished me."[33] Wigglesworth's sin was clear—a sin of prideful disobedience, before governors both of heaven and of earth. His failure to submit was inscribed in the dream of Judgment Day, and his sin compounded by his inability to bring the dream to good spiritual account.

Despite his persistent despair over these many failings, before a decade was out, Wigglesworth had written the most famous literary work of seventeenth-century New England, his poem about Judgment Day, *The Day of Doom*, fulfilling and somewhat obsessively elaborating his dream vision of October 1653. He offered, in the words of a biographer, "a picture in two hundred twenty-four stanzas as stark and vivid as the medieval sculptures [of *Dies Irae*] around the cathedral doors of Europe," crafting in words an almost medieval vision of hell.[34] Wigglesworth "had not been experiencing a fantastic nightmare, but had been envisioning the eschatological event—the end of history—which puritans believed literally was man's fate."[35] Sadly, as another commentator reminds us, success did not buoy Wigglesworth's spirits. Instead, he remained an invalid for much of his adult life, shut in his house and locked in persistent struggle with a congregation that resented having to support him and his family in addition to the assistant minister who carried out the actual duties of the job.[36]

Wigglesworth was certainly an unusual man, but his dilemma was grounded in the major religious preoccupations of his day. What did he express that others struggled with in silence? How many other young men castigated themselves for their wet dreams? How many others suffered from nightmares in which they were treated to a graphic picture of Judgment Day? We know, for example, that at least one New England minister told of a similar experience: "I heard him say," (wrote Nicholas Noyes of his father's friend, Thomas Parker, who had preached and kept school at Newbury until his death in 1677), that he once "had a very terrible representation in a dream of the devil assaulting of him, and he wrestled with him, and had more than once like to have prevailed against him; but that when he was most likely and most near to be overcome, he was afresh animated and strengthened to resist him; till at length the devil seemd to break abroad like a flash of lightening, and then disappeared." This dream had occurred just before a terrible temptation arose, and the dream's prediction of Parker's successful struggle "was so remarkable, that every day he had lived since that time, he had given thanks to God particularly for his assistance of him in that temptation, and his deliverance out of it," remembering it vividly and retelling it some twenty years after the fact.[37]

But where Parker was cheerful in his victory over the devil, Wigglesworth instead comes across as relentlessly dour, grim, and quick to judge both himself and others: "Wigglesworth thought that all pleasure apart from delight in God's grace was dangerous."[38] As Morgan noted wryly, whenever we start to imagine the puritans "as rather hearty, warmhearted creatures after all, in fact very much like ourselves," we eventually "have to reckon with a man like Michael Wigglesworth."[39] Finding ourselves face to face with Wigglesworth's dream record poses anew the problem of reading historical dream reports through a modern, post-Freudian lens. We psychologically minded moderns are tempted to see a son beaten down by his father (a man who criticized and caviled without restraint, if not perpetrating something much worse) so that the son, filled with anger, inevitably rebelled. But, living in a society in which disobedience to a parent was utterly unacceptable, the younger man then turned the anger back, castigating himself for his disobedience.

These struggles give us a glimpse of what may have been a common emotional constellation in this society.[40] In a society where a failure to honor father and mother could sometimes bring criminal prosecution, the failure of a father to temper his parental critique with love put the son in an awkward position indeed.[41] Love, the son notes in his private reflections, "covers a multitude of infirmitys, but this [his father's criticism] rakes them open to the bottom."[42] It might seem odd for an abused son, rubbed raw by paternal criticism, to heap yet more abuse on himself. And yet, in modern terms, it is a commonplace observation that those who have suffered abuse will internalize the abusive other, and, without intervention, will eventually recreate a variety of victim-victimizer interactions, including vicious attacks on the self.[43] And Wigglesworth took it all on himself: "God makes my father an instrument of so discovering my weak and silly management of every business, that he makes my savour [my achievements] to stink in my owne nosethrils." But, the son mused, "whether he be to blame or no; surely I am, in causing such things and in looking so much at man in the reproving them with discontent."[44] Little wonder that his nighttime rest was disturbed ("dream'd of the approach of the great and dreadful day of judgment") or that his hopeful improvement of this dream was dashed the very next day ("I found my self unable to make any work of it").[45] Wigglesworth's later invalidism was foreshadowed here in a paralyzing writer's block, fueled by what seems to have been, by his own report, an intense sense of shame and inadequacy.

While such a psychological explanation may indeed transcend the decades between Wigglesworth and Freud, it is also worth noting that everything in Wigglesworth's society would have encouraged him to interpret things exactly as he did. His "filthy" dreams were the result of his own "carnal lusts," "the sin of my youth" (one presumes, masturbation, though the presence of venereal disease points to other sexual experience as well), and, in a rare instance of someone acknowledging a dream inspired by Satan, "the power of that evil one." His other reported dream—the vision of Judgment Day—left him "exceedingly awakened in spirit" and inspired. This was a divinely sent wonder, in other words, despite (or because of) its terrifying content. In this way, we can see more clearly the seventeenth-century context that not only shaped the interpretation of dreams but also determined the images and story lines of the dreams themselves. It is fortunate that even bad dreams could be used for good. Wigglesworth struggled to let his dreams soften a hardened heart. He used his literacy for this relentless self-scrutiny, creating a private confessional space in which he poured out his struggle with these shameful dreams, albeit in a secret and intensely private code.

For Samuel Sewall, a lifelong diarist and unusually prolific dream reporter, we have already seen that dreams offered an avenue for spiritual self-reflection. In Sewall's dreams, as in Wigglesworth's, strong emotion found expression even as dream images and themes afforded opportunities for disciplined self-reflection. Sewall's dream reports met critical selfobject needs, helping him to tame and contain intense feelings, in a pattern that would continue throughout his life.

But as a young man, two especially important dreams, each with strong spiritual themes, show us how dreams might serve as signal spiritual experiences, giving us a clue as to why these were recorded and what meaning the dreamer might have taken from them. Sewall's earliest reported dream—which was recorded during King Philip's War of 1675, like Winthrop's dream of his family's salvation, Wilson's dream of a great church arisen, or Wigglesworth's awakening dream of Judgment Day—had manifest content centered explicitly on the central dilemma of puritan society, the issue of one's election or salvation. Given both its religious themes and its appearance just as the young man was launched into marriage and adulthood, this dream seems an example of something we might think of as a chartering dream—a dream recorded because of its potential to portend a future life course for the dreamer. In addition, the dream's central images encode important spiritual concerns in this society, revealing how central theological controversies might be woven into the dream's narrative.

This dream centered on a journey in which Sewall literally made his way to heaven. Given the preoccupation with heaven and hell, it is perhaps not unusual that they would show up in puritan dreams quite often, and the young Sewall treated the dream with both anxious hope and cautious restraint. In the dream, he climbs a "pair of stairs going to heaven," while carrying a young child in his arms. He reports, "I went up innumerable steps and still saw nothing, so that I was discouraged, doubting with myself whether there was such a place as *sedes beatorum* [seats of the blessed]".[46] "Yet I strengthened myself as well as I could, considering how apt things only heard of are to be doubted . . . though they be never so true." Eventually he arrived at "a fair chamber with goodly lodgings," but he felt disappointed not to be in heaven: "When I saw that was all, I earnestly prayed that God would help us, or else we should never get to our journey's end. Amazed I was, not being able to conceive how furniture should be brought up those stairs so high." Discovering that the room was a "chamber in the N[ew] Building" (at Harvard College) and that "part of an old [house] . . . joined to it, of the same height," he was told by "a scholar" that the furnishings had been "drawn up by a pully, and so took in at a window which was all ranshacled like that in Goff Colledge over the Fellows' chamber, and all things began to seem more vile [of little worth]." He then notes, "Hereabout I waked, being much troubled at the former part, and much wondring at the latter of my dream."[47]

By way of explanation of the dream's absurd juxtapositions, he quotes some lines from Horace "'Desinit in piscem mulier Formosa superne [A woman, beautiful above, has a fish's tail],'" a rather conventional aphorism describing the absurd, which has often been used to describe a work of literature that begins well but ends in disappointment. He then offers a prayer in Latin: "Deus det, deus misericors et benignus, me, et comites meos, non tantum et de somnis, sed vere tandem divinis gradibus ad coelum usque ascendere," or, in English, "O God, compassionate and kind, grant me and my comrades that we may ascend to heaven on the divine staircase not only in our dreams but also in truth."[48]

A Freudian might observe that climbing stairs could be associated with the rhythmic thrusting of male sexual intercourse, keeping the sexual and emotional turmoil of young manhood in mind (Sewall was twenty-three); but, unlike Wigglesworth's struggles with lustful dreams and wet dreams, there is no explicit evidence of sexual turmoil in Sewall's dreamt experience.[49] A better reading emphasizes the pervasive splits between things of God and things of the world. The upper stories that Sewall at first took to be heaven turned out to be just "vile" ("worthless," but also meaning "base") man-made rooms. Even the image of the mermaid, which he adds in order to highlight the ridiculous juxtapositions, contains within it the idea of upper and lower regions—a division between mind and body, human and beast, the heavenly and the quotidian, the glorious and the vile, the covenant of grace versus the covenant of works. References to the feminine and the sensual still creep back in: Mrs. Richardson, the young mother whose baby Sewall carries, "herself following me up a pair of stairs"; and in the longed-for arrival "at last, I came to a fair chamber with goodly lodgings," although, alas, Sewall immediately realizes he cannot stay there. In addition, there is the mermaid, whose traditional role in early modern travel literature is as a feminine trickster, a seductress, luring mariners to their deaths on disastrous rocky shoals.

Various connections can be made to a common fund of imagery. In Thomas Hill's 1576 dream dictionary, "To clyme to heaven" had signified "a great tradition," while John Bunyan famously placed his "Pilgrim" on a similar spiritual quest just a few years later.[50] But the main imagery of the dream includes multiple references to height and verticality: "I went up innumerable steps"; "not being able to conceive how furniture should be brought up those stairs so high"; "those things were drawn up by a pully"; "Goff Colledge over the Fellows' chamber"; "part of an old [house] . . . joined to it, of the same height." At this point in Sewall's life—newly graduated from "the College" (Harvard), before his marriage, and in the context of a fearful "rebellion" of the Indians against the colonial government—questions of gaining and keeping authority, of "rising" in the world (especially a world dominated by vertical images of social hierarchy, those "above" and those "below") may likely have been on this young man's mind. Taken as social comment, the issues of achievement—the literal "climb" that might be on the mind of an ambitious young man—stand out.

The highs and lows of the dream also capture powerful emotional swings. A repeated sequence of hope (climbing) versus doubt (despair) recurs throughout the dream in the "innumerable steps and still saw nothing"; in arriving at the "fair chamber" that was still not yet heaven; and in the disappointing discovery that the furnishings had been "brought in at a window." Perhaps heaven (and other good things, such as worldly achievement or success or a comfortable home with a "fair" consort) will, in fact, be shut to him, or worse still, turn out to be a chimera. Indeed, the adjective *ranshacled*, from the word *ramshackle*, had the meaning of being loose and shaky, as if ready to fall to pieces, rickety, tumbledown, in a state of severe disrepair, all terms that could refer not just to the state of the window but to a state of mind—or of soul—Sewall's own shaky hopes.[51] Yet to doubt would be itself a sin, as was also his ambition, in the dream, to reach heaven through something as quotidian as climbing (a covenant of works), clearly man's efforts, not God's grace. This alteration of ups and downs even continues into the Latin lines at the end of the dream report, which speak about the beautiful woman above (*superne*) that ends (*desinit*) (literally "stops," "leaves off") in a fish (the implication is the parts below the waist, like a mermaid). And so even as Sewall tries to close off the pressing movement of the dream's imagery, it recurs again in the Latin that he uses to close the report.[52]

In a second dream, recorded about ten years later, Sewall wrestles once again with questions of theology. This dream appears to have engaged a particularly intense emotional and spiritual struggle against ambition, with additional feelings of rebelliousness at his subordination. We can only imagine, given this society's particular emphasis on paired relationships of authority and submission, that this set of concerns might have been shared by many other young men, particularly dependent sons-in-law such as Sewall had been. On January 2, 1685/6, Sewall reported:

> Last night had a very unusual Dream; viz., That our Saviour [Jesus of Nazareth] in the days of his Flesh when upon Earth, came to Boston and abode here sometime, and moreover that He Lodged in that time at Father Hull's; upon which in my Dream had two Reflections, One was how much more Boston had to say than Rome boasting of Peter's being there. The other a sense of great Respect that I ought to have shewed Father Hull since Christ chose when in Town, to take up His Quarters at his House. Admired the goodness and Wisdom of Christ in coming hither and spending some part of His short Life here. The Chronological absurdity never came into my mind, as I remember.

Sewall was making his way in the world by this point.[53] He was thirty-three at the time of this second dream report (not incidentally, the age of Christ at his crucifixion, a fact that perhaps signaled a special link between Sewall and the figure of Christ in the dream). He had been married to John Hull's daughter Hannah for about ten years. Hull himself had been dead for several years, since October 1683. But the peaks and valleys of anxiety over authority seem clear: a son, albeit the exalted Christ, chooses to live at "Father Hull's" (the very place where Sewall, a "son," or rather son-in-law, resided on his marriage to Hannah). Upon this news, Sewall has two reflections. One betrays considerable grandiosity: "how much more" had Boston to boast of than Rome, which claimed only the residence of Peter; the other, a sense of deflation, shame, and regret, perhaps borne of guilt: "a sense of great Respect that I ought to have shewed Father Hull." Such an oscillation between certainty and anxiety, and the attempt to control it is certainly typical of Sewall and recurs again and again in his diary. As Merle Curti noticed half a century ago, Sewall often suffered from dismal dreams, but they "were not always an occasion for distress. In one fantasy of grandeur, he was chosen Lord Mayor of London!"[54] Indeed, the diary itself at times seems to function as a repository for strong emotions.

The shift between grandiosity and shame—or, put another way, between superiority and inferiority—while an individual experience, also appears in many facets of New England society and links to that major preoccupation of puritan thinking, the sin of pride (we saw Wigglesworth beset with shame over this same impulse). Individuals struggled with pride both inwardly and outwardly. Thus, in New England one might be censured for an "intolerable pride in clothes and hair." Sumptuary laws regulating dress and demeanor were designed to reinstate a proper sense of shame in the overly proud, through restrictions on the wearing of lace cuffs or silk dresses. Or, men of standing could be prideful, which was tellingly glossed as "high." For example, when the lay delegate Master Wheelock of Medway complained in the 1679 synod that ministers were not taxed, Solomon Stoddard called him a liar. When Wheelock tried to settle the matter with a private apology, Stoddard refused to soften. "Mr. Stodder was high," noted one witness.[55] Proper governance of the self thus was linked directly to proper ordering of society, and men walked a daily tightrope between the proper exercise of authority and the dangerous shoals of arrogance. The weight of authority required that responsible husbands and fathers pay constant attention to duty, self-sacrifice, and self-control—a task that weighed heavily on the individual. Sometimes that weight manifested itself in the psyche, creating judge, jury, and executioner to deal with guilty wishes. Thus, in 1705, Sewall dreamed: "Last night I had a very sad Dream that held me a great while. As I remember, I was condemn'd and to be executed. Before I went out I read Dr. Arrowsmith's Prayer, p. 274 [professor at Cambridge under Cromwell, author of several theological works] which was a comfort to me."[56]

Sewall recorded other dreams, and more will be discussed later (Chapter 5). But even though his diary represents a relatively rich source, both in terms of the number of dream reports and the detail with which he recorded them, these still represent just a tiny number of the dreams he must have had over the course of his long life. These are the ones that he chose to write down and to ponder, often, one presumes, as a means to stir himself to better behavior. Far from being a liability, however, the select nature of the record is all the more meaningful for being carefully chosen. After all, these were the dreams that reveal Sewall at his most "awakened" and, as such, they remind us that the most important aspect of their meaning lies in what seventeenth-century colonists chose to make of them. These two recorded dreams placed Sewall in proximity to Christ or to his heavenly kingdom, implicitly posing a question that was central for every puritan: whether Sewall might, one day, indeed be elected to reside with the saints.

*   *   *

L ike Sewall, the young Cotton Mather also dreamed about his future. Mather's chartering vision, however, was just that, a wondrous waking vision
of an Angel imbued with overflowing emotion, an awe-inspiring heavenly aspect, and, most striking of all—a special message regarding Mather's future.
Mather was a member of the third generation of an important New England
dynasty, so he bore the weight of family tradition on his shoulders. At the time
of his 1685 angelic vision, he had served as assistant minister in his father's
church (a position of obedient submission) for four years. Like Wigglesworth
and Sewall, this youth in his twenties (he was twenty-two) extolled the awakening powers of what was clearly a strange vision. Following on the hours of de-
votions spent in "outpourings of prayer, with the utmost fervour and fasting,"
Mather had suddenly seen "an Angel, whose face shone like the noonday sun.
His features were those of a man, and beardless; his head was encircled by a
splendid tiara; on his shoulders were wings; his garments were white and shining; his robe reached to his ankles; and about his loins was a belt not unlike the
girdles of the peoples of the East."[57]

Mather's angel told him "that he was sent by the Lord Jesus to bear a clear
answer to the prayers of a certain youth, and to bear back his words in reply."
The young man did not write down the specific words (he recorded the entire
vision in Latin, in order to keep its contents private from the prying eyes of a
casual reader), but he noted that "among other things not to be forgotten he
[the angel] declared that the fate of this youth [Mather] should be to find full
expression for what in him was best." The angel first quoted Ezekiel, chapter 31,
verses 3–5, 7, and 9, which Mather rendered: "Behold hee was a Cedar in Leb-
anon with fair branches, and with a shadowing Shrowd, and of an high Stature,
and his Top was among the thick Boughs."[58] The scriptural verse foreshadows
the young man's concern with achievement, position, and place, emphasizing,
once again, a superior height, but one imbued with erotic overtones as well:
"The Waters made him great, the Deep sett him up on High, with her Rivers
running about his Plants. His Heighth was exalted above all the Trees of the
Field, and his Boughs were multiplied, and his Branches became long, because
of the Multitude of Waters, when hee shott forth." And then the angel explicitly
linked Mather to the figure from Ezekiel: "And in particular this Angel spoke of
the influence his [Mather's] branches should have, and of the books this youth
should write and publish, not only in America, but in Europe. And he added
certain special prophecies of the great works this youth should do for the
church of Christ in the revolutions that are now in hand." Mather ends his

report with the acclamation, "Lord Jesus!" and a question, "What is the meaning of this marvel? From the wiles of the Devil, I beseech thee, deliver and defend Thy most unworthy servant."[59]

Visions like these three seemed to arise unbidden, but in each case, the dream or vision inspired strong feelings in its recipient, whether loathing and self-recrimination, wondering amazement, or swelling hopes.[60] Each young man struggled to understand these dreams or dreamlike experiences and to interpret their special meaning for his own life course. Each sought an awakening message, to be preserved from Satan, and to turn these visions to good account in their lives. As good Congregationalists, they knew not to place too much store in these wondrous events. In fact, they kept these dream visions private, committing them to diaries—in Mather's case in Latin, and for Wigglesworth, in a shorthand code. Had they been Catholics or Quakers, they might have gained social renown for visions with such public or communal implications. Instead, each of these visionary experiences was personalized and individualized through private writing. Steeped, nevertheless, both in wonder lore and in the providential worldview from which it sprang, these young men were primed to see their own dreams as significant communications. The only trick was to determine if they had been sent by God to warn, or by Satan to mislead. And thus, each man was plunged back into the anxious struggle—so familiar, so centrally a preoccupation of the faithful in this culture—to determine whether he might take assurance from his vision or not. Salvation or damnation? Justification or despair?

It is hard to know how far to generalize the experiences of these three exceptional young men, or to know whether others experienced chartering visions that simply were never recorded. While the early modern period frequently saw dream reports circulated as communal wonder tales (one thinks, for example, of the visions of Lucrecia de León, discussed in Chapter 1), the conventional mistrust of dreams may have discouraged these New England men from more publicly sharing them, leading them instead to record prophetic visions in private journals, often in a foreign tongue or code to protect them from prying eyes.

However, dream reporting did have a more public form, even among the mainstream Congregationalists. Brief anonymous dream reports were retold as oral wonder tales, allowing communal discussion of God's providence, as has been amply shown by historian David D. Hall. Particularly popular were predictive dreams or dreams in which God's vengeance was apparent. A few publicly circulated reports seem to have functioned as cautionary tales, passing from person to person until the specific individuals behind them disappeared into generalized personae.[61] The themes in these reports echoed those found in among Wigglesworth, Sewall or Cotton Mather, including themes of superiority versus submission, prideful self-aggrandizement cut off by swift judgment, or predictions that later came true.

The diary of John Hull, Sewall's father-in-law and one of the wealthiest men in New England, records just such a wonder, a divinely inspired message of warning. Hull's entry for November 1665 records the tale of a man on Long Island who "told his sonns he dreamed he fought with diviles & they took his hatt from him." The poor man "was soon after found dead in the way from his meadow home[,] killed as supposed by lightining & his hatt some few rods from him cutt as iff it was by art."[62] It was alleged that the story had been recounted first by his sons.

That the Boston merchant wrote this bit of oral culture down is no surprise. Many were fascinated by such wondrous portents and strange ends. Indeed, Increase Mather (Cotton's father) included an entire chapter in his 1684 book of wonders, *Illustrious Providences*, "Concerning Remarkables about Thunder and Lightning," which included many sad and sudden judgments in which individuals met their end by a sudden stroke of lightning, such as the "worthy" Captain Davenport, veteran of the Pequot War, struck down "as he lay upon his Bed asleep," or the story of fourteen people struck (three fatally) in a house in Marshfield in 1666.[63] Such a sudden and arbitrary judgment deserved a record. (Mather noted of Davenport's fellows, "God spared their lives.")[64] But this particular dream text encodes the concerns of Hull and others with symbols that were known to connote authority: the hat knocked off the head (so many contempt of authority cases involved hats not coming off heads); or, in this case, the hat cleaved in two by lightning (perhaps a reference to God's chastening power, or even to an actual beheading, that of King Charles I). This act abrogating monarchy had greatly troubled Hull, notwithstanding his puritan sympathies, and the restoration of the monarchy with Charles II in 1660 still preoccupied New England in 1665, which (rightly) worried about retribution from the crown, just at the moment that Hull recorded this "wonder."[65]

It is indeed just imaginable that Hull's story was intended to reference the Quaker threat—Quakers being known for their failure to remove hats before lawful authority. Issues of authority and submission had thus become rather urgent when, in the mid-1650s, this much-despised dissenting sect had begun an aggressive campaign to proselytize New England, setting up toeholds in Rhode Island and Long Island. Increase Mather asserted that "all wise men . . . observe the blasting rebukes of providence upon the late Singing and Dancing Quakers, in signal Instances, two or three of which may be here Recorded, that so others may hear and fear and do no more so wickedly."[66] Indeed, Mather père appeared to be firmly of the opinion that many Quakers, if not most, were actually possessed: "They are indeed to be pitied, in that they themselves know not that an Evil Spirit doth possess and act [in] them. Yet others should from that consideration dread to come among such Creatures, lest haply [it should happen that] the Righteous God suffer Satan to take possession of them also."[67]

In the midst of the controversy over Quaker proselytizing, the sect's open use of dreams as revelation took a central place, exacerbating tensions between Rhode Island, which received them, and Massachusetts, which attempted to exclude them. The Quakers, after all, adhered to the distinctive—and in many quarters, heretical—belief that God might well speak to individual believers through dreams, visions, or other direct means. This tenet cast Quaker converts into considered scrutiny and public sharing of dream experiences in a way not seen among Protestants since, perhaps, the dreadful days of the Marian persecutions. Quaker proselytizers looked to dream experience as an active indication of God's intended course for them. Quaker meetings and missionary preaching offered opportunity for renewed and sustained public attention to dream experience in what non-Quakers thought was a frighteningly unwise embrace of the dream, itself long thought inherently unstable and untrustworthy.

Quaker approaches to dreaming constitute another variety of dream belief and practice in midcentury New England, even though Quaker believers were much vilified by the Massachusetts leadership precisely for particular approach to dreams. It is hard to get behind the polemic to see what reported Quaker dreams were actually like, however. Most of our evidence comes from the scurrilous reports made by Mather and other hardened adversaries. The only direct source regarding regional Quaker dream reporting in this period is found in the records of a key Rhode Island convert to the new Quaker belief, Peter Easton. Son of one Rhode Island governor and brother of a second, Easton wrote down three dreams in the 1660s. This rare documentation, together with his other writings, give us an unparalleled window into the political, personal, and spiritual preoccupations of this man, and they suggest the richness of Quaker dream reporting. The remainder of this chapter is devoted to analysis of the three dream reports, along with the history of religious and political persecution that played a critical role in his self image. It would seem that Easton, like Wigglesworth and Sewall, experienced powerful struggles with intense emotion, and it may be that, as for them, the act of writing dreams down served as both reminder and container of these unruly passions. Beyond this, it is hard to know how these dream reports were used, or what Easton's intentions had been in recording them. Did he speak from them to his meeting? Did he pray over them, or ask other Quakers for help interpreting them?

It may be that Quaker dreams did not diverge greatly in their themes or imagery from those of contemporary puritan dreamers. Rather, what riled Mather and the critics would have been how literally these dreams were seen as revelation. Because the records of the Newport Quaker meeting do not contain description of dream reporting in this early period, we cannot know how Easton actually used his recorded dreams. But the narratives themselves are still notable for their richness of detail, fertile imagery, and connections to the contemporary political controversies, both between Quakers and their Massachusetts opponents, and between the Quakers and the larger experiences of civil war and Restoration.

Quaker proselytizers had arrived in Rhode Island in 1657, and they found there a ready audience of potential converts among the heterodox population of antinomians, Baptists, and seekers of all kinds. Since Quakers believed that direct and immediate divine revelation might come to them through dreams, these assumptions certainly inform and shape Easton's three dream texts. So too, the history of persecution--first as Baptists, and later as Quakers—emerges strongly from the narratives. Some of the dreams—together with Easton's other extant writings—reveal the ways in which his night visions were seamlessly bound to the epochal religious and political struggles of New England. Easton had little love for Winthrop or others who had harried his family out of Massachusetts Bay back in the late 1630s, and both his dreams and his surviving historical reflections provide a keenly felt counterpoint to the puritan hegemony that so often dominates New England histories. But the Easton dream records contain similar themes to those we have examined in the reports of other male dreamers. Although Easton was already in his middle years and therefore beyond the sort of chartering dreams we saw for Wigglesworth, Sewall, or Cotton Mather, concerns about male potency, displays of male prowess, and a tension between greed and restraint remain prominent messages of his three recorded dream texts.

Easton carefully recorded his dreams on the blank pages at the back of annual almanacs that he used as diary and notation books. Those pages were eventually sliced from their original volumes and placed in a reconstituted diary at the American Antiquarian Society. As its origins in the backs of separate almanacs might suggest, this diary is disjointed, fragmented, and hard to follow, more a collection of notes than a consecutive narrative. Reading it, one longs for the uniformity and wholeness of narration offered by Samuel Sewall's journal.[68]

Easton's recording of these dreams would perhaps have allowed him to fulfill a larger Quaker goal of discerning outward action from night visions.[69] Quakers valued the individual's exploration of "interior" realms as a source of more authentic discernment of divine truths, which in this early period of Quaker activism were inextricably linked to critiques of temporal authority and state power.[70] The themes of Easton's dream narratives suggest the importance of locating them within the context of his biography (including both his particular experience as a middle-aged man and his family's history of religious dissent). But his dream reports—when combined with his other writings—also lead us to anxieties about local political rivalries, intercolonial New England politics, and the larger Atlantic histories of the English Civil Wars and Restoration that so preoccupied this Rhode Island dissenter. In this way, these three reported dreams were indeed Quaker dreams, but they also expressed cultural norms that were commonly found across early modern English society. Because these texts are so rich, so intricate, and so little known, I have chosen to quote each dream in its entirety.

Of the first dream, from 1663, Easton wrote:

> I dreamt that I was in a strang[e] place with other of my neer frends and by the folk of the hous[e] were. . . kindly as [and] freely entertained with puding and milke[.] and after had a publik and a free gratuety wher all threw in silver at will as an acknowledgment of their love wher was so [illegible] and suche aboundanc that I beeing agoing to be on[e] of the orderers or apointing my self[,] found whole handfuls of muny beyond expectation and [I] had a mind to be fingering of sum[.] at length the party that lookt on me by whome I was stopt[,] willingly

absented on purpose and when I had libarty in ougt [?] all came
to naughthing[.] presently I had a mind or covetious Desier
though in my power [he had a mind to finger the money again,
but he kept it in check].[71]

This dream contains at least two paired themes: the first, of unrestrained
love and goodwill—"freely entertained," "free gratuety," "acknowledgment of
their love," "suche aboundanc," and "whole handfuls of muny beyond expectation." In this, the scene appears almost like an idealized Quaker meeting, filled
with love and generosity among brethren. But this theme is quickly opposed by
a second: of a sober, even rigid restraint, either by "the party that lookt on me
by whome I was stopt," or by the dreamer himself, first in his "apointing my
self" to be "on[e] of the orderers," or later, when he notes "covetious Desier[,]
though in my power."

This dream lends itself easily to a dynamic analysis as a struggle between
desire and restraint (with accompanying feelings of lust, shame, and pride in
self-control). But the placement of this dream report suggests other historical
and social contexts, including the emotional experience that followed a history
of persecution. Easton frequently used his "diary" pages as practice sheets,
copying out the same phrases and amusing sayings over and over, as if practic-
ing them. In this case, the dream is immediately preceded by a set of sums
(perhaps the day residue for the images of "muny beyond expectation," or for
the "ought" and "naught" that appear in the text). And just above these, two
phrases written out, in which he complains of the behavior of the magistrates
of Massachusetts in making a law against Quaker proselytizers, who had been
aggressively targeting that colony since 1657: "In new England there hath beene
a law made of [illegible] the quakers so called and of deth in case of returne is
well knone in these parts but what inclined them hereunto && [etc.]& what
iust grounds and reason they had [for] it many are not acquanted with but are
very much dissatisfied concerning there [their] proceedings therein fereing
[fearing] that thay have dishonored god [and] brought a reproach upon the
name of christ and his gospel."[72] In this context of a harsh repression of dissenting faiths, the tension between "free gratuity," "such aboundanc," and "liberty
in ought" versus restraint and self-control ("the party that lookt on me by
whome I was stopt") takes on a new and somewhat darker tone.[73]

\*    \*    \*

In the second reported dream, from 1668, Easton and a neighbor—his foster brother, James Barker—are transported to the deathbed of "the Lord Protector Oliver" (Cromwell), where "we handled him to and fro and he seemed to me his limbs like an olive branch al green and in his flower[.] I pittied the loss of such a plant and admired the bidgness[?] and largeness of his limbs and we were teling on[e] another he had been a frend to the anabaptists and others in his lifetime[.] After a while Jam[e]s was prety urgent for us to speedily tell of his being ded[.] I wisht him not to be to[o] forward for I thought that would shew a kinde of gladness and as I was puting on my cloathes me thought oliver started up and was well and alive[.]"[74] After Cromwell springs back to life, Easton is left to wonder that "maybe he did so dispos[e] of himself [i.e., perhaps Cromwell chose to play dead] to hear what we countrymen would say then."[75] Some fragmented pieces at the end include an awakening, still within the dream, where Easton continues, "and then my wife caled to come quickly and I came and [a] man was a dying." Finally someone (the name is not legible) "knockt at the doores and awaked me."[76]

This dream contains images both of dissenting religion ("the Anabaptists") and of state authority (largely cast as beneficent, but the Cromwell figure, of course, contains the opposite, harsh, repressive, and violent authority). Far more prominent, though, is the feeling of amazed and sensual wonder ("he seemed to me [though dead] his limbs like an olive branch al green and in his flower"). Indeed, a widely accepted dream dictionary would have suggested that this dream foretold happy events soon to come: "He that dreameth that he speaketh with a deade body, betokeneth goodnes that is to come. . . . To se[e] a dead body, and therwith to speke, betokeneth joye, & gladnes[s]."[77]

Perhaps the most intriguing and insistent image throughout is the image of the olive branch, which recurs in two other forms—as the Lord Protector himself (it is hard not to read this as a reference to God as well), who is "Oliver" (never "Cromwell") and through the word and image "alive" ("was well and alive"). Oliver, olive, alive: three iterations of the same message, repeated in the dream's imagery, in which a corpse suddenly springs back to life, "al green and in his flower." While it is tempting to focus on the sensual images that are so prevalent in this dream ("we handled him to and fro"; "admired the bidgness[?] and largeness of his limbs"), one need not segregate sensuality from devotion, as Richard Godbeer and others have shown regarding nonconformist prayer, which was quite sensual, both in metaphor and in practice.[78] If we remember that Cromwell's own body was dug up after the Restoration, his limbs severed, and his head placed as a dire warning to other traitors, the image of admiring the "bidgness and largeness of his limbs" takes on yet another layer of meaning, one saturated with the problematics of authority, submission, rebellion, and betrayal.[79] And as the "Lord Protector" easily references not just Cromwell but also Jehovah, we have a stew of imagery here that points to Easton's enthusiasm for a truly vibrant, resilient, and living faith, albeit a faith under siege from oppressive authority.[80]

But what to make of that revenant figure at the end of the dream, the "man . . . a dying"? The dream begins and ends with death but seems to tell of a struggle between death and life ("alive," "al green and in his flower") and, thus, a resurrection of sorts, or a triumph over death. Here we should consider the "olive branch," an image itself so resonant with religious and political meanings. It is an olive branch that Noah receives to tell him he has reached safe harbor in the divine flood that swept away evil from the world; the olive branch image conjures up the green tree ("al green and in his flower") in the common proverb about God's chastening power: "and if these things be done to the green tree what shall be done to the dry[?]."[81] It is the olive branch that is at once an ancient symbol of victory and a promise of perpetual peace, both of which might have seemed most welcome to this Rhode Island dissenter so preoccupied with the repression of dissenters and the destruction of the Protectorate, with all its meanings of protection.

However, peace itself seems to have been elusive for Easton. The scars of his early experiences, as a child, of being expelled and exiled—first from England, then from Massachusetts Bay to New Hampshire, then Portsmouth, and finally to Newport—seem to have stayed with him. Nearly the entire contents of the diary for the weeks before this dream report are preoccupied with conflict, aggressive attack, deceit, and slander. Easton loved puns and tongue twisters, and he wrote a favorite one here: "Thay that think (right men) doe wrong wilbe redy to think wrong men do Rig[ht]."[82] Just above the dream report he included another frequent stock phrase, one that conjures up a struggle to contain the forces of murder or lust: "I never tooke away the life of a man nor never made life in any woman but one P[eter] E[aston]."[83] And on the reverse and the next page, though likely written some time before the dream report, we find these phrases: "When John shews Richard how to wrong tom it makes tom learne then to wrong John[.] When John shews Richard how to wrong tom he little thinks tom learns by it to wrong John." To the left on the same page: "He that hatcheth mischiefe is like a stone at low water mark"; and, midway down the page: "Some are angry without a cause and the[y] would willingly be pleased and cannot."[84] Finally, he inserted a more personal recollection, almost in a rhyming form, having to do with the emotional struggles Easton faced: "When I have done a thing that wilbe greatly talk[ed] of it make[s] me as sick as a dogg and not becaus ther is harme in it but becaus I feare it [being talked of]. January 24 when I had the fight [several words crossed out] the terrors of the night put me in a fright and tooke me of[f] from sleeping so much by suden stalls [?] and signs [?] in the night and thoughts[.]"[85] Easton's dream about Cromwell is itself punctuated by sudden oscillations between wonder and urgency, between amazement and being called away to another death. Easton's was not a tranquil or placid state of mind but that of a man contending with storms of feeling.

While such storms may have been exacerbated by his membership in a persecuted minority, in this, these reported dreams are not so different from those of Wigglesworth, Sewall, or Mather, and, indeed, one gets the sense from reading Easton (due to his overt mentions of conflict and use of repetition and imagery) that a major benefit of written expression for him as for the others lay in containing and managing otherwise ungovernable and potentially troublesome emotion, particularly angry feelings about "wrongs" and "hurts." Indeed, later in his life, Easton would split from the Quaker meeting hosted by his brother in an angry rift that divided the tiny Quaker meeting of Newport into two separate meetings for a time—an enactment, or reenactment, of the rifts that the family had experienced in Massachusetts Bay.[86]

In the third dream report, recorded in 1670, Easton wrote:

> I dremt I two eagles catcht when I was aslepe yet thought I watcht[.] I espie the 2 eagls sitinge on the water as on firme land [and I] creapt for to get them boath in [hand] . . . [I] felt for my gun and had none then I stan-ded upright as to fright them[.] on[e] of them came hovering close over my head I catcht him and goeing round the little pond to gard[?] for he was [where?] I first began to crepe[,] I provokt the male eagle [faded] in suche maner as he made a nois[e] as if he had been treding of[f] the fem[ale?] which the female hearing came gently towards me [words missing] I taking hould of her . . . Likewise which was bidgest [*sic*] of the two [?] and brought them boath home wher

> was my wife[,] my brothers wife and some strangers and after I
> had related how I catchd them[,] put them ... [on] the porch
> and beeing awakt went to get them and then found it had beene
> a dreame.

The most prominent aspect of this dream appears in Easton's interaction with the two eagles, in which the male eagle arouses aggression and competition, while the female eagle suggests gentle seduction and erotic longing. Note Easton's resourcefulness in catching a flying male as well as how Easton "provokt him;" at the same time, he displays stealth in enticing the female, who moved "gently towards me." As a resourceful hunter, he brought both home, and not to just one wife, but to two: ("my wife[, and] my brothers wife)." Beyond these suggestively gendered constellations of emotion, the meanings of these dream images remain elusive—slipping out of our grasp, as it were. The eagle was, in general, a potent symbol in the English imaginary, having been frequently incorporated into the carved lecterns from which the Bible was read in the Church of England because of its association with John the Apostle. The bird signaled both evangelism and the unflinching Christian's acknowledgment of divine truth.[87] But a well-known sixteenth-century dream dictionary points us back toward the erotic: "A man that thynketh that he taketh byrdes, betokeneth [taking] wymen."[88] The sensual, the religious, the political—these dimensions that appear potentially separate are, in all of Easton's dream reports, thoroughly entangled.

We can imagine that many, if not most, dreams intertwined personal preoccupations, emotional experience, status anxieties, and spiritual concerns with considerable abandon, just as Easton's clearly did. But Easton was a Quaker, and that signaled to contemporaries a profound difference both in terms of belief about the status of the dream and particular practices of dream recording and dream interpretation. Easton's dream reports gain additional context when read together with the rest of the Easton archive. Most prominent was his fascination with a particular historical narrative that insistently interweaves the Easton family story both with the story of Quaker persecution and with the midcentury struggle between crown and Parliament. We gain a sense of the history in the diary, to be sure, but it emerges more forcefully from some precisely placed annotations that Easton made inside a copy of Nathaniel

Morton's 1669 *New England's Memoriall* (held by the Redwood Library of New-port).[89] Other important evidence includes the marginalia inside the "diary" almanacs themselves; the public record of his family's service to Rhode Island Colony (his father and brother each served as governor, and Peter served as both treasurer and attorney general); and the writings of his brother John Easton, who, in 1675, composed a blistering attack on the United Colonies' handling of Indian relations, blaming them for the outbreak of King Philip's War.[90] An examination of the dreams in conjunction with the rest of this his-torical and familial narrative offers unique access to a densely layered sense of self-identity, and the way that identity was inseparable from familial, confes-sional, and political or economic aspirations. These layers of meaning provide additional context for the interpretation of the dream reports, and this context helps explain their significance both as forms of nascent self-representation and as pieces of dissenting religious expression.

Clearly, Easton and his family were no friends to Massachusetts orthodoxy, nor were they held in good repute by that colony's leaders. Tensions had emerged from the start. Nicholas Easton had immigrated to New England in 1634 when his two boys, Peter and John, were just twelve and ten, settling first in Ipswich then moving to Agawam (Newbury) the next year. In 1638 they left for Winnaconnet, now Hampton, New Hampshire (near Exeter, where the dis-senter John Wheelwright had settled), but in May 1638 were warned out by the Massachusetts General Court, to be removed by force if necessary.[91] And so the family moved on to Portsmouth, Rhode Island, to settle with Anne Hutchinson and her followers. In May 1639, according to Peter's own notes, "this year the Eastons came to Newport in Road Iland and built ther the first English building and ther planted this year."[92] The impact of Peter's unsettling adoles-cent years is uncertain, but there may have been some lifetime emotional dis-turbance in a boy whose natural mother had died when he was young and whose father was unable at first to find a secure base within the new polities of New England.

Easton Sr. was almost immediately caught up in the free grace controversy. In a 1641 entry complaining that "those who were gone with Mrs. Hutchinson to Aquiday fell into new errors daily," Governor Winthrop mentions Nicholas Easton specifically, writing: "Other troubles arose in the island by reason of one Nicholas Easton, a tanner, a man very bold, though ignorant. He using to teach at Newport, . . . maintained that man hath no power or will in himself, but as he is acted by God, and that seeing God filled all things, nothing could be or move but by him, and so he must needs be the author of sin, etc., and that a Christian is united to the essence of God."[93] Winthrop described this error as "not apprehending" how God could make man in his own image, "and yet no [not] part of his essence." Winthrop cited "familiar instances," as examples of the distinction, such as "the light is in the air, and in every part of it, yet it is not air, but a distinct thing from it."[94]

Peter remembered this period of the family's life with bitter intensity. His annotations on the copy of *New England's Memoriall* explain the moves further and further to the north, followed by the move to Rhode Island, "but bee-ing put by our purchas [having their purchase invalidated] by the Disention in the Contry when Mr Vane was tur[ne]d out from being/governor they [we] went unto Road Iland in June . . . and built at porchmuth at the Cove and planted ther this yeare 1638."[95]

The later marginalia contain a dramatic record of the progress of the civil wars, intertwined with a few landmarks in Peter Easton's establishment of his own household. Since Morton organized his history as a year-by-year chronicle, it was easy for Easton to follow along with his own commentary about annual events. Like most chroniclers of the times, including Morton, Easton's narrative focuses on providential events. What is noteworthy for us, however, are the ways in which the personal trajectories of Nicholas, Peter, and John Easton (introduced against a framework of struggle against rigid puritan authorities) are interwoven with providential twists and turns in the English Civil War, itself a struggle of nonconformist believers against rigid authority.[96]

Easton's history developed a vigorous and sustained protest against the orthodox leaders of Massachusetts Bay with their high-handed and (implicitly) illegal treatment of dissenters within their own borders. Easton's account mixes local signs with wartime events abroad, as if God were signaling in New England the triumphs and tribulations then occurring in Old England. Thus, for 1640, he notes: "This year 3 d 9 m the long Parliament began," continuing down the left margin: "This year bulls marsh was a fier 9 d. 11 m the king leaves London."[97] Bull's Marsh, of course, belonged to Henry Bull, a prominent neighbor and close associate of the Eastons, a man who would eventually marry Nicholas Easton's widow Ann. But the significance of this great conflagration is set out as if equivalent to, and a sign of, the momentous events then "ablazing" through England.

The marginalia continue on to chronicle the fights at Edgehill, Newberry (both the first and second battles), and Hull; the installation of Sir Thomas

Fairfax as general of the Parliament's army; the flight of the king and his beheading; and "the Prentices Rise against the army."[98] Against this backdrop of momentous events, however, proceed the New England events of Morton's text, and then a second, still more personal narrative of Easton's life, including the launching of his marriage to Ann Coggeshall and the birth of his first child: "This year the 12 of November yong Nicholas/Easton was borne at Newport in 1644."[99] Some other notable personal events included a providential recovery with an unusual intervention: "This year I was sick[;] the French docter."[100] There was also a legal memorandum: "1665 This Aprill 13th day Peter Easton went to the new country to view the new purchas wher of I was one of the purchasers."[101] In the appropriate place, Easton notes, "This month the lord protector [Cromwell] was proclaimed," and then made a series of entries documenting the progress of Quaker belief and tribulations of Quaker proselytizers: "This year [1654] frends first began in the north of old England;" "27 d 10 m this yeare [1656] Jams Nailor Bored through the tongue and stigmatized."[102]

Mention of a Quaker martyr like James Nayler links the Easton family's earlier troubles with Massachusetts's puritan leaders to the more contemporary struggle of Quaker proselytizers with the last days of puritan rule, just before the Restoration. Here Easton enters into his most vigorous dialogue with Morton's orthodox narrative. In the section where Morton eulogizes Governor William Bradford, Easton writes of the arrival of Quaker preachers: "This year frends came over first to Plimoth[:] John Rous Christophe[r] houlder. Robert fowler Robert Houghton."[103] When Morton eventually notes the arrival of the proselytizers, using pejorative terms ("There arrived in the said Colony many of that pernicious sect called Quakers"), Easton's marginalia remove the sting, noting simply, "Quakers came to new England 1657."[104] The Easton annotations of Morton's account call our attention to the nuances of abusive authority from a Quaker perspective. While royal authority earlier in the century may have been a nemesis for all varieties of nonconformists, that struggle culminated in the dramatic beheading of the king. The chaos which later developed during the Interregnum left radicals like the Quakers oddly in the debt of the king, who, in Massachusetts at least, represented a check on the worst excesses of the puritan orthodoxy. (In England, of course, many Quakers were jailed during the Restoration.) This local valence of royal authority as protective trumped other concerns, however. Indeed, the account of King Philip's War written by Peter Easton's brother John in the winter of 1675/6 asks throughout that the king be sought as an arbiter who could put to rest the grievances between English colonists and Indian landholders, and he places the blame for escalation to war squarely on the puritan United Colonies: "I am so perswaided of New England Prists thay are so blinded by the Spirit of Persecution . . . that thay have bine the Ca[u]se that the Law of Nations and the Law of Arems have bine violated in this War."[105]

The figure of Oliver Cromwell, who surfaced as a central figure in Easton's 1668 dream, also appears in the history Easton wrote in the margins of Morton's book. Easton records the date that "the lord protector was proclaimed." In the right margin, near a line of funeral oratory stressing hopes for a reunion in heaven ("Shall meet, embrace, and shal not part for ever"), Easton noted, "23 d 9 m this year oliver Cromwell was buried with very great Cost."[106]

In short, the archive of Easton's life and letters, though often fragmentary and incomplete, describes dynamics of intercolonial politics that Easton's three dream reports deepen and elaborate in unique ways. The dream reports give us unusually intimate access to Easton's emotional world. They suggest rich and fluid interconnections between inward vision and outward politics in this early modern society and offer a rich picture of one man's sense of his place in history. They unpack for us afresh the holistic links among religion, politics, institutions, gender relations, intergenerational experience, and individual psyche that could otherwise be overlooked. A reading of these dream reports must attend to all these contexts, without privileging some as more primary than others. That said, we should not neglect to note the sensual, even sexual, images and emotions that saturate Easton's recorded dreams. "Fingering" money, handling and admiring limbs for their "bidgness and largeness," or miraculously catching a female eagle right out of the sky—especially given the period reference that linked dream images of catching a bird to catching a woman—all these dreams offer glimpses of a middle-aged man in the grips of powerful physical and emotional desires, even as they speak about his attempts to control and order these desires and, as well, to make sense of images he believed represented a directly revealed divine communication.[107]

But above all, it is his identification with a history of religious persecution that stands out. This was not just something to be struggled against, but, I would contend, an integral part of an emotionally resonant religious experience. It might be a bit much to say that the Quakers needed their persecutors and relished them as foils through which they could convey their message, but few things could convey with as much dramatic effect their Christ-like commitment to an alternate path. While Easton emphasized his own experiences of persecution at the hands of Massachusetts authorities—and his own triumphs over those authorities with the help of the "Lord Protector"—Easton's record of his inward visions helps us to see more clearly the emotional import of Quaker political critique of New England orthodoxy, and, in turn, of the repression of that critique.

It is ironic, but perhaps not unexpected, that this history of struggle did not shield Easton from strife within his family and community. We might fantasize about a harmonious, peaceful, and nonviolent community of Quaker believers set up in opposition to external persecutors. But the records of the Newport meeting tell a different story. Whether in their intense animosity toward Massachusetts officials for their treatment of dissenters, or in the fascination with the great drama of midcentury, the civil wars, Easton's reported dreams condense and overlap imagery, themes, and emotional power in a way that conveys, as no other source can, the intensity of inward affect that accompanied the outward events of the day. They speak to a central dilemma of his life: how to manage unruly and unwanted feelings of selfishness, greed, and aggression even as one embraced a religious identity that invited persecution.

The study of these dream reports allows us to glimpse the variety of approaches to dreams among the English colonists at midcentury. Despite a rhetoric which cast dreams as untrustworthy, even elite and well-educated men sought out dream experience throughout their lives. Whether they looked for predictions of their future or simply recorded the wondrous dreams being told and retold in the neighborhood, dreams were not dismissed as wholly without meaning. Dream reporting helped fashion new selves and to manage intense experiences looking first to record and then to understand, moderate, and exercise restraint—whether over sexual impulses, covetous desire, prideful ambition, unrestrained rage, or fears of being condemned. Some struggled with worry about the attainment or loss of power, as well as with moderating their joy as they anticipated a successful reward depicted in the stairways leading heavenward. When read in context, reported dreams provide a new way for historians to understand some of the emotional dilemmas of life in this colonial society. For most English reporters, dream phenomena demanded a sober and restrained approach, even as the dreams themselves spoke to strong and nearly ungovernable feelings. The exception was Quaker practice, which allowed a more fulsome view of dream experience and may have involved public discussion of these night visions. Recorded dream texts document personal, societal, and confessional preoccupations, and they were always produced—as were the emotional valences embedded within them—in the cultural context of the mid-seventeenth century. This was true whether one embraced restraint, discipline, and self-governance, or whether one looked within for the divine, as did Quakers.

While Massachusetts Bay authorities thought Quakers were persecuting them, Quakers like Peter Easton held tightly to their identities as victims of a tyrannical priesthood. For Easton, this took the form of obsessive recollection of historical events and the placement of those events in the operations of the invisible world. For both Easton brothers, a focus of critique was also the behavior of Massachusetts Bay authorities: Peter felt the persecution of Anabaptists and Quakers most keenly; in John Easton's most memorable writing, the persecuted were the Indians.

King Philip's War would become a key turning point for these narratives of persecution, and dreams and dreamers would play a key part in that conflict—Quakers, Congregationalists, and Indians alike. But the war also signaled a change in attitudes toward dreaming. Colonial elites had long advocated cautious restraint in relationship to their dreams. Approaching dreams with a sober and cautious reserve was both a Christian and a masculine duty. A measured control, a manly reserve in relation to the dream, was embraced. Anything else—a too-credulous use of dreams—would only expose the weakness and penetrability of the human mind. It was this enthusiasm and penetrability that had led the Quakers to be overcome by Satan, at least in the view of Increase Mather and other critics. And it would be a similar attribution of credulous and misguided dreaming that would cement the links between Indian visionaries during the war and Satan's meddling. But that was yet to come.

At midcentury, most English colonists, steeped in the older medieval traditions of wonder lore, continued to regard dreams as potentially valuable, if sometimes dangerous, communications. Some, like Peter Easton, subscribed to theologies that encouraged, even required, the dreamer to scrutinize night visions for divine messages and guidance. But even among those such as Cotton Mather, Samuel Sewall, or Michael Wigglesworth, who confined revelation to scripture alone, dreams were sometimes so powerfully awakening and so explicit that they might be drawn into enacting them, whether by writing a poem or following a prophecy.

In all, the midcentury dream reports suggest that dreams were treated with greater significance than puritan proscriptions suggest. Colonists still believed in wonders, and the emotional power of some dreams spurred individuals to record them, along with the feelings they encoded; those who recorded dreams often hoped to better govern themselves or others. By recording the strange juxtapositions and what Samuel Sewall would have called the surprising "absurdities" of these dream experiences for later reflection, colonial dreamers validated older ideas of the dream as carrying important and spiritually potent messages. The dream reports of this chapter also suggest some of the special dilemmas facing the male dreamer, particularly the young and ambitious male dreamer struggling to temper covetous desires or rebellious rage. The dream reports—whether for the orthodox Congregationalists or the Quaker radical Easton—suggest that concerns over hierarchy, position, destiny, and, most of all, spiritual estate might emerge along with potentially painful and extraordinarily powerful emotional states. Insofar as dream reporting could locate this emotion in a fixed text through acts of reflection, prayer, and written expression, English dream practices served hidden selfobject functions for the dreamer, allowing for the management and integration of potentially disruptive experiences, and for the maintenance of an idealized masculine restraint in the face of destabilizing feelings and awe-inspiring wonders. Midcentury dream reports suggest that a variety of approaches to dream experience were employed by English colonists, and they point to the emotional dilemmas and rich cultural contexts in which dream experience was always embedded. It is not surprising, therefore, to see many of the key political, economic, and doctrinal controversies of the day echoed in reported dreams. Belief in one's dreams was not just the province of Indians, women, or Quakers. But the unruly and unbidden emotion found in dreams did have to be channeled, recuperated, and contained. Dream reporting was one means for that, and along the way, it furthered new forms of self-representation, emotional expression, and spiritual practice.

# Chapter 4

## *Dreams and Visions in King Philip's War*

In response to John Easton's indictment of the United Colonies for their role in precipitating King Philip's War, the Reverend Increase Mather wrote his own history of events. Fascinated by wonders of all kinds—including dreams, witchcraft, possession, apparitions, and other unusual events—Mather's account of the Indian war underscored its role as a warning to the English from Jehovah. He intended his account, which was written just as the war came to a close in the summer of 1676, to highlight this message and serve as a spur to the reformation of the English colonists. His narrative is thus somewhat ambivalent. On the one hand, he offered a vigorous defense of the United Colonies against Easton and other critics, taking care to portray the English as victims of the Indians' perfidy. This was the defensive recuperation of trauma described by Jill Lepore in her book on the trauma of King Philip's War and its consequences: the "victory of words," which was at least as important as the "victory of wounds" waged to win the war in the first place.[1] On the other hand, Mather wrote a jeremiad. He trusted that his history would outline "so dreadfull a Judgment" on the English, especially of the second generation, "which hath not so pursued, as ought to have been, the blessed design of their Fathers, in following the Lord into this Wilderness." While Mather clearly believed that the Indians were Satan's agents, he explicitly hoped that the English would heed God's call and reform their own ways.[2] Thus Mather's narrative wends its way between these two competing goals: to defend English conduct from all sorts of critics, both Quaker adversaries in New England and royal officials abroad, and, at the same time, to try to amplify God's message so that no one could miss the judgment on the English that was contained in these awful events.

Although he finished his history after King Philip had been slain (the Indian sachem's head and hands cut off and exhibited, intended to be a dire warning about the fate of "traitors"), Mather argued that the war itself was far from over. Framing it all in the language of wonders so familiar to him, the minister knew better than to suggest that all would now be fine. Following Philip's death, New England's English colonists sat uneasily between "the River Indians"—that is, the Connecticut River peoples—who had moved north and westward, and the various groups of Algonquian Indians "to the East" in Maine, where the violence would continue for at least another year. "Whilst they and others that have been in hostility against us, remain unconquered," Mather intoned darkly, "we cannot enjoy such perfect peace as in the years which are past. . . . there seems to be a dark Cloud rising from the East . . . yea a Cloud which streameth forth blood."[3] Mather's apocalyptic language reveals a search for supernatural portents, omens, visions, and signs, a search that had been pursued by ordinary English men and women during the war itself.

Behind this ominous cloud, the Indians searched for guidance from supernatural sources of their own. Indeed, as anthropologist William Simmons has remarked, "If the Indians had written their history of King Philip's War, they might have emphasized the importance of shamanistic divination in the formulation of strategy."[4] The narratives of the English captive Mary Rowlandson, the local commander Benjamin Church, and several others reveal that shamanistic divination rituals were commonly used prior to major Indian attacks on English settlements.[5] For example, early on May 8, 1676, a group of more than three hundred Indians surrounded Bridgewater, Massachusetts, and began to besiege it and its twenty-six defenders, led by Tispaquin, who was a great shaman as well as a warrior. But "according to a legend told in the area long after King Philip's War, the warriors 'had a Pawaw. . .[and] the Devil appeared in the Shape of a Bear walkg on his 2 hind feet.'" When Ezra Stiles later collected this legend, he was told that had they seen a deer; "'They would have destroyed the whole Town & all the English,'" but on the appearance of the bear they suddenly withdrew.[6] Similarly, on one expedition involving the Connecticut militia, "Major Symon," an Indian who was fighting on the English side, slept peacefully, "'but towards Morning he fell into a Dream, wherein he apprehended the Indians were upon him, . . . but presently presenting his Gun against them, he so frighted them, that they gave him an Opportunity to make an Escape from a Multitude of them.'"[7] Earlier sources, like Samuel de Champlain's account of the 1608 attack on the Iroquois, and later ones like Frank

Speck's early twentieth-century informants in Maine and eastern Canada suggest considerable stability in the connection of insightful dreaming to Algonquian practices of predictive visioning and divination in advance of hunting expeditions or wartime attacks, though doubtless there are many facets of this tradition obscured by colonialist misunderstanding.[8]

King Philip's War had also been a movement of nativist revitalization, a coalition among the many separate indigenous groups in the region. In at least one case, a set of visions explicitly inspired and propelled the Indian resistance. New England had seen such a movement before; Miantonomo of the Narragansett had led a resistance effort in the 1640s that was cut short by his murder, a death engineered by his Mohegan enemies and sanctioned by the English. But before his execution, the Narragansett sachem had worked to forge a pan-Indian alliance, including "all the Sachems from east to west, both Moquakues and Mohauks," who were prepared to attack the English. They planned to "kill men, women, and children," but that was all; they would preserve the cows, "for they will serve to eat till our deer be increased again."[9]

While Miantonomo's movement had failed, evidence from the Maine frontier suggests that visions were once again afoot in the 1670s, some years before Philip of Pokanoket, an influential sachem of southern New England also known as Metacom, began sending emissaries to try to build his pan-Indian revolt. These northern traditions had a trajectory of their own. One man, a paramount sagamore (political leader) named Squando, proved a particularly influential visionary.[10] A likely Christian convert before the war, it was a specific act of violence against his child that supposedly drove Squando into implacable resistance against the English at the war's beginning. As perpetrator of several "outrages" against colonial outposts, Squando was just one of many Native visionaries who were guided by spirit helpers throughout the conflict. After the war was lost, Squando's visions continued, leading him, supposedly, to end his own life in an act that his spirit helper assured him would be followed by a Christ-like resurrection.[11] Other Eastern Woodland groups would experience revitalization efforts centered on visionaries like Squando in later decades. The best-known examples include the "Delaware prophet," Neolin, whose involvement underlay Pontiac's Rebellion of 1763; the movement led by Handsome Lake among the early nineteenth-century Seneca; and the visions of Tenskwatawa, brother to the resistance leader Tecumseh, just before the War of 1812.[12]

But it was not just Indians who sought revitalization. As Mather's account makes clear, some, perhaps most, English colonists framed the war as a divine warning—and as a spur to future cultural reformation. As Lepore noted in her skillful study of puritan rhetoric, "Everywhere, the English found God writing his judgment onto New England's landscape or onto English bodies. He had made New England into 'a looking glasse' whose ravages reflected the colonists' own corruption."[13] While Mather was expansive on the subject, even the more subdued William Hubbard, Mather's nemesis and competitor as historian of the war, saw the message in these horrific events: "God in his Wisdome suffered so much of the rage of the Heathen to be let loose against his people here [the English], as to become a Scourge unto them, that by the wrath of men, praise might be yeilded to his holy Name."[14] Imperfect though his history might be, Hubbard hoped that it "might be of use to posterity, as well as to those of the present Generation, to help them both to call [to] mind, and carry along the memory of such eminent deliverances and special preservations granted by divine favour to the people here." He trusted, as well, that it would remind them that God, "in his abundant goodness restrained the remainder that it should not consume."[15] And on an individual level, Mary Rowlandson—an Indian captive from February to May 1676—gratefully embraced the "heart-sinking tryals" that eventually awakened her to a new appreciation that God was behind all her suffering: "Oh I may see the wonderfull power of God, that my Spirit did not utterly sink under my affliction: still the Lord upheld me with his gracious and mercifull Spirit."[16] Mather, who introduced her account, hoped that these providences would become crystal clear to the reader: "Once and again you have heard, but here you may see, that power belongeth unto God; ... That our God is in the Heavens, and doth whatever pleases him."[17]

Thus, both English and Indian leaders thought the war might inspire recommitment to core cultural values, and each saw the war as an event of significance in the invisible world, quite apart from its origins in more quotidian—though crucial—conflicts over land, resources, and political power. It should therefore be no surprise to find that dreams and visions played critical roles at key moments in the conflict. Anxious colonists looked for signs and wonders with which to predict the next events of the war. Authors like Mather appropriated reports of wondrous dreams among the Indians—including a dream that supposedly came to King Philip on the very morning of his death—as a way of containing the chaos unleashed by this conflict. Wonder lore offered a critical context through which the unnamable suffering of war found language. If "acts of war generate acts of narration," as Lepore has argued, the language of dreams, both divine and diabolical, was one grammar that Mather and other English colonists used to contain their experience and to endow it with meaning.[18]

Sad to say, containment of this social violence lay in turning the language of wonders to its oldest sectarian purposes: the enlistment of God's judgment to "prove" who was right and who was wrong. Locating excessive, irrational emotion in their Native opponents would advance racialized stereotypes that could justify postwar dispossession or worse.[19] Indian leaders' supposed reliance on dreams and divination seemed abhorrent diabolism to English observers, yet many English men and women searched for signs that would indicate God's intentions, signs they found in odd visions, apparitions, or other wonders. Puritan authors also turned to Biblical typologies to structure the chaotic and terrifying events of war. Casting Indian leaders like Squando as visionaries deluded by Satan allowed the English to displace their own uncertainties onto Natives, hardening racial boundaries and moving internal doubts onto newly demonized others. The conclusion of Mather's story—the death of Philip in 1676 and the purported suicide of Squando in the early 1680s—wrapped up the chaos unleashed by the war into a neat, reassuring package; the implication of the suicide was that this bad end was a just punishment from God, a construction fully in keeping with New Englanders' providential view of events. With Squando's fate resolved, Mather could turn his attention away from the Natives' grievances and toward casting the war as an object lesson with which to encourage reform among the English.[20]

This tidy lesson seems too neat, however. Some scholars believe that Squando did not die at all; he simply moved inland after the war, exploiting the possibility of dealing with the French. These experts cite "Atecouando" as the sachem's real name, dismissing "Squando" as an English corruption and the suicide as a bit of English wishful thinking.[21] Other scholars make no such link, noting that Atecouando first appears in the records in 1688 and does not serve as paramount leader until 1701, suggesting a separate person altogether.[22] If this demonized figure reappeared having dealings with the English in Maine, as Atecouando does, would not these Englishmen have remembered the famous protagonist from Mather's history? Would not Cotton Mather, who writes his own history of these events in 1702, have corrected the story based on fresh news of his father's old protagonist? The linkage between Squando, last mentioned in 1684 as having died in 1682, and Atecouando, first appearing in the records in summer of 1688, is therefore hard to prove. If Squando and

Atecouando are one and the same, he would have had a career of over sixty years, as Squando was first recorded in the 1660s, and Atecouando disappears from the records in 1726—such a career is not impossible, but it is unlikely.

While Squando's fate remains open-ended, the story—as a story—can end in other ways besides, and those as well suggest that Mather moved too soon for too neat a close. The issues underlying Squando's protest certainly did not go away. Indian resistance did not disappear, either in the wake of Philip's death or after Squando's reported suicide. These alternatives will be considered at more length below.

But regardless of the real outcome, by turning his reader's gaze to the condensed stories of these awful ends, Mather manages to redefine King Philip's War as a victory designed by a chastening God. Squando and Philip are dead, and, as symbols of all Indian resistance, Mather and his readers could remain assured that this Indian resistance would die as well, as long as his English readers continued to reform their behavior. This belief flew in the face of abundant evidence that the Indians had very nearly destroyed the English, driving them out of Maine altogether. Indeed, these "eastern" parts would continue as "Indian Country" and hotly contested borderlands well into the eighteenth century.

With the story of Squando's suicide, Mather invited his reader to resonate with the defeat and destruction of false prophets. Even if it turned out to be untrue, Mather needed a death—and a suicide at that—to end his narrative. There is no reason to believe that Mather intentionally misled his readers. He was in regular communication with Joshua Scottow, a prominent trader and militia leader, and the report appears in Mather's diary as well as in his history.[23] But the mode of death (by hanging) is itself unusual, conveying a surprising acculturation of English practice. Poisoning was generally a more likely choice among the eastern Indians.[24] Modern testimony tells us of the many burdens faced by visionaries, and that, rather than actively welcoming visions, the recipients often experience themselves as burdened by them. Sometimes visionaries have to exercise considerable courage in following them.[25] Mather appropriated these visions, working them into his jeremiad about social decline as a harbinger of his hoped-for New England cultural reformation. Indeed, while English men and women during the war paid close attention to omens, images, wonders, and signs, what emerges most forcefully in the major accounts of the war is a sense of pervasive diabolic influence among the Indians, nowhere more prominent than in the stories of their dreams and visions.

When dreams are discussed in Mather or Hubbard, they are either examples of biblical judgment renewed in the present conflict—showing God is on the English side—or they are unequivocally represented as misleading visions inspired by Satan. This chapter opens with an extended discussion of Squando and his visionary movement before turning to other accounts of dreams and visions, including Philip's supposedly predictive dream, and investigating the ways that Indian revitalization struggles were portrayed by English authors as proof of their irredeemable link to the Devil. The resort to biblical imagery and language in these English accounts was designed to cement this link.

In Mather's telling, Squando first experienced visions well before the war. In his 1676 *Brief History*, Mather described the appearance of a spirit helper: "God appeared to him, in the form of a tall Man, in black Cloaths," and "commanded [him] to leave his Drinking of Strong Liquors, and to pray, and to keep Sabbaths, and to go to hear the Word Preached, all which things the Indian did for some years, with great seeming Devotion and Conscience observe."[26] Mather's later account in 1684's *Illustrious Providences* is a bit more fulsome, describing Squando's story, supported by "sundry accounts," to be "Remarkable." Mather wrote, "Many years ago he was sick, and near unto death, after which he said, that one pretending to be the English-mans God, appeared to him in form of an English Minister; and discoursed with him, requiring him to leave off his drinking of Rum, and religiously to observe the Sabbath day, and to deal justly amongst Men, withal promising him that if he did so, then at death his Soul should go upwards to an happy place; but if he did not obey these commandments, at death his Soul should go downwards, and be for ever miserable."[27] Mather presents the story as a curiosity, but not as a divinely inspired vision, noting that, "this pretended God said nothing to him about Jesus Christ," something a divine vision would have included.[28]

From an Algonquian perspective, the "English minister" who appeared to Squando might have been regarded as a manitou that, because of his repeated appearances, may have been a guardian spirit. Something quite powerful emerged from these syncretic visions, as Mather reported: "This Apparition so wrought upon Squando, as that he left his Drunkenness, and became a strict observer of the Sabbath day; Yea, so as that he always kept it as a day of Fast, and would hear the English Ministers Preach, and was very just in his dealing."[29]

To the English, then, this could still seem a hopeful sign of the progress of Christianity among the peoples of the Maine coast, and, what is more, this was a triumph of English Protestant Christianity in a border region hotly contested by both France and England. As the Reverend William Hubbard of Ipswich reported, both Squando and another sagamore, Madockawando of Penobscot, were "a strange kind of moralized savages," who were "Grave and Serious in their Speech and Carriage, and not without some shew of a kind of Religion."[30]

But as quickly as these potential converts appear in his account, Hubbard dismisses them (using language borrowed from Paul's second letter to the Corinthians) as deluded prophets of a faith, "which no doubt but they have learned from *the Prince of darkness,* (by the help of some papist in those parts) that can *Transform himself into an Angel of Light*; under that shape, the better to carry on the designes of his Kingdome."[31] As did Mather, Hubbard utterly rejected the visions: "It is said also, they pretend to have *received some Visions* and *Revelations,* by which they have been commanded to *worship the great God,* and not to *work on the Lords day.*" But, he added knowingly, "We know where *that Fountain* hath its Rise, that sendeth forth at the same place *sweet and bitter waters.* And from whence their hearts are inspired, that join blessing of God, with cursing and killing his Servants."[32]

The exact significance of Squando's visioning is hard to discern, both because of a lack of details and because his experiences were, without exception, recorded by his enemies in a foreign language. We clearly have too little information to assess the particular nature of the apparition that Squando saw. Did his apparition appear in nighttime dreams? In induced trance states? As a visual hallucination? Despite these gaps, by attempting to locate Squando within the contexts of Algonquian visioning practice and the pressures of English colonial expansion, we fulfill one scholar's call to place shamanic practice within specific local cultures, to avoid reductionism, and to plumb "the connections of shamanic practices to wider social processes."[33] Squando's visions both reflected and extended the tensions and opportunities of intercultural exchanges in prewar Saco.

Squando was a powwaw as well as a sachem. Hubbard notes elsewhere that this "Enthusiastical, or rather Diabolical Miscreant; who yet hath put on a garbe of Religion, and orders his People to do the like," was reported to be "performing Religious worship amongst the Indians in his way," and was "supposed to have very familiar Converse with the Devil, that appears to him . . . in some shape or other very frequently."[34] There are recorded examples of New

England sachems that also served as powwaws.[35] Indeed, Squando's very name (if it was not solely an English corruption of Atecouando) may have associated him with powerful and somewhat dark forces: Squantum was a personage associated with death, night, the northeast wind, the dark, the color black, and the underworld. As we saw above (Chapter 2), shamans did sometimes take on the names of powerful personages from Algonquian cosmology, merging with these guardian spirits to incorporate a guardian soul.[36] Even if he was Atecouando, and Squando was only an English corruption, both possible derivations of the name link the person to considerable spiritual power: Gordon M. Day, the respected ethnographer of northern New England peoples gives two possible etymologies for Atecouando, one translating to "the Deer Spirit-power" and the other to "the Dog Spirit-power."[37]

Visions that incorporated European figures or objects were one response to colonial contact. These seem to have offered a way for established Native leaders, especially religious specialists like powwaws, to absorb the manitou of the English spiritual specialist without disrupting the existing Native system of cosmological understanding.[38] New England Indians also appear to have incorporated whatever source of spiritual power might prove most efficacious: thus, when Uncas—an English ally throughout the war—despaired of his powwaws being able to bring forth rain in a time of drought no matter what "hideous and diabolical howlings" they employed, Mather reported in his *Brief History* that they turned to Mr. Fitch, the teacher of the church at Norwich. Fitch refused to try his hand until Uncas and his son Owaneco "had done with their vanities and witcheries."[39] So, too, Indian captive Quentin Stockwell reported that, when Indian powwaws could not achieve successes in hunting, his captors asked the English captives to pray, so they could "see what the English-man's God could do."[40]

Evidence suggests that the Saco Indians found Squando's visions compelling. Indians of New England valued both visions and visionaries, and Squando's status as a sachem may have made his visions all the more substantial in the eyes of the Saco Indians. Indeed, Hubbard notes that some English "that came lately from those parts" (presumably released captives) reported "that the Indians there do as yet refuse to have any peace with the *English*, and will not as yet return any of our captive Friends, till God speak to the foresaid *Enthusiasts*, that are *their Leaders*, that they should *no longer* make *warr with us*, and the like."[41]

Nor was Squando a lone visionary. Even before the outbreak of war, a

sagamore at Kittery had asked on his deathbed for some of his land to be conveyed by deed to his children, because "he knew there would shortly fall out a
War between the Indians and the English all over the Country, and that the
Indians at the first should prevail, and do much mischief to the English, and
kill many of them; But . . . after three years, all the Indians which so did, should
be rooted out, and utterly destroyed."[42] And again, near the end of the war, in
early 1677, Major Waldron's party, frustrated in its attempt to negotiate the return of English captives, chased the sagamore Mattahando and about twenty-
five of his men, shooting and killing seven, among whom was "an old Powwaw,
to whom the Devil had revealed, as sometimes he did to Saul, . . . that within
two days, the English would come and kill them all."[43] But if he was not the only
visionary in Mather and Hubbard's accounts, Squando and his story became
the personification of such practices, as well as of virtually the entire Indian
resistance movement on the Maine frontier.

During the war years, Squando led raids on the English settlement at Saco,
in which thirteen English colonists were killed and the town burned.[44] One
explanation for his anti-English actions is found in a story that, before hostilities broke out, three drunken Englishmen had intentionally overset a canoe in
which Squando's wife and child were traveling. Hubbard, whose account of this
is the most detailed, wrote that Squando's "squaw" (woman, wife) was "abused
by a rude and indiscreet act of some English Seamen in the last Summer, 1675,
who either overset the Canoo wherein said Squaw with her Child were swim-
ming [riding] in a River thereabouts, or else to try whether the Children of the
Indians as they had heard, could Swimme as naturally as any other Creatures,
wittingly cast her Child into the water."[45] In other words, the sailors may have
intentionally thrown the baby into the water to see if Indians, like animals,
could swim on instinct alone. The mother rescued the child, but, in Hubbard's
account, it died a few days later. In Mather's account, the war in Maine had
begun in revenge for this horrific interracial incident, although he does not
explicitly mention Squando as the father, explaining "that some rude English
did purposely overset a Canoe wherein was an Indian Lad; and that although a
Squaw dived to the bottom of the River and getched [sic] him up alive, yet the
Lad never came to himself again."[46]

Squando, in these stories, vowed revenge: "Squando Father of the Child
hath been so provoked thereat, that he hath ever since set himself to do all the
mischief he can to the English in those parts, and was never as yet since that
time [as of Hubbard's writing in 1677] truly willing to be Reconciled."[47] Mather

added a stern rebuke to the English: "It is greatly to be lamented that the heathen should have any ground for such allegations, or that they should be scandalized by men that call themselves Christians."[48]

Whether or not it was really Squando's wife and child in that canoe, this report was used to explain his sudden antagonism to the English. More important still, this incident distills a much larger set of struggles between English and Algonquian peoples over land and resources, using the power of narrative to convey them in a highly condensed form. English agrarian economies were incompatible with the hunter-gatherer organization of northern New England Algonquian society over the long term. When interethnic economic tensions were added to an English sense of superiority over the Indians, the result was the type of racial violence suffered by Squando's wife and child.[49] As Philip's men arrived from the south to enlist the assistance of the Maine Indians in the growing resistance, these northern groups had numerous reasons to join in warfare that might drive the aggressors out of their homelands. Suggestions from the invisible world—Squando's visions, for example—thus mirrored other more material factors undergirding resistance to English colonialism.

The visible and invisible worlds now moved in concert with each other. With the first hostilities in the spring of 1675, Philip managed to mobilize a widespread pan-Indian struggle that, while it raged in part in the invisible realm, nevertheless had devastating effects on everyday life. Indians very nearly destroyed the English colonists' society. More than half the English towns were destroyed or evacuated. The war itself was only ended by the intervention of the Algonquians' rivals, the Mohawks, who saw advantage in an alliance with the British officials in New York and against the New England Algonquians.

William Hubbard's *Narrative* located several causes for the conflict. Given the long and peaceful relationship in southern New England between Massasoit and the English colonists, the accession of Philip to the sachemdom after the death of his brother Alexander in 1662 brought sudden strife and discord to the "league"—in part because of "his ambitious and haughty Spirit," which was, Hubbard said in a bit of post hoc interpretation, why he was nicknamed "King-Philip," brother to Alexander the Great.[50] Hubbard describes the great "correspondence" between Philip and the English over the next years and defends the colonists from blame, "no cause of provocation being given by the English."[51] The frustrated historian finally falls back upon events in the invisible world to explain the continued hostility: "What can be imagined therefore, besides the instigation of Satan, that either envied at the prosperity of the

Church of God here seated, or else fearing lest the power of the Lord Jesus, that had overthrown his Kingdome in other parts of the World, should do the like here."[52] Indeed, by 1671, "the Devill, who was a Murderer from the beginning, had so filled the heart of this salvage Miscreant [Philip] with envy and malice against the English, that he was ready to break out into open war . . . pretending some petite injuryes done him in his planting land."[53]

In northern New England, Hubbard cited English colonists' squabbles among themselves as a hindrance to the development of robust and unified colonial settlements in this borderland, which prevented a quick and fair response to Native complaints; "a well ordered Government" with "absolute or positive and unquestioned power of Rule in their hands," would have been able to avert "the present mischief that is come upon those places."[54]

But to those who laid the blame for conflict at the feet of "the Ruder sort of the English, by their imprudent & irregular acting" (a direct reference to Mather's frequent laments at English misbehavior), Hubbard held up the Indians' natural perfidy: "Yet is it too evident, that the said Indians (who naturally delight in bloody & deceitful actions) did lay hold of any opportunity that might serve for a pretence to be put upon their barbarous practices."[55] Elsewhere he complains, "Subtilety, malice, and Revenge, seems to be as inseparable from them [the Indians], as if it were part of their Essence."[56] Hubbard hoped that the English would learn from this betrayal, but in contrast to Mather's pronouncements about the importance of reformation among the English, Hubbard argued they ought to learn "to beware *this subtle Brood*, and *Generation of Vipers*."[57] The quoted phrases (Matthew 23:33) speak of scribes and Pharisees who reject true belief, but earlier in the same book (Matthew 12:34) this "generation of vipers" is castigated, saying, "how can ye, being evil, speak good things? for out of the abundance of the heart the mouth speaketh."[58] In short, neither things from the visible world (complaints over land and mistreatment) nor things from the invisible one ("deluding" visions) could sufficiently explain these events. Indians, for Hubbard, were not to be trusted, because they were manipulated by Satan himself. This is a potent moment of transformation, a moment in which the rhetoric of diabolism begun with the first descriptions of Indian dreaming and powwowing began to be translated into real-world consequences, shaping racialized English policies toward the Indians.

As Lepore pointed out, only a few English men "recognized that such acts of 'cruelty' were also a form of communication, not from God, but from the Indians themselves." And though "most colonists" would deny it, "Algonquian attacks and Algonquian tortures were not random or arbitrary."[59] Indeed, one period observer, Benjamin Church, thought that the English provoked the Indians early in the war by taking some "eight-score" (160) Indians who had "surrendered themselves" and carrying them away to Plymouth, where they were "there sold, and transported out of the country" as slaves. Church thought that "had their promises to the Indians been kept, and the Indians fairly treated, 'tis probable that most, if not all the Indians in those parts, had soon followed the example . . . which would have been a good step toward finishing the war."[60] Church even lost "the good will and respect of some that before were his good friends" because he so vociferously "opposed" this betrayal of trust.[61]

But most colonists experienced the Indians' actions as inexplicable, and therefore, for them, the war was doubly terrifying. As Mather put it, quoting from Psalm 124, "The Heathen . . . rose up against us, thinking to swallow us up quick, when their Wrath was kindled against us. [But] Blessed be the Lord, who hath not given us [as] a prey to their Teeth."[62] Instead, paraphrasing Numbers 24:8, Mather added, with Old Testament fervor, "This Israel in the Wilderness [the English] hath eat[en] up the Nations his Enemies, he hath broke their Bones, and pierced them through with his Arrows."[63] Yet privately, Mather despaired that these awful events might ever lead to true reformation. He confided to his diary in October 1675: "N.E. [New England] is in the most Lamentable state that ever was. The Indians risen almost round the countrey. God doth not goe forth wth o[u]r Armies. Many cutt off by the enemy. There [is] like to be scarcity of p[ro]vision. Some speake as if the spotted Fever were in Boston. No Reformation wrought by thes[e] Judg[men]ts."[64] By February 1675/6 he lamented, "People are not Humbled & Reformed. Full of murmurings, & unreasonable Rage agt the enemy. . . . It is to be feared that there is guilt upon the Land in resp[ect]. of the Indians yea Guilt of blood in resp[ect]. of the Indian so treacherously murdered at Chelmsford. I am afraid God will visit [judgment on the English] for that g[rie]f."[65]

If Mather himself was afraid, at home in Boston, it is little wonder that English men and women closer to the action also searched for signs, portents, and other wonders with which to make sense of these chaotic and terrifying events. Thus, at the beginning of the war, when Daniel Henchman's company set out on an evening march against Philip's forces, they were forced to stop by an eclipse of the moon, and to wait "till the moon recovered her light again." As Hubbard noted, "some melancholy Fancyes would not be perswaded, but that the Eclipse falling out at that instant of time, was ominous, conceiving also that in the centre of the Moon they discerned an unusual black spot, not a little resembling the scalp of an Indian."[66]

In the spring of 1676, some of the inhabitants at Plymouth saw "the perfect form of an Indian Bow appearing in the aire," and "(at least some of them)" had interpreted this as "a Prodigious Apparition."[67] While Mather noted that another similar sight occurred "a little before the Fort Fight in the Narragansett Countrey," he cautioned that no one could know "but that it may be an Omen of ruine to the enemy, and that the Lord will break the bow and spear asunder, and make warrs to cease unto the ends of the earth."[68] In his private diary he was excited but skeptical, noting that those collected "at Lieut Howland's Garison in Plym[outh]" had "seen in the air an Indian bow pointing from East to West!" but cautioning, "Perhaps the edge of a cloud illuminated by the rising or setting sun. I have seen divers appearances of the like kind."[69] Hubbard reported that at the beginning of the war, "some had imagined they saw the form of an *Indian Bow*," noting more laconically that "the mischief following was done by [Indians'] Guns, not by Bows."[70]

But if Mather and Hubbard tried to downplay these wondrous signs, it was because most colonists took them quite seriously. Even Mather himself remarked, "It is a common observation, verified by the experience of many Ages, that great and publick Calamityes seldome come upon any place without Prodigious Warnings to forerun and signify what is to be expected."[71] Elsewhere in his account he noted, "Certainly God would have such providences to be observed and recorded; He doth not send such things for nothing, or that no notice should be taken of them, And therefore was I willing to give a true account thereof, hoping that thereby mistakes and false Reports may be prevented."[72] Indeed, Mather then reported, he had heard of several strange events from "serious, faithfull, and Judicious hands, even of those who were ear witnesses;" that "no less than seven years before this warr there were plain prodigious Notices of it," when, on the morning of November 30, "being a very clear, still, Sun-shine morning there were diverse Persons in Maldon who heard in the air on the Southeast of them [in the direction of Mount Hope], a great Gun go off, and as soon as that was past, they heard the report of small Guns like musket shott, discharging very thick," and, most amazing of all, "the flying of the Bullets which came singing over their heads, and seemed to be very near them, [and] after this they heard drums passing by them & going Westward." On the same day in Scituate and other towns in Plymouth Colony, reliable individuals "heard as it were the running of troops of horses." And, just a year before the war actually broke out, "Hadly, Northampton, and other Towns thereabouts [on the western frontier]" heard "the report of a great piece of Ordinance, with a shaking of the earth, and a considerable Echo, whenas there was not ordinance really discharged at or near any of those Towns at that time."[73]

The war had two fronts, one in southern and central New England that raged from 1675 to 1676, and the other along what is now the Maine coastline. That latter conflict began a bit later and stretched longer, to the 1678 Treaty of Casco Bay, but the Maine frontier did not quiet until well into the eighteenth century. Although there was a brief lull in the 1680s, violence would break out with renewed vigor just a few short years later with the arrival of King William's War in 1689 and would continue largely unabated through Queen Anne's War of 1713.[74] Cultural conflicts along the Maine coast were long-standing, even before the 1676 eruption of violence, and frequently, these prewar incidents had been quite brutal, as Hubbard's account makes abundantly clear.[75]

King Philip's War was characterized by a shocking cycle of violence and retaliation.[76] English garrison houses were overwhelmed, the men put to death, infants killed, and the women and older children taken captive.[77] When the English had the upper hand, Indian attackers were gunned down or clubbed to death and Indian survivors were sold into slavery. The killing extended over many months, with reverberations well into the next century.[78] Hundreds of English men, women, and children were killed; period estimates put the number between five hundred and eight hundred.[79] During the war some twenty-five English towns were destroyed: "More than half of all the colonists' settlements in New England . . . and the line of English habitation had been pushed back almost to the coast."[80] Maine was completely evacuated. After the fall of Arrowsick Island in August 1676, Hubbard reported, "All the Plantations of the English in those parts were soon after left, and forsaken by degrees."[81] As Hubbard noted of the refugees, "When People have once been frighted with Reports and Sense of danger, they are ready to fly away like a Hart before the Hunter or his Hounds."[82]

At the height of the conflict, in January 1676, Francis Card, an escaped captive, reported that Squando was telling the Indians, "God doth speak to him, and doth tell him that God hath left our Nation [the English] to them to *destroy*, and the Indians do take it for a Truth all that he doth tell them; because they have met with *no Affront*."[83] In his discussion of Card's news, Hubbard suggested it was best "not to trouble our selves farther with those Ministers of Satan. . . . We know better how to understand the mind of the great Lord of

Heaven & Earth then to depend on such lying Oracles."[84] Indeed, the Indians "since their *delusions*," were, if anything, "*two fold more the children of Hell* then they were before."[85] As if to moderate the stream of vituperation, Hubbard tacked on a prayer: "That God who hath at present turned their hearts to hate his People, and deal subtilly with his Servants; we hope in his time, will either *turn the stream*, and cause them [the Indians] to deal *friendly* and *sincerely* with his People, as *heretofore*, or," he burst out, "give us an opportunity to *destroy them*."[86]

A s much as the English suffered, the Indians suffered more; and, ultimately, it would be the Indians who would lose the struggle. At the end—their leaders dead, towns destroyed, the people hungry and discouraged—the coalition of Philip's supporters fell apart, and various sachems began to make their own arrangements for peace. Philip himself was slain in August 1676. Squando signed the Piscataqua Treaty between the English and the Pennacooks and Wabanakis at Cocheco on July 3, 1676.[87] Eventually returning to war, a year later, in June 1677, he renewed his promises of peace and returned an English girl, the only survivor of the attack on Waterly's house at Casco Bay, who had been taken captive in September 1675.[88]

Other sachems remained at war, and the fighting in Maine dragged on past Philip's death, extending well into 1677. Even Hubbard was cautious: "The Dispensations of the Almighty have been very *awful* towards us, for a long time, not seeming to *go forth with our Armies*, nor helping us in *defending* our selves, or defeating of our Enemies, as if he had a purpose and designe to bring a *sharp Scourge* upon us, by that means to *humble us* . . . and then (as we trust) to *do us good in our latter end*: acting therein as wise *Parents* that after they have *corrected* their *Children*, to *cast the Rod* into the Fire."[89] Nevertheless, Hubbard wrote, the tide seemed to have turned; "Justice" was "by degrees pursuing those *perfidious Villains*, and one after another they are brought under the Wheel of Destruction."[90] It had been much "hoped" by those who participated in a February 1677 offensive that "the Enemies" would be "so *scattered and broken*, that they will not be able to *rally again* suddenly."[91] Indeed, among the Indians of southern New England, "by this occasion, (quarrelling with us without cause) themselves in a manner [are] all destroyed by the special hand of God," and those that were "at the beginning of these Troubles, possessed of many goodly Havens, many rich and Fertile places, as at Mount-Hope, and all along the

Narrhagansit Country," were now "their *Posterity* quite *rooted out*, as were the Pequots before them, whereby it may be gathered as we hope, that God is making way to settle a better people in their rooms, and in their stead."[92] And, proclaimed Hubbard, "Thus have our Enemies themselves many of them *fallen into the pit, which they have been digging for others*."[93] As if his words could make it so, the biblical reference here is doubled, recalling both Psalm 7, verse 15: "He hathe made a pit and digged it, and is fallen into the pit that he made," and Psalm 9, verse 15: "The heathen are sunken downe in the pit, that they made: in the net that they hid, is their fote [foot] taken."[94] Mather concurred, invoking Psalm 9 as well: "The Heathen are sunk down into the pit that they made, in the net which they had hid, is their own foot taken; the Lord is known by the Judgment which he executeth, the wicked is snared in the work of his own hands."[95] Racialist rhetoric takes center stage in Hubbard's account: "Barbarous Enemies," a "Salvage Villain," "a *nest of Hornets*," "*this subtle Brood*, and *Generation of Vipers*."[96] Having recounted what seemed to him an obvious instance of Indian treachery, Hubbard pronounced this judgment on the Indians: "Subtilety, malice and Revenge seems to be as inseparable from them, as if it were part of their Essence."[97]

In 1682, Squando was reported to have experienced another vision, in which the English minister urged him to kill himself. There was a promise that he would be resurrected soon: "The pretended English-mans God, appeared to him again, as afore, in the form of a Minister, requiring him to kill himself, and promising him that if he did obey, he should live again the next day, and never die more."[98] When Squando told his wife "and some other Indians" about this new vision, "they most earnestly advised him not to follow the murderous Counsel which the Spectre had given." Nevertheless, Mather reported, "He since hath Hanged himself, and so is gone to his own place" (i.e., damnation, hell).[99] Joshua Scottow, the military commander who relayed news of Squando's death to Mather, was more direct, offering the simple invocation (from Judges 5:31): "Soe let all thine enemies perish, Oh Lord!"[100]

If the English seemed sure of its meaning, Squando's death still leaves modern readers puzzled. While we know little about his mental state, any of the circumstances (the death of his child, the ongoing dispossession of Native peoples in this part of New England, violent and bloody raids during the war, the subsequent Indian defeat) point to the presence of massive trauma. Many question the story's veracity; hanging stands out as not quite true to Woodland Indian practices, which would be more likely to attribute a death to poisoning or simply to soul sickness. Yet many, if not most, revitalization movements blend elements of Christianity (Christ's death and resurrection) with nativist goals; the sudden appearance of a Christlike death and resurrection to remobilize this defeated and doubtless traumatized community is in keeping with other similar visionary movements. If Squando viewed himself as a visionary called to action by a manitou, it would be a summons that one had best obey.

If the records are puzzlingly inconclusive for recapturing Native perspectives, we can at least focus on what such a report of suicide would have done for the English. Mather's diary for 1682 notes only, "This winter Simon & Squando, the bloody Eastern Indians, died; the latter of wh hanged himself."[101] Joshua Scottow's letter to Mather in October 1683 stresses that Squando was "dumpish [sad] & melancholique" before his death.[102] This seems more a suicide and less a "spirited resistance." Or rather, it was a suicide as a form of resistance. And yet, Cotton Mather suggests this was no suicide at all: in his version, Squando was simply following the promises of his spirit helper, "assuring him that he should revive in a Day or two, never to die any more."[103] On the English side, Scottow's summation ("Soe let all thine enemies perish, Oh Lord!") rings a bit hollow, given the mortal danger the colonies had faced and, in fact, would face once again in just a few years along this same coast.[104] With convoluted syntax, Mather noted: "That [a] Remarkable Judgement . . . [has] fallen upon those who have sought the hurt of the People of God in New-England, is so notorious, as that it . . . [has] become the observation of every Man."[105] Indeed, although these "Adversaries" had "escaped longer unpunished than others," Mather remarked, "their ends have been of all the most woful, and tragical at last."[106]

Mather was very interested in endings. But Squando's end, though remarkable and strange (and quite possibly, entirely fictional), paled in comparison to that of Philip, whose end—according to Mather's pen—involved a predictive dream that was truly biblical in scope. "For one of Philips men (being disgusted at him, for killing an Indian who had propounded an expedient for peace with the English) ran away from him."[107] The turncoat came to Rhode Island and told the English "that Philip was now returned again to Mount-Hope, and undertook [the next day] to bring them to the Swamp where he hid himself."[108] Thus far, Benjamin Church's account corroborates Mather's version: one of Philip's men had indeed gone over to the English side, after Philip had murdered his brother "for giving some advice that displeased him."[109] Church then recounts how he followed this man's instructions to find Philip, splitting his men into separate parties, and creeping forward in order to preserve the surprise. According to Church, one of his men, thinking (wrongly) that they had been discovered, let loose a shot that began a volley that passed just over the heads of the Indians, who had not yet "had time to rise from their sleep."[110] Philip, in this account, raced "foremost" into the swamp, where he was felled.

In Mather's account, Philip had a predictive dream on this very morning: "It seemeth that night Philip (like the man, in the Host of Midion) dreamed that he was fallen into the hand of the English; and just as he was saying to those that were with him, that they must fly for their lives that day, lest the Indian that was gone from him should discover where he was, Our Souldiers came upon him, and surrounded the Swamp (where he with seven of his men [had] absconded)."[111]

Mather references the dream of the Midianite, from the book of Judges 7:13–15. In this story, which was a staple of the biblical canon on dreams, God guided Gideon to the camp of his enemies the Midianites at night, where he overheard one Midianite tell another his dream: "Behold, I dreamed a dream," said the Midianite while Gideon secretly listened, "and, lo, a cake of barley bread tumbled into the host of Midian, and came unto a tent, and smote it that it fell, and overturned it, that the tent lay along [fell down on the ground]."[112] And once Gideon heard the dream, which had the interpretation that the Midianites would be easily overcome, he gave thanks to God, and then took his inferior force of three hundred men and crept down to the Midianite camp, and all at once, when Gideon blew his trumpet as a signal, the men surprised the Midianites, who, in the confusion, slew each other—and so the Lord designed the victory of Gideon and his men.[113] As the Geneva Bible notes underscore, the "whole victory" was the Lord's, and Gideon was but his servant in achieving its implementation.

Through this story, Mather stressed once again the proper relationship of man to God in New England: the Indians were, like the Midianites, infidels and (as Mather and Hubbard made abundantly clear to their readers) had been manipulated by Satan. In each of their accounts, King Philip's War had been unleashed by God himself for a very specific reason: to provoke a reformation of the English. New England's victorious English Christians were, therefore, but a faithful Gideon, and the destruction of the Indians was, like their rising, just a part of God's plan. God even arranged it so that an Indian ally called Alderman—not an English soldier—fired the fatal bullet (although, according to Church, only after the English soldier, whose gun had misfired, gave him permission).[114] Alderman, according to Mather, had remained loyal to the English from the beginning, a detail that was important to the biblical parallel that Mather now developed. Quoting Isaiah 33:1—a text that offers a powerful plea from the faithful against those that would destroy them, and which promises that God will deal harshly with his enemies—Mather wrote: "Thus when Philip had made an end to deal treacherously, his own Subjects dealt treacherously with him. This Wo[e] was brought upon him that spyled when he was not spoyled."[115] But that was hardly all. Philip met his end "in that very place where he first contrived [to begin] his mischief."[116]

Church ordered that Philip's body be dragged out of the swampy ground where he had fallen and pulled onto the upland, "And a doleful, great, naked, dirty beast he looked like."[117] Noting that, "he had caused many an Englishman's body to lie unburied and rot above ground," Church ordered, "that not one of his bones should be buried."[118] Calling "his old Indian executioner," Church ordered the man to behead and quarter Philip. But when the man came forward, before he struck, "he made a small speech" to the body, "directing it to Philip," saying "he had been a very great man, and had made many a man afraid of him, but so big as he was, he would now chop his ass for him. And so went to work."[119] Such a speech suggests a special care taken in approaching this potent manitou. Church's account then reveals that the head and hand of Philip—a hand quite "remarkable," for "being much scarred," were then given to Alderman, "to show to such gentlemen as would bestow gratuities upon him. And accordingly, he got many a penny by it."[120]

Mather's account elevates these actions to the level of scripture once again, stressing the ways that New England's unfolding history merely fulfilled the experiences already revealed in the Bible. He noted that although the English had vanquished Philip and his men, "the Lord . . . to prevent us from being lifted up with our successes, and that we might not become [too] secure, so ordered as that not an English-man but an Indian (though under *Churches* influence) must have the honour of killing Philip."[121] Mather also likened Philip to another biblical foe, writing that Philip was here "taken and destroyed, and there was he (like as Agag [King of the Amalekites, captured by Saul] was hewed in pieces before the Lord) cut into four quarters, and is now hanged up as a monument of revenging Justice, his head being cut off and carried away to Plymouth, his Hands were brought to Boston."[122] Mather ended with the familiar invocation from Judges 5:31: "So let all thine Enemies perish, O Lord!"[123]

While Church's family later complained that the captain had received no recompense from the colonies for his efforts in tracking down Philip and his remaining confederates, his account suggests that the Indians were very careful to honor his victory over the sachem. Philip's counselor Annawon, who was captured some days later, presented Church with a pack containing Philip's wampum belts "being nine inches broad, wrought with black and white wompom in various figures and flowers, and pictures of many birds and beasts," as well as "two horns of glazed powder and a red cloth blanket." And "speaking in plain English," the man said, "Great Captain, you have killed Philip and conquered his country . . . so [I] suppose the war is ended by your means; and therefore these things belong unto you."[124]

The war's end seemed to many to reveal the final triumph of English spiritual power over Indian powwaws despite their visioning, soul flight, and various magical protections. One of Philip's counselors—Tispaquin, "a great captain"—was among the last to be captured. In his story, people on both sides might have marveled that the English God seemed to vanquish Indian foes so easily, even those protected by powerful manitou. The Indians had said "that he [Tispaquin] was such a great Pouwau that no bullet could enter him."[125] Being a practical sort, Church hoped to capture him alive, "for there was a war broke out in the eastern part of the country [Maine], and he would have him saved to go with them to fight the eastern Indians."[126] But though Church "laid a trap," by capturing "his wife, children and company" and carrying them to Plymouth as hostages for his surrender, the Englishman returned from Boston only to find that the Plymouth men had already executed him, and "that the heads of Annawon [and] Tispaquin [had been] cut off, which were the last of Philip's friend's."[127] Hubbard reported that, although the Indians had reported, "that the bullets glanced by him and could not hurt him," once condemned to death, "he was found penetrable by the English gunns, for he fell down at the first shot, and thereby received the just reward of his former wickedness."[128] While Englishmen such as Mather or Hubbard may have found this to be a welcome restoration of God's order, Church considered it a waste of a useful resource in the continuing struggle in Maine. It is hard to know what Philip's surviving people made of this shocking assault on the powwaw's body.

*    *    *

King Philip's War posed a challenge to both of New England's peoples. To the Indians, it represented an attempt to push back against English colonialism, with its daily assaults on Indian persons, property, and beliefs. It made sense that powwowing and potent visions both served a critical role during wartime. The experiences of Squando may be our best-documented instance of the influence of a visionary leader in the region, but Squando's experiences were clearly not isolated events. In such troubled times, many powwaws sought, and received, visions with which to guide their actions. If they were divided over the best course, their attempts to enlist powerful manitou in their cause were nearly universal.

For the English, the search for omens, signs, and other "wonders" was a natural reaction to the terror and helplessness of the wartime assaults. But in the language of wonders, we see a subtle shift. It was the Indians who received dreams or visions, not English men or women. What emerges most forcefully in the major accounts of the war is that the war deepened English convictions that Indian dreamers primarily suffered from diabolical influence. The earlier characterizations of powwowing with their animalistic imagery continued and, if anything, became more firmly entrenched in the colonial imaginary. English dreams disappear from the record; Indian dreams move to center stage—and yet, these dreams now can only be conceived as diabolically inspired.

There can be no question that New England's people looked at the war, as Hubbard indicated, for its significance as a sign of "God's mind." And if it was an act of revitalization for the Indians, it was as well for the English, who felt they had not lived up to the aspirations of the immigrant generation. It was hard to see the war as anything but the chastening hand of God—as a dreadful judgment on God's people. As the numerous scriptural quotations in Mather's and Hubbard's accounts make clear, both Squando's visions and Philip's dream linked the actual events of 1675 and 1676 to the more deeply meaningful events in scripture. The layers of this language tune our ears to the authors' attempts to discern God's mind—his message for his people—and to find a reason for the terrible events unfolding all around.

Try though they might to put the horrible events of 1675 and 1676 to rest, such traumatic encounters would not resolve as neatly as either Mather's or Hubbard's accounts might have suggested. While Squando and Philip suffered remarkable ends, their deaths—and those of so many other Indians—would not put to rest the fears of the English. In his diary for 1681, Mather noted that the year had begun "awfully" that is, with awe-inspiring portents. "The latter end of last year," had seen a comet, "a fearful blazing star whereby the whole earth hath been alarmed." Now, in Connecticut, "We hear rumors as if some prodigies [are] observed. . . . Tis reported that at Wallingford an Indian appeared in the star (probably a phantasy)[;] Guns & drums heard at Middletown & Guildford." In the margin, he noted with some relief, "(The report occasioned by a drum which somebody did really beat but was supposed to be an invisible hand.)" This could not quell the terror resurgent, however, as the entry continues, "Rumors & great fears lest N.E. should be involved in another War with the Indians."[129] Clearly, the death of Philip—while a remarkable ending by anyone's account—could not, by itself, provide resolution.[130] Would reports of Squando's supposed suicide the next year provide a better reassurance? The "awful" events of the Indian war would continue to resound in strange drums and prodigious stars—in terrifying dreams—and, in the northernmost parts, in resurgent conflict for years to come.

# Chapter 5

## *Emotion, Embodiment, and Context*

Despite the increasing demonization of Indians, Quakers, and others as "deluded dreamers," English colonists at the end of the seventeenth century still embraced all sorts of wondrous experiences, from visits by specters and apparitions to dreams in which they communed with the dead or with relatives far from home. One problem they faced lay in how to discriminate a dream visitation from a material apparition, and another lay in how much weight to give to knowledge gained from their dreams. Because seventeenth-century magistrates allowed testimony about ghosts and apparitions to be offered in evidence, determinations about what had been a true visitation (either in sleep or in a waking state) and what had been a deluding dream sometimes became crucial. Nowhere does this appear more clearly than in the trials for witchcraft that occurred at Salem in 1692. Here, events that might, under other circumstances, have been taken for "frothy" or malicious dreams became compelling evidence of diabolical wrongdoing. Historians have wrestled for years with the reasons that events at Salem blossomed into crisis. But as participants looked back on these dreadful events, they acknowledged that many individuals had been hanged on no firmer grounds than mere dreams and fancies.[1]

Events that modern observers would class as dreams or sleep disturbances were often defined differently by colonists, and this usually depended greatly on the surrounding context, including the dream's manifest content, and most important, the feelings embedded in the dream. Whether dreams brought useable insight, vain hopes, or authentic connection to divine power remained very much in question during the latter decades of the seventeenth century and throughout much of the next. What was classed as dream experience, what was understood as waking experience, and which of these were seen as "real" was also deeply dependent on context.

Therefore, we might say that the English could never fully colonize dreams, at least not in the sense of either being able to contain them or to render them completely powerless. But certain forms of experience—apparitions, spectral visits, or conversations with the dead—might be classed as dreams (and therefore as something subject to question), or they could be determined to have really occurred. How wondrous experiences were defined depended on many factors, including who had experienced them and the nature of the feeling embedded within them. For some on the margins of colonial society—women suspected of witchcraft, for example—such dreamlike experiences would have consequences that were only too real. But a great deal also hinged on the sleeper's emotional experience on awakening: being soothed, enlivened, or happily "amazed" was a sign of a wondrous dream, worthy of scrutiny or even some active fulfillment, but not a cause for criminal action. Terrifying experience was another matter and might result in legal action or scrutiny by the community. Whether happy or fear-inducing, such startling experience remained worthy of examination and reflection.

At the very end of May 1692, William Stacy, a man of middle years, swore a deposition that accused his neighbor Bridget Bishop of being a witch, based on events that had happened some fourteen years before (about 1678). The suspicious events included: when Stacy had smallpox, he had received a strange visit from Bridget in which she had rather excessively "Professed" her love; money Bishop had paid to Stacy mysteriously disappeared right out of the "Pockett where he put it"; the wheel of a cart full of grain had become sunk in a hole, but later, on looking again, the hole was nowhere to be found.

And then, "sometime after, "in the winter about midnight ~~being awake~~ this Deponent felt something betweene his lips Pressing hard agt his teeth: and withal was very Cold: insomuch that it did awake him so that he gott up and sat upon his beed." As Stacy sat, "he at the same time [at once] seeing the said Bridgett Bishop sitting at the foot of his bed: being to his seeming, it was then as light as if it had been day." There is a period here, as if the clerk paused while someone asked a question, and then went on: Stacy averred that it was Bishop, "or one in the said Bishop[s] shape: she having then a black cap, & and black hat, and a Red Coat . . . then she the said Bishop or her shape clapt her coate close to her Leggs, & hopt upon the bed and about the roome and then went out."[2]

Immediately after the nighttime visitation, Stacy told his friends about the apparition and the neighborhood began to talk. At this, he received a visit from Bishop herself, who "asked him whither that [which he had reported] was true," as "he had told to severall: he answered that was true & that it was she, and bid her denigh it if she dare." She did not deny it, but went away angry, complaining that he did her a great "Mischief" because "folks would believe him before anybody Elce."[3]

Bishop's fears proved all too true. One of the first to be accused of witchcraft at Salem, she would also be the first to be executed. In her April 19 examination before the court, Bishop protested her innocence; but accusers produced proofs of mischief done by Bishop in spectral form. Asked to show the court her coat, the justices found "it cut or toren two ways." This was apparent proof of the story told by witnesses Jonathan and Mary Walcot. Tormented by a specter that only Mary could see, her brother Jonathan had taken up his sword, still in its scabbard, and struck at the air.[4] Mary testified that "she saw that he had tore her [Bishop's] coat in striking, & she heard it tare," and now the rent garment confirmed the deed.[5] The court pressed Bishop repeatedly to explain her specter's acts: "Who is it that doth it [torment the victims] if you doe not[;] they say it is your likenes that comes and torments them and tempts them to write in the booke," and "have you not given consent that some evill spirit should doe this in your likenes[?]" When Bishop continued to profess absolute innocence, Marshall Herrick asked, "How came you into my bedchamber one morning then and asked me whither I had any curtains to sell[?]"[6]

All this was enough to hold Goody Bishop over for trial, but in the eyes of her neighbors, her "shape" continued to make mischief even while she was at the jail, held in irons. At the trial in June, Mary Warren complained that around April 19 Bridget Bishop "did appear to this depon[ant] tempting her to signe the book & oft times . . . the sd Bridgett did torture & afflic[t] this depont," despite being in jail at the time; indeed, Bishop was always "in Chaines" when Warren saw her.[7] On June 1, Abigail Hobbs said she had seen Bishop, among others, "at the generall meeting of the Witches in the field near Mr. Parrisses' house."[8] On the same day, Sarah Churchill, a confessed witch, said that Bridget Bishop "appeared" to her and confessed to having killed a child, and later that she "saw Goody Olliver [Bishop] sitt sate vpon her knee."[9]

In early June, Bishop was tried and convicted, and she was hanged on June 10, 1692.[10] Of the testimonies presumably used against her at trial (excluding those of the afflicted girls), those of William Stacy, John Cook, John Louder, and Richard Coman centered on descriptions of mysterious visitations from Bishop in the nighttime or very early morning, while Susannah Shelden said that Bishop's "Apperishtion" had appeared to her, followed by "t[w]o little children . . . [who] said that they ware Thomas Greens two tiwins [*sic*] and tould Bridget Bishop to hir face that she had murthered them in seting them into fits whereof they dyed."[11] A final nail in Bishop's coffin was John Bly Sr. and his son William's testimony that they had "found seuerall popitts made vp of Raggs And hoggs Brusells [bristles] with headless[s] pins in Them with the points outward," stuffed in "holes" in the cellar wall of her "owld house she formerly Liued in."[12] The accusations against Bishop in the first trial of the 1692 outbreak offer a classic witchcraft case in which nighttime visitations, strange illnesses (especially in helpless children and animals), and odd apparitions seemed to follow on interactions with an angry or vengeful neighbor.

The Bishop case offers important links to the study of dreams, dreaming, and visions because it brings folk understandings of the person and her alters (specter, shape, likeness, apparition) into the open. In no other set of records do we see the thinking of ordinary men and women, or their experience of the invisible world, quite so dramatically exposed. The Bishop case is especially important for the ways that the deponents stressed nighttime visitations by the woman—visits that verge closely on English folk beliefs about the nightmare, but that were almost without exception carefully marked as events experienced in a waking state. Just as New England Algonquians' dream souls were thought to travel at night, so, too, careful study of witch belief exposes a remarkable complexity of English theories about the soul and the body, consciousness and corporeality. In particular, the picture that emerges is one in which the person's shape (likeness, specter), could move separately from the corporeal person. The shape then interacted with real, substantive persons as well as with the specters or shapes of others. The Salem crisis would eventually end because elite men decided both that spectral testimony was legally suspect and that the Devil might take the shape of anyone, without their consent, thus implicating otherwise innocent men and women.[13]

This chapter looks at several different forms of dream experience and dreamlike events, beginning with the witch's specter, her familiars and the nightmare, which was intimately connected to witchcraft belief. The analysis then moves to nighttime apparitions of all sorts, including visitations from the dead and at least one dream involving an angel. An examination of these strange visitations reveals a social history of dreaming and its connections to ideas about the relationship of body, mind, and spirit. Social status, individual identity, and the experiential context could determine whether visitations were interpreted as dreams or as other sorts of events. But above all, the emotional tone of the visitation seems to have determined its fate. Extended discussion of dreams reported by Samuel Sewall suggest that happy or amazing experience might actually satisfy significant emotional needs. Modern interpreters would term these selfobject experiences. Usually not frightening, these sorts of positive experiences rarely became sources of controversy or conflict. Terrifying, assaultive, or otherwise troubling experience sometimes demanded further investigation. Context was therefore key in discriminating wondrous dreams from diabolical activity. In the Salem trials and other legal actions that open the chapter, dreamt evidence could be presented, but only if all were convinced that it had not been just a dream. But other dreamt wonders—visits from the dead, from angels, or other providential occurrences—occurred in less charged contexts. These sorts of dream visitations might arouse the dreamer and his intimates to action or, alternately, soothe, instruct, and inspire. Colonists depended on the dreamer's identity and circumstances as well as the content of the night vision to make these crucial distinctions. But powerful—even wondrous—experiences (a visit from a dead friend, relative, or mentor, for example) were taken as positive signs and worthy of reflection, while a frightening apparition (of a neighbor or even of a stranger) might be cast as a dreadful and only too real visitation by a witch, a ghost, or the Devil himself. Social stress resulted in scapegoating of various "others," English as well as Native, as had happened with Mather's interpretation of Squando's visions. In the increasingly stratified world of the late seventeenth century, so-called credulous dreaming was now located in Indians, witches, and the weak-minded or spiritually vulnerable—while those who expected happy or spiritually enriching visitations through dreams might get exactly what they wished for.

Several instances of "supernatural" visitation are outlined here, many of which, in their day, became the sources of controversy. Next, we turn to those events that were clearly identified as dreams, looking for the odd and sometimes fascinating ways in which New Englanders chose to interpret or to transform dreamt experience into action. This chapter considers dreaming as an embodied emotional practice, and it includes examination of the ways that dreams helped experience of the self to take form. Finally, the chapter addresses the dreams of Samuel Sewall, looking at the emotional experience and spiritual beliefs embedded in his night visions. The discrimination of dreams from other sorts of spectral events hinged largely on the social status and social context of the individuals involved. In this way, dreaming and dream reporting is intimately linked to other processes of social stratification at work in late seventeenth-century New England.

Because of the dream's ambivalent status, context was everything. Credibility hung on reputation. For some, the diabolic nature of strange events was obvious—one only had to look at particular aspects of the individuals' character and history to determine its likely meaning. For others, strange visitations were inconceivable as anything but divinely authorized. Particular interpretations of dream experiences were closely tied to social status, with influential factors including the dreamer's ethnicity, gender, or personal reputation. From these essential details, the correct interpretation of a dream or dreamlike event could be discerned. The differences were critical and could lead to it all being dismissed as a bad dream or, as in Bishop's case, to a hanging.

In many, if not most, circumstances, testimonies against Goody Bishop such as those offered by Stacy, Cook, Louder, and Coman would have been classed as nightmarish dream events rather than as malevolent witchcraft. In fact, the earliest and most vivid incidents had occurred as much as fourteen years earlier. Had they constituted clear-cut proof of diabolical activity at that time, Bishop might have experienced legal discipline much sooner.

Such nighttime visitations could have been taken as perfect examples of that which early modern English men and women knew as the "night mare." As Janine Rivière has noted, "one of the nightmare's most horrifying aspects was the victim's encounter with a strange malevolent presence, or being, that attacked while he or she lay in a paralytic state . . . [lying] on the chest preventing the victim from moving or breathing."[14] Being "hag ridden"—experiencing an incubus or succubus who sat on your chest, cold and heavy—was a common occurrence well known and much talked of in contemporary folk culture. The hag "oppressed" the victim, who lay helpless in her grip. While Richard Coman attributed his experience to a witch's visitation, the language that he used—"he could not speake nor stir[;] noe not soe much as to awake his wife althow he Endeauered much soe to doe itt"—could just as easily have described a classic instance of being hag ridden.[15] But an episode of nightmare did not usually provoke a witchhunt.

Instead, it more often indicated ill health. As Rivière notes in her discussion of the dream in early modern England, it is curious that historians have mostly overlooked the relationship between dreams and diagnosis of various ailments. "As medical experts of the time knew, natural dreams occurred in a state of sleep and were products of the physiology of the sleeping body and mind.... Early modern writers ... drew from Galenic medicine to suggest that physicians could utilize dreams as important clues to the health of the individual."[16] Drawing on popular tracts such as Thomas Elyot's 1539 *The Castel of Helth*, reprinted in fourteen editions until 1610, Thomas Cogan's 1584 *The Haven of Health*, or Nicholas Culpeper's *The English Physitian* (1652), Rivière concludes that "early modern writers believed that in sleep we are particularly vulnerable to a host of external and internal stimuli beyond our control," and that "dreams—their dominant emotions and symbols—could assist in the diagnosis of disease and identify both the humoral imbalance and overall temperament of the dreamer. Since the inner workings and complex balances of the body were hard to discern, dreams were construed as a useful means of finding clues to the physiological and psychological imbalances of the body and mind."[17]

Some late seventeenth-century thinkers attributed nightmares to natural phenomena or dismissed them as dream events. The alchemist Thomas Tryon described such nightmares thus: "And tho the Vulgar, when they are thus affected, conceit it some external thing [the incubus] comes and lies upon them, which they fancy to be some Ghost, or Hob-Goblin, yet the truth is, it proceeds from inward Causes. This Disease being an obstruction of Motion, or an interception, especially of Breathing and Speech, with a false apprehension of some heavy thing lying upon their Breast and as it were stifling them, occasioned, by means the free penetration of the Spirits to the Nerves, is hindred, the passages being stopt by a surcharge of the aforesaid [melancholic] Humors."[18] Tryon continued: "This happens most to such as use[d] to lie upon their Backs; and Whilst it is upon them, they are in great Agony, being unable to speak, but strive to do it with imperfect groans, but if any person speak to them, and call them by name, the animal spirits being excited, force their way [out], and the oppression ceases."[19]

Two approaches to the nightmare thus coexisted: a medical discourse that attributed these events to "disease or disorder of the body," in which there was "a deception of the senses into believing what was dreamed was in fact real," versus a "hag-riding tradition" which saw the nightmare as "the real assaults of witches, demons, or spirits"—the incubus, or the succubus, who literally sat on one's chest.[20] And thus, "at the heart of debates about the nightmare experience was the problem of discerning between dreams and reality, as well as doubts concerning the reliability of the senses."[21]

Although ordinary folk might not have known about the scientific theories of the day, the educated men of Massachusetts Bay did. Unlike Tryon, however, authors like Increase Mather believed in the active presence of Satan and chalked up these dream events to his deluding influence. The nightmare may not have been an actual visit from a witch or other malevolent being, but it was still Satan's doing.

While Mather never doubted the existence of witches, he explained many witchcraft "experiences" as diabolically inspired dream events. In his encyclopedic catalogue of wonders, *Illustrious Providences*, published in 1684, Mather railed, "What Fables are there concerning Incubi and Succubae, and of Men begotten by Daemons?"[22] He then retold a story from the German physician and demonologist, Daniel Sennert (1572–1637), casting Satan as the instigator of these events:

> A certain Woman, being in Prison on suspicion for Witchcraft; pretending to be able to turn herself into a Wolf, the Magistrate before whom she was brought promised her, that she should not be put to death, in case [i. e., if] she would then in his presence so transform her self. Which she readily consented unto. Accordingly she anointed her head, neck, and arm-pits; immediately upon which she fell into a most profound sleep, for three hours; after which she suddenly rose up, declaring that she had been turned into a Wolf, and been at a place some miles distant, and there killed first a Sheep, and then a Cow; the Magistrate presently sent to the place; and found that first a Sheep and then a Cow had there been killed.[23]

Mather continued, "It is then evident, that the Devil himself did that mischief, and in the mean time the Witches who were cast into so profound a sleep by him, as that they could not by any noises or blows be awakened, had their Phansies imposed upon by Dreams and Delusions according to the pleasure of their Master Satan."[24] As to the specifics of this witch's story, Mather dismissed as "extreamly Fabulous" any notion that such transformations from human to animal and back again could be other than a delusion, terming beliefs about witches transforming themselves into animals "a blind Heathenish phansie: And yet Stories of this nature have been generally believed; and I have not without wonderment seen grave Authors relating them, as if the things had been really so."[25]

From the perspective of modern sleep research, scholars have identified a continuum of consciousness that stretches from REM sleep on the one end to possession trance (with impersonations) on the other, with trance (with hallucinations) "as the midpoint between them." In the hypnagogic (sleep onset) or hypnopompic (awakening) periods, those "twilight zone[s] between waking and sleeping," it has been demonstrated that many individuals "experience unusual bodily sensations, including the inability to perform voluntary movements, known as sleep paralysis ... , and visual, auditory, and kinesthetic imagery of various sorts known as hypnagogic hallucinations."[26] Many of these premodern accounts "often associated with witchcraft" may fairly be "attributed to incidents of sleep paralysis."[27]

But while we moderns might dismiss these events as having an explanation rooted in the laws of nature, judicial officials at Salem took pains to distinguish the experiences described by Bishop's antagonists from frightening dream events. For one thing, both witnesses and court clerks seem to have taken care in identifying whether these events took place while the deponent was awake or asleep. Stacy at first testified that he had been awake, but this was struck out, as later his narrative made it clear that he was awakened from a sleep state by Bishop's strange appearance: "About midnight ~~being awake~~ this Deponent felt something betweene his lips Pressing hard agt his teeth: and withal was very Cold: insomuch that *it did awake him* so that he gott up and sat upon his beed" (emphasis added).[28] John Cook (who was eighteen when he testified in 1692 but talked about an event that had taken place "fiue or Six yeares agoe," when he was still a boy) made it clear that he had been awake, though still in bed: he said that "one Morning [it was the Sabbath] about Sun rising as I was in bed before I rose," Goody Bishop was standing at his window, and "she looked On me & Grinn'd On me & presently Struck me on the Side of the head wch did very much hurt me."[29] Goody Safford did not specify, but seems to have thought she was awake, when she was visited early one morning by the apparitions of Bishop and Elizabeth Howe. When Joseph Safford was kindling the fire in the other room, his "wife shricked out"; he ran to where she was, and she cried out,

"Ther be[e] [th]e euill ones teke [them]"; he asked her where, but she ran to the window and said "ther tha went out," both being "biger then she," but "thay went out ther [that way, through the tiny spaces around the window] but shee c[o]uld not."[30]

John Louder, having had some controversy with Bishop about "her fowles that used to Come into our orchard or garden," also made clear that he had been awake when he experienced his terrifying encounter with Bishop: "I goeing well to bed; aboute the dead of the night felt a great weight upon my Breast and awakening looked and it being bright moon: light did clearly see sd Bridget Bushop—or her likeness sitting upon my stomake." Louder tried to defend himself, "puting my Armes of[f] of the bed to free myselfe from that great oppression[,] she presently layd hold of my throat and almost Choa[ked] mee and I had noe strength or power in my hands to resist or help my selfe, and in this Condittion she held mee to almost day."[31] Louder told his mistress, Susannah Gedney, and Gedney and Louder confronted Bishop over the orchard fence: "My Mistress told sd Bridget. that I said or afirmed that she cume one night & satt upon my brest as aforesd which she denyed and I Afirmed to her face to be tru[e] and that I did plainely see her. upon which discourse with her she Threatened me."[32]

William Stacy was awakened from sleep; Cook was just waking up, it being dawn; Louder "went well [not sick] to bed," but "aboute the dead of night" felt a great weight on his chest "and awakening" looked out to see Bishop. Samuel Gray "had ben asleep some time" but awakened to find the house brightly lit and a woman standing near the bed side who "vanished or disappeared" after he rose up. Finding the door locked, he opened it and looked outside, and seeing the same woman in the same clothing, "he said to her [']in the name of God what doe you Come for,[']" but she "vanished away." Locking the door and getting back into bed, he judged he was "between sleepeing & wakeing" when "he felt some thing Come to his mouth of lipes cold, & there vpon started & looked vp againe did see the same woman with some thing betweene both her hands holding before his mouth." She moved away, and the baby in the cradle "gaue a great screech out as if it was greatly hurt" and could not be comforted. From that moment, the child "did pine away and was never well, althow it Liued some moneths after, yet in a sad Condition and soe dyed." These events had happened some fourteen years before, on "one Lord's Day night," and now, fourteen years later, he know "both by her Countenance & garb" that his visitor had been Bridget Bishop. The only problem with Gray's testimony was that it seems to have been a fake, albeit a fake that reveals the cultural norms. He himself later recanted it.[33]

Richard Coman, whose testimony about events eight years before was in some ways the most dramatic, was fully awake, and therefore, perhaps among the most convincing. This had been no dream. He had been already in bed and had "a light burneing in our Roome," affirming "I being awake," when he saw Bishop and two other women come into the chamber although he had locked the door. (After the visitation, he would check it again and find it still tightly latched.) The light went out, and the bed curtains opened, and "presently" she came "and lay upon my Brest or body and soe oppressed him that he could not speake nor stur noe not soe much as to awake his wife althow he Endeavered much soe to doe itt." The next night was even worse, as Bishop "tooke hold of him by [the] throate and almost haled him out of the bed." Not surprisingly, "haveing beene telling of what I had seene and how I suffered," his "kinsman" William Coman offered to come sleep in his house, and suggested Richard keep his sword across his body. While the two men were still awake and talking, the three women arrived again, and Richard cried out, "W[illia]m here thay be all Come againe." William was "immediately strook speechless & could not move hand or foote." The women tried to disarm Richard, but he held his sword fast and when he could again speak, he called out to William and to his wife and Sarah Phillips who lay together in another bed, but they "all told mee [that thay heard] mee, but had not power to Spea[k or stir]. When Sarah Phillips was finally able to call out, "in the name of god Goodman Coman what is the Matter with you[?]" all the three women "vanished away."[34] This terrifying encounter, Coman made clear, had been no dream. New England colonists wrestled carefully with discriminating between dreamt and waking experience of the extraordinary.

While New England colonists believed that the witch's specter, "likeness," or "shape" could walk abroad, not all visitations came from witches. Court documents and wonder tales described all kinds of visitations from apparitions and ghosts. When Rebecca Cornell was murdered in 1671, her brother testified that her "aperition" visited his bedchamber. He "being in a Dreame of Mrs. Rebeca Cornell Deseased and being betweene Sleeping and Wakeing," he "felt something heave up the Bedclothes twice and thought some body had beene coming to bed to him, where upon he Awaked." Turning around, "he perceived A Light in the roome, like to the Dawning of the Day, and plainely saw the shape and Apearance of A Woman standing by his Bed side, where at he was much Afrighted."[35] While this case begins with a dream, in order to carry any weight in court, John Briggs, like Coman and the others who accused Bridget Bishop, had to affirm that they had been fully awakened by the apparition. As Elaine Forman Crane notes, the apparition offered a medium for an indirect accusation, admissible in court, shielding Briggs from prosecution "in a situation where the narrator was reluctant to take responsibility for the information conveyed."[36] While in a Protestant worldview in which there was no purgatory, "ghosts could not be the souls of dead people," they could be construed as "the spirits of the dead who always had a reason for their appearance."[37] Rebecca came back—and Briggs testified about it—in order to subtly suggest "that Rebecca's death was not accidental."[38]

The uncertain and ambivalent meanings of such encounters were what lent them a unique fascination. Discerning between diabolical or divine sources fascinated Increase Mather. Visitations were a part of the world of wonders that was most frightening and strange (Mather would have said most "awefull"), but it was in the careful scrutiny of such wonders that one could best see what pleased God. *Illustrious Providences*—a vast compendium of wonder tales—was undertaken by Mather in 1681. It was based on a manuscript begun some 26 years before, which had been sent from England to Reverend Samuel Davenport of Boston's third church. When Davenport died, Mather proposed to the colony's ministers that they complete the manuscript, extending its scope to include events in New England. Among the "Remarkable Providences" to be included were "Such Divine Judgements, Tempests, Floods, Earth-quakes, Thunders as are unusual, strange Apparitions or what ever else shall happen that is Prodigious, Witchcrafts, Diabolical Possessions, Remarkable Judgements upon noted Sinners: eminent Deliverances, and Answers of Prayer."[39]

*Illustrious Providences* contains very few reported dreams. But it is chock full of eerie visions, strange visitations, and awesome judgments. Some parts of the manuscript betray its recycled origins: the very beginning includes typical examples of "several Remarkables about Apparitions," all from England, including the story of a certain Dr. Frith of Windsor, "[who] . . . lying on his Bed, the Chamber Doors were thrown open, and a Corps with attending Torches brought to his Bed-side upon a Bier; The Corps representing one of his own Family: After some pause, there was such another shew, till he, the said Dr. his Wife and all his Family were brought in on the Bier in such order as they all soon after died."[40] While Frith's experience was given a patina of authenticity, like many modern urban legends, because of its "as told to" bona fides (relayed via his son to the third party, "a Person of great integrity," who in turn related it for the compendium), other reports derived from the realm of anonymous legend. Such a one was the story of a scholar who signed a bargain with the Devil but then became suicidally despondent. When a group of ministers gathered to pray with him, a strange cloud appeared and out of it "the very contract signed with the poor creatures Blood was dropped down amongst them; which being taken up and viewed, the party concerned took it, and tore it in pieces."[41]

While not questioning the veracity of these older stories, Mather hoped, in the expanded version, to rely on New England's ministers, who "have been improved in the Recording and Declaring the works of the Lord," to "diligently enquire into, and Record such Illustrious Providences, as have happened in the places whereunto they do belong." In other words, he hoped to verify each story by ensuring that the testimony of "the Witnesses of Such notable Occurrents" would "be likewise set down in Writing."[42]

The text that results has a strange bifurcated quality, careening at times between third- or fourth-hand fables versus those stories that can be verified from local court records as happening to Mather's near neighbors. Thus the cases of Goody Morse, Ann Cole, Elizabeth Knapp, and others in New England involved with witchcraft all make an appearance in these pages.[43] The Quakers are a frequent foil, as he believed "that some of the Quakers are really possessed with Infernal Spirits."[44]

Wherever possible, Mather introduced a moral to these stories of possession, supernatural assault, and remarkable judgment. So, for example, in his lengthy discussion of Quakers on Long Island and in Plymouth Colony, he wrote that he was including it, "inasmuch as the publication of it [this story of possession], will make appear unto all Mankind, that Quakers are under the strong delusions of Satan; [thus] I think myself bound to acquaint the World, that not many Moneths ago, a Man passing under the name of Jonathan Dunen (alias Singleterry) a Singing Quaker, drew away the Wife of one of Marshfield to follow him; Also one Mary Ross falling into their company, was quickly possessed with the Devil, playing such Frentick and Diabolical tricks, as the like hath seldom been known or heard of."[45] Other "sad" examples came from the unhappy ends visited on those who had used unlawful means and dark methods to heal themselves, rather than "by the prayer of Faith to betake themselves to the Lord Jesus, the great Physitian both of body and soul, and so to wait for healing in the use of lawful means, until God shall see meet to bestow that mercy on them."[46]

In some cases, God brought about certain wondrous occurrences to inspire faith in those who doubted, and Mather's purpose in documenting and republishing such tales was similarly meant to reinforce piety, even as it doubtless served as a sort of entertainment. Thus, he told the story of a Mr. Watkinson of Smithfield (in England), whose daughter, on parting from him, expressed "her fears that she should never see him more." But he promised "that should he Die, if ever God did permit the Dead to see the living, he would see her again." About six months after his death, "on a night when she was in Bed but could not sleep, she heard Musick, and the Chamber grew lighter and lighter, she then saw her Father by the Bed-side." He spoke to her, saying, "Moll, did not I tell thee that I would see thee again? He exhorted her to be patient under her afflictions, and to carry it dutiful towards her Mother; and told her that her Child that was born since his departure should not trouble her long. And bid her speak what she would speak to him now, for he must go and she should see him no more upon Earth."[47] As Mather explained, such wonders were intended to cure uncertainty: "Sometimes the Great and Holy God, hath permitted, and by his Providence ordered such Apparitions to the end that Atheists might thereby be astonished and affrighted out of their Infidelity."[48]

The ultimate goal of the book was to excite and amaze, and thus to awaken the reader with the many examples of God's power. Hence, in the story of a man terrified by thunder (recycled from Ambrose's *Treatise of Angels* and Clark's *Examples*), his wife, a puritan, remained calm and collected. "At which the Man was amazed, concluding with himself, these Puritans have a divine principle in them, which the World seeth not, that they should have peace and serenity in their Souls when others are filled with dismal fears and horrors."[49]

As David D. Hall suggested a generation ago, New England men and women who had been nurtured on such tales would shape their own experiences according to this pattern. This shaping process applies to dreams as well—which in turn became part of this fabric of wonders. The wondrous, therefore, helped colonists explain some of the mysterious aspects of dreams, both in how they took shape and what they might signify. Take, as an example, a dream of Thomas Minor, who emigrated very early to New England, possibly on the *Arbella* with John Winthrop, and who moved into Connecticut in 1645 as part of John Winthrop Jr.'s New London venture, eventually settling in Stonington by 1652.[50] In 1662, Minor recorded a curious coincidence in which he and his wife dreamed at the same time, two dreams with almost the same content. The full report is challenging because of the lack of punctuation, but I include it in full here to allow readers to parse it for themselves: "I & my wife dreamed at one time my wife dreamed that I struck her & said that I strucke at a dogg & I dreamed that I was going by a red bich [*sic*] which had a puppie and shee bit at me & I struck her & struck my wife in the face either with my hand or fist which waked my wife & shee waked me & asked me what I did doe."[51] It is perhaps not too far-fetched to note that while Minor offered a culturally acceptable act of violence toward the "red bitch" in his dream, this dream experience resulted in an inadvisable (if not entirely unacceptable) act of violence and loss of control toward his wife (perhaps, sometimes, herself another sort of "bitch"?), which she duly protested ("& she waked me & asked me what I did doe").[52] The repetition of the phrases "I struck her" in the dream report, first when Grace Minor dreamed "that I struck her" and later when Thomas Minor says that the bitch bit at him "& I struck her" further entwines these two female figures (dog, wife). Minor makes no other comment about this dream, a circumstance that leaves modern readers almost in the dark. We know that it was important enough to him to write it down and to note the startling coincidence between the two dreams. This was enough to make it a wondrous event.

What historians have not recognized to date is that such wondrous dreams also functioned as elegant means to emotional containment. In a society where anger was conceived as a dangerous and divisive force and was often repressed and redirected outside of the household (or displaced onto the person of the vengeful witch or implacable Indian), Minor's sleeping mind seems to have redirected his anger (at his wife?) at the snarling "red bitch."[53] This word had the same double meaning then as it does today. Note that two figures in this dream are angry—first the dog, and then Minor himself—a narrative doubling that would seem to reinforce the central affect of this brief dream report. Anger among intimates was tricky, and, as explored above (Chapter 3), recorded dreams often presented dreamers with a challenging array of feelings, feelings likely to disrupt attempts at mastery and control. Subordinates (like a dog . . . or a wife) were supposed to submit quietly to male authority, but male authority was also supposed to stay its hand from excessive violence. And thus, second, this brief and unelaborated report still offers a snapshot of Minor's emotional life, perhaps related to his wife, or to females protective of their

pups. The evidence is only suggestive, however, more tantalizing than revealing. It is interesting, though, that while he records that he literally struck his
wife, awakening her and provoking her to ask "what he did do," that his only
feeling on awakening appears to have been "wonder," not anger. It is also noteworthy that he expresses no remorse, either to her, or, more privately, in his
record of the incident. This gives us a sense of an early modern household in
which the wife literally became "one flesh" with the husband—*feme covert* in a
cultural and emotional as well as legal sense. Grace Minor's feelings, other than
her indignation or amazement at being struck by her sleeping husband, were
not important enough to her husband to be recorded as well. We do, in the end,
though, have the sense that the couple did awaken and, perhaps, they marveled
together at the strange event and its possible meaning.

One other couple is recorded to have worked together on a wondrous
dream, a dream that once again involved an apparition, this time of an angelic
nature. In October 1702, amid a health crisis that would prove fatal, Abigail
Mather, who had been sick ever since a miscarriage in May, had a notable
dream.[54] The dream occurred the very first night after a late-night fast and vigil
that her husband Cotton had kept, during which he lighted on a particular
psalm that encouraged him to "resign the Condition of my Consort, at last,
unto what shall be done in the future State [to focus more on her spiritual estate rather than on whether she lived or died in this visible world]."[55] Closing
his fast with the simple invocation, "Lord, Thy Will be done!" he continued,
"Behold a strange Thing! On the Night after the Fast, my Consort had appearing to her, (she supposes, in her sleep) a grave Person, who brought with him, a
Woman in the most meager and wretched Circumstances imaginable." In this
dream, he continued, "My Consort fell into the Praises of God, in that her Condition was not yet so miserably Circumstanced as that woman's now before her.
The grave Person then told her, that inasmuch as there were at this Time, a
Couple of Symptomes become insupportable to her, he would propose a Way,
wherein she should obtain some Help for them." What followed was a very
specific recipe: "First, for her intolerable Pain in her Breast" (perhaps she had a
breast infection, mastitis or cancer), "said he, lett them cutt the warm Wool
from a living Sheep, and apply it warm unto the grieved Pain. Next, for her
Salivation, which hitherto nothing had releeved, said he, take a Tankard of
Spring-Water, and therein over the Fire dissolve an agreeable Quantity of Mas-
tic's, and of Gum Icinglass: Drink of this Liquor now and then, to strengthen
the Glands, which ought to have been done a great while ago." Abigail reported

the dream, presumably first to Cotton and then later ("on Friday"), "She told this to her principal Physician; who mightily encouraged our trying the Experiments."[56]

Cotton Mather first reports this all as if it were only his wife's fascination with her own dream vision. But now he joined her in the experiment: "We did it [followed the instructions]; and unto our Astonishment, my Consort revived at a most unexpected Rate; insomuch, that she came twice on Saturedary out of her sick Chamber, unto me in my Study; and there she asked me to give Thanks unto God with her, and for her, on the Account of the Recovery in so surprising a Degree begun unto her."[57] In a sad turn of events, however, Abigail Mather would sicken again, and, continuing unwell, she would die on December 1.[58]

This dream's significance lies in the ways in which the couple interpreted and acted on its message, but it is also noteworthy for the fact that no diabolical inspiration was suspected, even though Abigail Mather had once, years before, seen a demonic specter.[59] Though "no credit nor regard" was to be given to dreams, Mather and his wife sought to implement a special cure brought to her through the medium of this "grave Person." Abigail actually reports the dream twice: once to Cotton, once to the physician, seemingly in that order. But the dream had a potent effect. Illness, suffering, and death were excruciatingly painful passages, then as now. This dream and its enactment took a situation in which the Mathers were largely helpless and gave them something specific to do, perhaps a psychological relief if not a lasting physical one. This is one explanation for the dream's prominent reception in this otherwise devoutly orthodox household.

Another explanation, and one more closely grounded in period understandings, has to do with the motif of the "grave Person" who appears suddenly, offers advice, and then disappears again. Cotton and Abigail Mather would have been familiar with this personage. Indeed, Increase Mather's collection *Illustrious Providences* contains two relevant cases that might well have been familiar to his son and daughter-in-law. The first was the story of Innocentia's breast cancer (taken from Augustine's writings): "In her sleep she was admonished to repair unto the Font where she had been Baptized, and there to sign that place with the sign of the Cross, which she did, and was immediately healed of her Cancer."[60]

The second story, reprinted from Clarke's *Examples*, is remarkably similar to Abigail Mather's reported dream, all of which suggests that this was a common folkloric motif of the day. In the story, as Increase Mather retold it, one

Samuel Wallas of Stamford in Lincolnshire, who suffered from consumption, was reading a religious book on a rainy day when there was a knock on the door. He opened it, and "a comely and grave old Man of a fresh complexion, with white curled Hair, entred; and after walking several times about the room, said to him, Friend, I perceive you are not well." Wallas told the man that he had been ill for many years, and was quite "past cure, and that he was a poor Man, and not able to follow their [the Doctors'] costly presecriptions, only he committed himself and life into the hands of God, to dispose of as he pleased."[61]

This pious answer pleased the visitor, who said, "'*Thou sayest very well, be sure to fear God, and serve him; and remember to observe what now I say to thee*; Tomorrow morning go into the Garden, and there take two leaves of red Sage, and one of Blood-wort; and put those three Leaves into a cup of small Beer, and drink thereof as oft as need requires; the fourth Morning, cast away those Leaves, and put in fresh ones, thus do for twelve dayes together; and thou shalt find e're these twelve dayes be expired, through the help of God they Disease will be cured, and the frame of they body altered.'"[62]

But the advice of this grave man was not at an end yet. Once Wallas had recovered his strength "somewhat," he would do well to "change the Air, and go three or four Miles off; and that within a Moneth he should find that the Clothes which he had on his Back would then be too strait [too tight] for him: Having spoken these things, he again charged Samuel Wallas to remember the Directions given to him, but above all things to fear God, and serve him."[63] The astonished Wallas asked, "'if he would eat any thing?'" but he was answered, "'*No Friend*, the Lord Christ is sufficient for me. Seldom do I drink any thing but what cometh from the Rock.' So wishing the Lord of Heaven to be with him he [the grave man] departed." Wallas, who must have run to the window to look, could see the Man "passing in the Street, but none else observed him, though some were then standing in the doors opposite to Wallas his House." There was another strange detail, indicative of the grave man's otherworldly origins: "Although it Rained when this Grave Person came into the House, and had done so all that day, yet he had not one spot of wet or dirt upon him."[64] Wallas tried the cure and found himself much improved.

The nature of his strange visitor remained to be determined. Mather (or Clarke) tells us that some ministers met at Stamford to discuss the nature of this man, and "concluded that this cure was wrought by a good Angel, sent from Heaven upon that Errand."[65] Mather père noted that it was "not impossible, but that Holy angels may appear, and visibly converse with some." Yet he added a strong note of caution: "For any to desire such a thing is unwarrantable, and exceeding dangerous. For thereby some have been imposed upon by wicked Daemons, who know how to transform themselves into Angels of Light." Indeed, Mather now cited "the sacred History of [the] dead Samuel's appearing to Saul" as evidence that, just "as the evil Spirit [Satan] will speak good Words, so doth he sometimes appear in the likeness of good Men, to the end that he may the more effectually deceive and delude all such as shall be so unhappy as to entertain converses with him."[66]

Absent a context of active witchcraft, the Mathers had no reason to view their strange nighttime visitor as diabolic. Indeed, the motif of the strange man, grave man, or shining man was a recognized phenomenon. In England, Bishop Joseph Hall's mother had encountered one in her illness and gained great relief from him in the sixteenth century (see Chapter 1), while one of the apparitions at Salem also proved to be "a angell from heaven," appearing in the deposition of Susannah Shelden against John Willard, she tried to go to Mr. Hathorne (the magistrate) to tell him of the specters that tormented her, but Willard's shape said "he would break my head and stop my leegs" so that she could not go; and just then, "did Appeared to Mee A shineing Man whoe tolde [me] I should goe And tell wt I had heard And seen," promising "that I should bee well goeing And Coming." Not trusting this shining apparition, Shelden asked that he prove she would be safe by chasing Willard's specter off, at which "that shining man held up his hand And Willard vanished Away."[67]

Context seems to have been the only determinant as to whether these tricky figures would prove to be angelic or demonic in origin. For the Mathers, a consultation with their physician was an essential step before taking any action related to the dream. Of course, consultation with a physician was also necessary in witchcraft cases, in which a natural cause was ruled out before a demonic origin could be determined. This couple's mutual search to implement the knowledge that arrived in a dream vision also offered them a shared way of approaching what was already a horrific illness—for the sufferer, it was something to do despite her fears and sense of helplessness about illness and impending death.[68] The period pun seems significant too: these "grave" personages usually appeared just as the person had resigned themselves to their future "grave"—the tomb awaiting them at their death.

\*    \*    \*

Samuel Sewall's recorded dreams offer a counterweight to the strange specters and awful apparitions of the court records, as well as to the amazing
angelic visitation experienced by the Mathers, suggesting another route by
which extraordinary experience might be incorporated into daily life. Indeed,
when compared with examples from Cotton Mather's 1702 history of New England, *Magnalia Christi Americana*, we see that authentic dream visitations and
the knowledge gained from dreams was commonly respected by the dreamers,
and sometimes retold in ways echoed in Sewall's own reported dreams. As Hall
notes, dreams played a central part in the lives of pious New England men
throughout the seventeenth century, despite their stated suspicions about
them. "Condemned in the case of Anabaptists, dreams returned to center stage
in the pages of the *Magnalia* as authentic promptings from the supernatural. . .
[as did prophesying]. Thus he (Mather) dared report that John Cotton and
John Wilson learned in dreams who would be selected by the Boston church to
succeed them."[69] Cotton Mather noted that prophetic dreams had come to
Thomas Parker, the minister of Newbury; his friend's son recorded, "I have
heard him tell . . . that the great changes of his life had been signified to him
before-hand by *dreams*."[70] And John Eliot, "the great preacher to the Indians,
'often had strange forebodings of things that were to come.' "[71] As these many
examples suggest, wonders generally appeared through dreams, and Sewall's
diary contains an especially rich trove of examples.

Although there is no way that the prolific diarist can be anything other than
an extraordinary source because of his amazingly detailed record keeping,
Sewall may nevertheless, in this case, represent the norm, as he seems to have
taken his dreams in stride, even though they occasionally included remarkable
or startling visitations. Nevertheless, Sewall's dreams were often emotionally
powerful; in modern terms, they seem to have served transforming selfobject
functions, satisfying needs for archaic merger states, and—in the case of visitations from mentors, fellows, or alter egos—providing gratifying and crucial
psychological experiences of twinship or merger.[72] Sewall recorded, pondered
over, and wondered at such visitations as spiritual messages with strong meaning. To write them down was another way to keep this desired experience near
at hand.

Of seventeen dreams that Sewall had over the years from 1676 to 1728,
three were wonders that have already been discussed: the 1675 dream about
climbing stairs to Heaven; the 1686 dream about Jesus living in Boston; and the
1728 dream about the boy stealing his watch, which opened this book. These,

along with the 1705 dream that he was judged and condemned and the 1706/7 dream that he had been chosen Lord Mayor of London (also described above, Chapter 3) played on themes of being chosen—elected, in the spiritual sense— or, at the least, were focused on position, status, and rank. His dream in February 1710/11, "Now I dream'd of being at the Commencement and seeing Mr. Leverett in Scarlet," came on the heels of a hard loss, just after he noted the death of a trusted Council colleague and offered prayer: "The good Lord prepare the rest, and me especially to follow after."[73] In short, Sewall seemed to be of two minds at least, dreaming of a "commencement" (a beginning), just after he had dutifully prayed for a sober and dignified ending.

Many of the remaining twelve dream reports had to do with loss, death of a loved one, or guilt over neglect of duty. These tended to be "heavy" in feeling (Sewall's own term) and somber or frightening in tone. Thus in June 1685 Sewall recorded a lengthy and troubling dream in Latin, presumably to keep its shameful contents private from other family members, particularly his wife, whom it concerned. Translated, Sewall wrote: "I had dreamt that I returned to Newbury or some other town, and that during my absence, my wife died at Roxbury or Dorchester. I took the tidings very hard, and repeatedly called her name out." He was surprised that his father-in-law was gone from home; "they said that he had started for England: since his daughter had died he was free to travel as he wished." Then another daughter, Sewall's own Elizabeth (also known as Betty), then four years old, "whispered that the death had occurred in part because of my neglect and want of love. When I shook off sleep, I embraced my wife for joy as if I had newly married her."[74]

While it is impossible at this remove to speculate about the cause or the full meanings of this particular dream, nevertheless, a few things are notable about the report. One aspect that jumps out is the varying volumes in which the dream "speaks." First, Sewall's dream presents Hannah as dead, but then the dreamer calls out her name "repeatedly." When guilty feelings surface in Elizabeth's message ("my neglect and want of love") they are only "whispered," a puzzling and incongruous detail. Add to that the fact that he recorded it in Latin, and the dream, whatever its other meanings, seems to talk about a conflictual set of feelings—a Sewall who shouts out his attachment to his wife, but who, in the figure of Betty and the mode of recording, "whispers" his guilt, and hides it in Latin. Could Sewall, like Father Hull, have felt tied down by his family obligations, and could he too wish to be "free to travel as he wished"?

This was not the only dream of Sewall's in which his wife had died. Indeed, this dream pattern appears again four years later, nearly word for word the same. Thus in June 1689—when Sewall was already six months into a journey to England—he had dreams on two successive nights, back to back, which betokened his wife's death. On June 16, the Sabbath, he wrote, "Last night I dreamed of my Wife, and of Father Hull, that he had buried somebody, and was presently intending to goe to Salem."[75] In the other, recorded on Thursday, June 20, but dreamed on Sunday, June 16, he noted, "Last Sabbath day night dreamed of the death of my dear Wife, which made me very heavy."[76] Sewall may have subscribed to the belief, discussed in Chapter 1, that dreams of loved ones far distant might, through some sympathetic connection or divine intercession, carry actual news of them.[77] These dreams appeared on the heels of having signed a petition "for leave to goe home." Sewall had also dreamed about a dead friend, "Mr. Adams" (William Adams, Sewall's classmate from Harvard College, who twice appeared in Sewall's dreams) and had busied himself with preparations to return. Thus it would seem the return to New England, and to Hannah, was very much on Sewall's mind.[78]

Sewall again may have been of two minds about his return to Massachusetts. Accompanying the sad scenes of death, Sewall the dreamer had imagined that Father Hull, already dead for five years, "had buried somebody" and then was planning another trip ("presently intending to goe to Salem"). The very next night, Sewall himself killed off his wife (at least figuratively), though he did feel "very heavy" at the prospect. An ambivalent message keeps pressing for our attention: did Sewall feel "heavy" (sad, depressed, worried) about losing his wife? Yes, ostensibly. But might he not also have felt heavy about heading back to family and responsibilities after the exciting and important work in England?[79] And, more complex still, could separation have caused the continued travel to feel heavy, occasioning a desire to return home? Ambivalence seems to saturate these dream reports, and what predominates is the recurring heaviness of mood.

For all these dreams, Sewall might have proffered a spiritual interpretation regarding a central challenge in a pious puritan's life. Where the modern analyst might emphasize the emotions of sadness, loss (both past and anticipated), hidden aggression, and ambivalence, the early modern interpreter would likely stress instead the spiritual dilemma encoded in these dreams of family: the spiritual obligation of all puritan believers to never place things of this world above those of the next. In this view, the journeys to be undertaken and separations to be endured were spiritual ones. The deaths and the guilt stemmed from one's "neglect" of a spiritual duty and one's "want of love" for God. While Sewall might not have recognized the emotional panoply presented by these dreams, I like to think that he would have embraced this second reading as containing a central dilemma of his life that he articulated directly on many occasions: the puritan principle that one should never be more attached to things of this world than to God.

Two additional dreams circle around this theme. One, the dream of March 1695, is well known: "Last night I dream'd that all of my Children were dead except Sarah; which did distress me sorely with Reflexions on my Omission of Duty towards them, as well as Breaking oft the Hopes I had of them."[80] The other, rarely cited, involved Sewall's grown daughter, Betty Hirst: "Last night I dream'd that I had my daughter Hirst in a little Closet to pray with her, and of a sudden she was gon, I could not tell how; although the Closet was so small, and not Cumber'd with Chairs or Shelves. I was much affected with it when I waked."[81] The first stresses feelings of loss and guilt, while the second carried a feeling of sadness and intensity even after Sewall woke up. One wonders if Sewall noticed a message in the second—that even when you have your loved one close (in a "little Closet," a space "so small") and even when you are knitted together in devoted prayer, even then you cannot safeguard against sudden and inexplicable loss. Perhaps it was feelings such as these that lingered on into the daytime, perhaps intertwining with worry about the actual fate of Betty Hirst or of all the paternal hopes she represented.

Three remaining dreams (which account for all the recorded dreams in the diary, except for one that we will examine later) centered on contact with the dead. In addition to the culturally sanctioned belief about the significance of visitations from the dead, additional themes hint that Sewall may have been wrestling with growing older, maturing as a father (at, respectively, thirty-three and forty-two years old), both for his family and in his duties to his community. In December 1685, just after the wrenching final illness and burial of his young son Henry, he wrote: "Dreamed last night of Mr. Chauncy, the President, and of Sam. Danforth."[82] Danforth was a classmate from Harvard who had died in London in 1676, nearly nine years before to the day.[83] Chauncy was Charles Chauncy, the president of Harvard College, who had died in office a few months after Sewall's graduation, eulogized by Increase Mather as "[']a venerable old man, most accomplished . . . most expert in the art of instruction, who devoted himself with exemplary and unfailing diligence to the instruction of the sons of the prophets.[']" Cotton Mather added, "The death of so great a man left the college crippled and well nigh crushed."[84] On another occasion, in 1695, Sewall dreamed of Harvard again and his dead friend, William Adams, this time the dream focused on disturbances in the proper order between fathers and sons: "Was somewhat exercis'd about my dream the last night, which was that Mr. Edward Oakes, the Father [of Urian Oakes, minister at Cambridge and president of Harvard College], was chosen Pastor of Cambridge Church. Mr. Adams and I had discourse about the Oddness of the matter, that the father should succeed his Son so long after the Son's death [Urian Oakes had died in 1681]." Sewall "excus'd my not voting, as not pertaining to me, though I had other reasons besides. Thus I was conversing among the dead."[85] It seems notable that each dream involves a pair of men: one junior, one senior. Each involves a Harvard classmate (Danforth and Adams, either of whom, as age-mates, could be a figurative representation of Sewall himself), along with a president of Harvard as the senior member (Charles Chauncy and Urian Oakes). In the second dream there is the additional father-son pair of Edward and Urian Oakes.[86] It thus seems not too far a leap to suggest that Sewall's dreams—in addition to bringing him close to the honored dead—were also wrestling with issues of succession and seniority, all potent issues in the male life cycle and particularly relevant to Sewall, who buried a son just prior to the first of these dreams and who reported a visit to his "Unkle Quinsey" just before the record of the second.[87]

The last dream we shall discuss here also plays with issues of seniority and succession, or achievement and aspiration, in potent ways. Perhaps the closest thing to an apparition that Sewall ever saw happened in a dream he had while at sea, bound for England, and just after hearing of the Glorious Revolution staged by William, Prince of Orange. In the flush of excitement that must have followed hearing the news at sea from a passing ship, Sewall reported this lively dream: "Last night I dreamed of military matters, Arms and Captains, and, of a sudden, Major Gookin, very well clad from head to foot, and of a very fresh lively countenance—his Coat and Breeches of blood-red silk, beckoned me out of the room where I was to speak to me [sic] I think 'twas the Town-house."[88] Sewall notes that in the evening (following the dream) he read "the Eleventh of the Hebrews [on faith], and sung the 46th Psalm [on God as refuge and strength]." He also notes, "When I waked from my Dream I thought of Mr. Oakes's Dream about Mr. Shepard and Mitchell beckening him up the Garret-Stairs in Harvard College."[89]

This dream offers a clear invitation to the ambitious Sewall, who was going to England hoping "to uphold the interests of the colony, now without a charter or a settled government, and to secure, if possible, a restoration of its privileges."[90] Not only did the auspicious news seem a hopeful sign, but now Major Gookin appeared, who, at his death in 1687 had been a vigorous defender of Massachusetts liberties. Auspiciously, he was "well clad," "of a very fresh, lively countenance" and arrayed from head to foot in "blood-red silk," a lively color if ever there was, and beckoned to Sewall. But more fascinating still is Sewall's waking reference to "Mr. Oakes' Dream," a suggestion of some prior dream sharing, that Sewall should know what Oakes had dreamed. Though its details are lost to us now, it seems to have been a similar dream of being invited in to take the place of a deceased predecessor (Shepard had been pastor of the Cambridge Church, where Oakes succeeded him), which has the effect of doubling (and thereby intensifying) the dream's message.[91]

Sewall's dreams—when read in context but with an eye to possible emotional meanings—give us a chance to explore more deeply the range of dream experience found among colonists in a maturing New England. While Sewall marked these sad dreams and visitations from the dead as nothing more than dreams, other members of this society sometimes experienced such events as literal visitations: from a neighbor or a sister or even an angel. The emotional experience embedded in these dream events and apparitions varied from terrifying to tantalizing. New England colonists embedded strong emotion within accepted frames or culturally sanctioned idioms and knitted expressions of the wondrous into a fabric of accepted spiritual experience.

This maturing colonial society thus had a range of approaches to dreams and dreamlike visitations. Meaning was assigned largely based in the context: a dream might be just that, —or it might be something much darker, and only the surrounding social fabric would determine its significance. Who dreamed it? Was there an ongoing crisis? Did it demand public expression? Was it part of a criminal action? Did it seem better suited to private reflection? The answers to these questions helped to shape responses to dreams, and the dreamer's approach to acting on dreamt experience, or not. In an increasingly complex, expansive, and segmented society, however, decisions about dream experience could have profound outcomes. In some cases—such as at Salem, or in the case of Rebecca Cornell's murder—they might even lead to capital punishments.

Specters, familiars, apparitions, wonders, and angels remained relatively frequent occurrences in late seventeenth-century New England, along with emotionally powerful, spiritually awakening dream experiences. The invisible world remained a frighteningly vibrant potentiality, and two major Indian wars had left colonists keenly attuned to their own vulnerability. When Bridget Bishop or other witches walked abroad, they made their neighbors painfully aware of this vulnerability and, as historian Mary Beth Norton and others have argued, they provoked a murderous response. Eager to kill off an external enemy—the threat of their Native neighbors—English men and women contented themselves with internal ones instead. As Sarah Osborne, one of the first women charged in the Salem crisis, had averred: "Shee was more like to be bewitched then that she was a witch." When asked by Justice Hathorne "what made her say so," Osborne responded: "She was frighted one time in her sleep and either saw or dreamed that shee saw a thing like an indian all black which did pinch her in her neck and pulled her by the back part of her {head} to the dore of the house."[92] As Norton remarked in relation to this, "That nightmare would have been hardly unusual for a woman in northern New England familiar with reports of scalping and the recent raid on York, and Hathorne did not explore it further."[93] But now, spectators in the meetinghouse complained that Osborne had told them, "Shee would never believe that lying spirit any more." Asked what spirit she meant, and whether it had been the Devil, Osborne said that while she did not know the Devil and "I never did see him," she had been troubled by "a voice that I thought I heard" that said "I should go no more to meeting."[94] Hathorne immediately pressed Osborne for an explanation as to why she had not been to meeting "thes yeare and two months."[95]

It is perhaps surprising that more New England colonists did not record troubling dreams about encounters with Indians on the order of Osborne's nightmare. The sources, however, are mute on this point. The closest we can come, besides Osborne's dream, is a nightmare that troubled Samuel Sewall in 1706, after several years of serious Indian disturbance during Queen Anne's War (the North American version of the War of the Spanish Succession, also known in New England as the Third Indian War). Sewall wrote on April 4: "Last night I dream'd I saw a vast number of French coming towards us, for multitude and Huddle like a great Flock of Sheep. It put me into a great Consternation, and made me think of Hiding in some thicket. The Impression remain'd upon me after my Waking. GOD defend!"[96] The links of this dream to the wartime context are plain: several diarists of the period make it clear that many in New England were anxiously tracking news from the northern front, where every major twist and turn was recorded.[97]

But the religious references fairly leap off Sewall's page as well: the Catholic French, who "huddle like a great Flock of Sheep," would have been a familiar image for the puritan Sewall, who was trained in the idea that Catholic adversaries and their Indian allies lived under the thumb of their priests. And yet, despite the incongruity, Sewall was scared by the dream—the "vast number" and "multitude" of enemies, "coming towards us"—which made him "think of Hiding in some thicket." It is hard, once again, not to think of the religious "thickets" (sinful retreats) that might have to be overcome on a regular basis in Sewall's demanding Protestant piety. There could be no retreat, no refuge, from God's enemies. Indeed, as diarist John Marshall of Braintree noted in 1707 of difficulties among the English militia at Casco, "I shall only remark that the disappointment of that design [attacking the French] speaks much of divine anger of which we are generally too insensible."[98]

Doubtless the English would have liked to reassure themselves that the Native threat was a thing of the past. But while they could destroy Bridget Bishop, they could do little about the Native peoples and their French allies that ringed the region, and who, from 1676 to 1713, regularly descended on towns in the various border regions, wreaking havoc on what were (from their own perspective) otherwise orderly English communities.[99] In the meantime, the English were left with apparitions and angels—frightening specters and helpful guides—whose role was to warn and to chasten, as well as to reassure and protect. The impact of colonialism was wide reaching, affecting not only its ostensible target—the Indians—but penetrating as well in the lives of English colonists, and even unto their dreams.

Try as they might, however, the English could not completely colonize their dream lives. As the dream reports of Thomas Minor, Samuel Sewall, or many others suggest, dreams would continue to startle, "exercise," and awaken dreamers, airing knotty feelings, raising surprising juxtapositions, and bringing uncomfortable knowledge. For many, dreams and dreamlike experience remained deadly serious and, in the right circumstances, might lead to deadly action. As it would happen, the English found that Native Americans, even those ostensibly "under governance," would continue to converse about difficult and momentous dreams as well.

# Chapter 6

## *Native Dream Reporting as Cultural Resistance*

In the opening decades of the eighteenth century, in a remote Wampanoag Indian community on the island of Martha's Vineyard, a woman lay in the grips of her final illness. Abigail Kesoehtaut knew that she was likely to die. After several days of anxious struggle, like any exemplary puritan woman on her deathbed she found a lasting peace when "the Spirit of God did bear witness with her Spirit, that she was a Child of God, and had a Right to the Inheritance laid up in store for his Children."[1] Abigail's sister (unnamed in the sources), who was caring for her in her last days, was very troubled by Abigail's impending death. She "long'd for a more full Assurance in her Sister's Wellbeing," and, in particular, she wondered whether Abigail would go "out of this World in a State of Grace."[2] One night, during the sick woman's last hours, this caretaker fell asleep and began to dream:

> As she thought, she [Abigail's sister] plainly heard a Voice in the Air over the top of the House, saying in her own Language, *Wunnantinnea Kanaanut*, the same being diverse times repeated, which Words may be thus rendered in English, tho they are much more emphatical in Indian, ["]There is Favour now extended in Canaan; there is Favour, &c.["] The person that in her Sleep thought she heard such a Voice, supposed it to be a Voice from Heaven by the Ministry of Angels, sent to give her Satisfaction in the Case that did distress her: and [still dreaming] she was exceeding refreshed with the good Tidings which she thought she had in this wonderful way received; but while

she was transported with the Thoughts of God's condescending Goodness thus manifested to her, and her Heart filled with unspeakable Delight, to her great Grief, some Person, as she thought, awaked her, and wake she did, but she could not find that any Person called her.[3]

Newly troubled by her thoughts, the woman appears to have consulted the Reverend Experience Mayhew, missionary to Martha's Vineyard, for guidance in interpreting this remarkable occurrence. The dream report appears in his 1727 book of Native biographies, *Indian Converts*. Mayhew appended a "Query" to the story, asking "whether the Person that dreamed the dream now related, ought to take any other notice of it, than she should of any common Dream; or what she should think concerning it?" And he attached a further plea to his readers, that "a Solution of this Problem would greatly satisfy both the Person that had the Dream, and him that has related it."[4]

Exchanges such as the one that took place between Abigail Kesoehtaut's sister and Experience Mayhew on Martha's Vineyard so long ago offer rich examples of the types of conversations about dreams that occurred between Indian people and their new spiritual advisors, English ministers, well into the eighteenth century. They also suggest that the English could not completely dominate either Native peoples or their dreams. Until recently, historians subscribed to various teleological narratives about the "disenchantment" of the world. In these models, the scrutiny of events for signs of providence declined in favor of increasingly rational explanations for natural phenomena, including dreams, which were now classed as such. In New England in particular, David D. Hall's book *Worlds of Wonder, Days of Judgment* ends with the assumption that the old "world of wonders"—in which ministry and laity alike emphasized the active presence of a divine hand—gradually gave way to explanations that no longer linked natural and supernatural phenomena. Instead, by the century's end "this vernacular religion, this culture of the Word, was beginning to fragment." At least some ministers began to emphasize that religion "was a matter more of 'reason' than of inward spiritual experience," a trend that "compromised the lore of wonders," and eventually set the stage for "tensions that eventually erupted in the Great Awakening."[5] In addition, Native Americans, who, at contact, had a completely different cosmology than Europeans, now began—in this view—to yield to Christian systems of belief and Western patterns of thought. Native peoples either disappeared entirely (after the Pequot

War, or after King Philip's War, or certainly by the eighteenth century) or, if they did survive, converted to Christianity and formed a part of a permanent racial underclass within New England's agricultural and maritime eighteenth-century economies that was, in all other respects, completely unremarkable.[6]

However, actual practices turn any tidy teleologies on their heads. For the colonists, older beliefs never vanished. Explorations of the Great Awakening of the 1740s and subsequent evangelicalism has revealed a resurgent interest in dreams and other supernatural phenomena that persisted throughout the colonial period. Indeed, the scrutiny of dreams as divine communications never disappears in Western cultures but remains a vibrant potential, ready to be tapped when conditions are right.[7]

This is especially true in the case of New England's Indian peoples, where dream belief and associated ritual practices retained their force well into mature colonial and even postcolonial contexts. The work of many scholars has proven that Indian communities in New England remained culturally as well as economically distinct through the eighteenth, nineteenth, and twentieth centuries, long enough to stage an impressive resurgence, beginning in the 1920s, that would fuel the recent movements to gain and regain, respectively, federal and state recognition. As Kathleen J. Bragdon has argued, the persistence of Native languages well into the eighteenth century gave Indians a lasting heritage of distinctive symbolic systems and ontologies, a pattern of meaning that undergirded their religious, social, and economic struggles throughout the colonial and into the early national periods and up to the present.[8] Once scholars abandon various narratives of Indian decline and disappearance, a different story emerges.

This new story reinscribes Native American identity as a constant presence in New England regional culture, albeit one that was often virtually invisible within the dominant culture—an "invisible world" of another sort. With this assumption at base, scholars have reappraised older texts and found tantalizing glimpses of Native alterity in exchanges such as the one that Abigail Kesoehtaut's sister had with Experience Mayhew. The period from 1700 to 1760 saw many such discussions, especially as the more enthusiastic theology and style of worship of the Great Awakening began to sweep through Indian enclaves, bringing some Native peoples to Christianity for the first time.

Native dream practices offered a viable alternative to European Christian worship throughout this period. Despite the assaults and the slurs that Europeans cast on shamans and their practices, or on the dream vision as a supposed "idol" of the Indians, practices of dreaming, visioning, communal "dances" and other gatherings—ranging from mere conviviality to sacred ritual—continued to be pursued along the many back roads and woodlots of rural Native New England. In some places, a more directly syncretic approach emerged, in which Indian Christians could explore their dreamt knowledge as wondrous communications. This chapter first turns back to the dream text reported by Abigail Kesoehtaut's sister and then explores other examples drawn from *Indian Converts*, which is, as an instance of the "deathbed conversion" genre, chock full of reports of strange visions, apparitions, premonitions, and bright, heavenly lights.[9] Finally, I suggest some other examples of distinctive eighteenth-century dream practices, though one that sometimes blended older Native traditions with the new evangelical enthusiasms of the eighteenth century.

Written in English, by a missionary rather than the dreamer herself, the dream reported by Abigail's sister is a highly compromised piece of historical evidence, at least in terms of its ability to provide direct access to the dreamer's experience. In addition to the normal censoring, revision, and narrativization of the dream report, Abigail's sister's dream was also translated from Massachusett to English, though, fortunately, Experience Mayhew himself was raised as fluent in both languages due to his upbringing on the island, which had an Indian majority until the 1720s.[10] Thus, despite its many limitations, this translated text is as close to the original dream report as we can possibly get at this point.

This dream clearly speaks of great losses: those of the past and those yet to come. In this regard, it reflects the immediate concerns of Native Americans of the late seventeenth and early eighteenth centuries. In the context of the virgin soil epidemics unwittingly brought by contact with Europeans, Native communities continued to suffer from bouts that Mayhew described as "Chronical Diseases" and that the eminent Boston ministers who introduced his book attributed to "a strange Blast from Heaven consuming them," by which "their Numbers are sensibly decreased."[11] As the century wore on, populations may have stabilized somewhat, but Native vulnerability to disease continued to be exacerbated by growing poverty.

In this context, then, Abigail's impending death filled her sister with considerable anxiety about the state of their eternal souls. Prior to the dream itself, Mayhew reported that Abigail found peace only when "the Spirit of God" bore "witness with her Spirit, that she was a Child of God and had a Right to the Inheritance laid up in store for his Children." As Abigail's sister nodded off, ostensibly worrying for Abigail's soul, she also anticipated a painful loss and perhaps experienced other complex feelings associated with the death of a sibling.

While there were real reasons for these women to be consumed with anxiety, their stance also accorded completely with the demands of puritan Calvinist teachings, which, as we have seen, required the cultivation of uncertainty and the difficult emotional path of strong oscillations between assurance and despair. In Mayhew's text, then, both the ardor of the missionary's message and the power of his orthodox teachings are at work. This makes sense, since the book, with its deathbed conversion narratives, was intended to convey the progress of sincere Christian conversion among the Indians as well as to inspire pious reflection in its readers.

This concern with salvation bespeaks a still larger internal struggle between anxiety and reassurance. Consider, for example, the "Voice in the Air over the Top of the House," which reassured Abigail's sister. Conveying a sense of safety and confidence, could the voice have reflected unacknowledged feelings of the dreamer herself? As Mayhew made clear, the woman's longing "for a more full Assurance"—her great anxiety "in the Case that did distress her"—was much relieved by this voice. He reported, "She was exceeding refreshed," and "Her Heart filled with unspeakable Delight" at this "Ministry of Angels, sent to give her Satisfaction." In opposition to the reassuring voice stood her fears as revealed in the latter part of the dream, when Abigail's sister was awakened "to her great Grief" by some invisible person. This awakening plunged her back into the state of worry, anxiety, grieving, and anticipation of loss in which she had begun the night and which the dream had temporarily relieved.

The sudden alteration in the scene—a shift from the reassurance of angelic voices to the sudden urging by an unknown person to "awake"—replicated the central tension in Abigail's sister's life. How could she find safety in a world of tormenting worries and afflictions? The fact that the voice urged her to "awake" was no accident, of course. Just as Samuel Sewall was prodded by his dream to keep a closer "watch" on himself (see Introduction), Abigail's sister appears, as would any good puritan, to have "awakened" to the uncertain state of her soul. The dream even used the same language as Mayhew might have done in speaking to Native Christians. The anxiety of the dream, then, in its intensity and mode of expression, represents not only the psychic fruits of puritan teachings but also the precarious situation of Native Americans in the colonized society of eighteenth-century New England.

There is a second key communication buried in this dream narrative, because the occasion of this dream report offered an opportunity for communication, contest, and collaboration between the dreamer and Mayhew himself. In this sense, Abigail's sister may have been continuing a practice common to Native American cultures. In seeking out someone to listen to her dream, she was acting on the dream experience to fulfill or complete the dream's message, a widespread approach to dreaming that, in many cultures, can require the performance of particular rituals.[12] The connection of dreams to ritual practices intended to resolve the dream communication is well documented among the seventeenth-century Iroquois to the west of New England, and similar observances took place among southern New England Algonquian communities, though here the evidence is considerably more sketchy.[13] As we have seen, New England Natives assiduously sought to share dreams and interpret their meanings (see Chapter 2). And almost from the very first moments of encounter, New England's Algonquian-speaking peoples sought to enter into conversation with colonists and missionaries about the meaning of their dreams—as, it will be recalled, when they asked the missionaries "whether they should beleeve Dreames" or when they were much concerned about "the evill of thoughts and dreames."[14]

So when Abigail Kesoehtaut's sister sat down with Experience Mayhew to discuss her unusual dream, she brought to the table a complex intercultural repertoire of imagery, interpretation, and ritual through which to make sense of this event. For his part, the missionary brought a long tradition of wonder lore, of anxious puritan self-scrutiny, and of deathbed observation with which to interpret the message of this Indian woman's dream. Mayhew, as a fully bilingual and fairly bicultural individual, would have had some understanding of traditional Wampanoag dream sharing and dream interpretation. It is hard to determine to what extent each of these cultural traditions contributed to the conversation that emerged, although clearly these different understandings had become fully entangled over the previous two generations of intimate colonial contact. Indeed, the conversation between this Wampanoag woman and the English missionary took place in a cultural terrain of dream interpretation that merged elements of both English and Algonquian traditions of dream practice. The conversation suggests that after three generations of colonial experience, initially separate and discrete dream cultures now interacted, engaged, or even borrowed from each other in a rich bricolage of meanings, even if Europeans were less interested in Indian ones than vice versa.

Of course, Mayhew himself did not dare to represent the full syncretism of this encounter. Instead, he recast the conversation as an orthodox Christian examination of a powerful dream event—a sign of his exemplary efforts on behalf of Indian Christians and further evidence of the successful conversion of a pious Indian family. It is significant that he shied away from venturing an opinion about the dream's worth, instead inviting his learned readers to participate in the missionizing process more directly by contributing their views as to whether this dream was to be believed, or even deserved "any other notice" than "any common Dream." Thus, in his report, the dangers of syncretic deviation were covered over, to be recast as evidence of orthodox, modest, and exemplary piety.

But there is a third message in this dream, one that pushes the modern reader well beyond the territory Mayhew chose to map. His discussion of this dream suggests the growing dominance of English culture, but it also reveals the Wampanoags' distinctive experiences as a colonized people. Dream reports like this one enabled Wampanoags to explore, both internally and in a safely veiled form in conversation with colonizers like Mayhew, an assertion of Native presence and Native self-worth despite Christian teachings and English dominance.

Consider once again the "Voice in the Air." In this respect, the dream and its context speak to the much larger questions of the Indians' place in eighteenth-century social hierarchies and assert the value, worth, and equality of all souls before God. The voice offered its words of comfort not in English but in Massachusett. Its message was translated only through Mayhew's intervention. The voice said, "Wunnantinnea Kanaanut," repeating these words several times. As Mayhew admitted, he toned down their meaning, rendering them "in English, tho they are much more emphatical in Indian," as "There is Favour now extended in Canaan." Canaan, in this sense, is God's promised land, God's reward for the saved (that is, heaven). Abigail's sister dreamed of this Christian redemption in the Massachusett language. This by itself was not so remarkable— quite likely the entire dream report represented Mayhew's translation of an experience told to him in Massachusett. Yet it is significant in that he left this one phrase in the original words: God apparently spoke the language of the Wampanoags with considerable fluency.

Abigail herself had found deathbed assurance that she, an Indian and (like every human) a sinner, would, at death, still be "a Child of God." God's Massachusett utterances in Abigail's sister's dream now hammered home to an English audience that Indians could achieve a place in heaven just as easily as Englishmen. The political power of this Christian egalitarianism would have fairly leapt off the page for Mayhew's contemporaries. Yet how could they have denied a communication if it had truly come from God's own messenger?

Though Abigail's sister reported a dream that, in every way, seemed to echo orthodox puritan practices, the strange voice, as reported, taught Mayhew and his readers that Natives might be both fully Christian and still fully Native—a rejection of the complete cultural conversion that English missionaries usually sought. Moreover, unlike earlier seventeenth-century missionaries, who had focused on translating Christian texts into Massachusett, translation tapered off in the early eighteenth century, and missionaries encouraged Indians to use English instead, thus obviating the need for costly and time-consuming translations.[15] The voice spoke, however, in a defiant embrace of Massachusett, speaking its Christian message with more vigor than could be found in English translation. In this way, the narration of Abigail's sister's dream expressed resistance to colonial hegemony. Historian Mechal Sobel has argued that dreams can provide individuals with "a protected place for negotiations with the other," including parts of themselves constellated as "other."[16]

Moreover, when Abigail's sister hurried to Mayhew to explore this wondrous voice, she "performed" her dream and carried this explicit (and defiant) message to his very chamber. God has laid up a store in heaven for those who have bravely endured the grossest earthly inequities. God's fluency in the Massachusett language opens, in metaphor, a place in heaven for all Natives who seriously seek after "Kanaanut."

Did her message get through? Apparently enough of it did to leave Mayhew himself worried by this curious dream. His final queries to the reader made this puzzlement quite clear. When he asked for guidance from his fellow ministers and other men of experience who might judge the significance of God's speech, he made it plain that the dreamer would not be the only person relieved to find an answer. As Mayhew noted, "A solution of this Problem would greatly satisfy" he "that has related" her dream in writing, that is to say, Mayhew himself.

Of course, the report we have before us is Mayhew's text, not one that the dreamer herself would have written. It is perhaps not surprising that, as such, it reveals at least as much about the anxious position of English missionaries in relation to exemplary Indian converts as it does about the cultural syncretism of eighteenth-century Wampanoag Christianity. Experience Mayhew long hoped to obtain his own sort of "Favour" (settled ministry) in "Canaan" (the English not infrequently referred to New England as "New Canaan." But neither Indians nor Englishmen would ever call him to a congregation, and he would instead content himself with peripatetic preaching to the Indians and administration of charity among the Wampanoags of Martha's Vineyard.[17] There is also profound cultural insecurity mingled with Mayhew's personal concerns. Missionary literature quite predictably lauded notable successes among the so-called "praying Indians." But missionary authors were also surprisingly vociferous in expressing their insecurities—including their fear that corrupt Englishmen had forever lost God's favor, and that they performed only the final errand of bringing Christianity into the wilderness. Perhaps, they feared, they were just the vessels by which the true Israelites—the Indians— would be delivered from a spiritual enslavement in sin and ignorance to a new Canaan.[18]

Surely we can now understand why Abigail Kesoehtaut's sister experienced a restless night. Her dream report reveals the complex, painful, and anxious situations of both Native Americans and English colonizers in this eighteenth-century colonial society.

That ambiguous and emotionally charged position is mirrored in a number of other startling visions, dreams, and apparitions recounted in *Indian Converts* and elsewhere. Sometimes these occurred in the form of visions, other times as true night dreams. Some, like the dream of Abigail's sister, spoke to the state of one's soul, other times such dream events simply offered foreknowledge of what was to come in the next world. In a few cases, we can see in these compromised texts the vague outlines of a syncretic, emergent Indian Christianity, or, shaded differently, the continuing influence of powwaws and their practices.

Such dream visions were varied, but usually, as with Abigail Kesoehtaut, they were associated with deathbed scenes. In 1698, Wuttinomanomin (also known as David), who was too much neglected in his last illness by "his Brethren of Earth," was attended by one fellow praying with him, when "there appeared in the Room where he lay far brighter Attendants, in human Shape, than any which this lower World could have afforded."[19] While this miraculous event had only been witnessed by one person still living, nevertheless it seemed a sign of assurance in Wuttinomanomin's salvation. In another case, Ammapoo (also known as Abigail) was attended by her daughter during her last sickness. The daughter, "much broken of her Rest . . . and her self not well," sat up "in the Room drowsy, with her Eyes well night shut, [but] suddenly saw a Light which seemed to her brighter than that of Noon-day; when looking up, she saw two bright shining Persons, standing in white Raiment at her Mother's Bed-side, who, on her Sight of them, with the Light attending them, immediately disappeared." Abigail remained unsurprised, telling both her daughter and, later, another person, "that her Guardians were already come for her."[20]

These sorts of events—associated with strange lights, music, or personages—dot the pages of Mayhew's compendium. Abiah Paaonit, another devout Christian, went out late at night during her last illness, and being "very suddenly refreshed with a Light shining upon and about her," she looked "upwards to see if she could discern from whence it came, [and] she saw, as she thought, as it were a Window open in the Heavens, and a Stream of glorious Light issuing out from thence, and lighting upon her." And as she "admired at it, in the twinkling of an Eye [it] disappeared."[21] At the deathbed of Margaret Osooit (also known as Meeksishqune) in 1723, "two Persons" affirmed "that they then plainly heard a melodious singing in the Air, over the House where this Woman lay."[22] Abigail Manhut's deathbed in 1685 was accompanied by a "marvelous Light" that "lasted several Hours," and which appeared just as her attendants were searching for something with which to make a light in the house.[23] Hannah Soopasun, who was just eleven years old at her death in 1723, insisted that she saw "a shining Person clothed in White standing by the Foot of her Bed," even though "none else in the Room saw any thing of that Nature." When her father told her "she should rather think upon God, and call upon him, than mind any such thing," she "prayed to God for his Mercy, and then, as it is to be hoped, went to *him*."[24]

In addition to these amazing deathbed visions, the Christian Indians chronicled by Mayhew also had night dreams, sometimes prophetic, sometimes offering warning. Thus, in the winter of 1715, Abigail Ahhunnut had a dream about the safe return of her two sons, both gone on a whaling voyage to Cape Cod. The dream showed "that they were come home, and that she was at the Point of Death." And things transpired just this way, "she being seiz'd with the Measles" just a few days after her sons' return.[25]

Those who died had often received intimations of death before the event.

These sorts of predictive dreams dovetailed neatly with European colonists' dreaming traditions, in which predictions of death were perhaps the most common sort of wonder tale circulating through New England's oral culture. Japheth Hannit, whose mother had received knowledge of the Englishman's God some years before the first Christian teachers arrived on Martha's Vineyard, had, a year before his death, himself left his sickbed to walk "alone in the Woods," and "there it was by God revealed to him, that he had but a little time to live in this World.[26] Stephen Shohkau, who died when his canoe capsized in October 1713, also had "some Apprehensions, that the time of his Departure was at hand for some time before his death," having told his wife that "if it did fall out as he thought it would, he would not have her discouraged, but continue to pray earnestly to God, and put her Trust in him."[27]

Sometimes deathbed experiences went well beyond foreknowledge. Elisha Paaonut, an Indian minister, suffered from a lengthy last illness. "A little before his Death he complained sadly of Molestation from evil Spirits," affirming that "they appeared in human Shape to him, to trouble and disquiet him." These spirits, he said, " 'continually come in so, that the House is filled with them, and they bring things and offer to me, but I do refuse to receive them, and do drive them away, and they quickly go out of the House again.' " When questioned, Paaonut said he did not know the spirits who tempted him, "but [except] one of them, and that is —— he is among the Devils." Mayhew refused to name the person Paaonut knew, except to say that he shortly after became "such an Apostate, that one would be ready to fear, that what was said of him had too much of Truth in it."[28]

The link between this sort of dream experience and English witch belief seems obvious (see Chapter 5). Under other circumstances, Mayhew or another minister might have fanned the flames of discontent or investigated this as a matter of witchcraft. This case may also speak to other continuing traditions of powwowing and dream soul contests alive in Indian communities of the late colonial period, now submerged within Christian belief.[29]

Some deathbed dreams took the form of a prophetic warning to the entire community. Jedidah Hannit, the daughter of the revered Christian minister Japheth Hannit, had a dream on the very night she was taken with her last illness. She dreamed that "there was a very dark and dismal time shortly coming on the Indian Nation; with which Dream being much distressed, she waked out of her Sleep, and had such an Impression made on her Mind that what she had so dreamed would come to pass, and of the Dreadfulness of the thing so apprehended, that she immediately prayed earnestly to God, that she might not live to see the thing feared, but that she might be removed out of the World before it came to pass." Upon going to sleep again, she became very ill and "after some time awaked very sick: and the Sickness whereof she was so seized, did in a few Days put an end to her Life."[30]

Relatives had obligations to memorialize and spread the deathbed warnings of their loved ones. Just before the teenaged Elizabeth Pattompan died in 1710, she asked her father to commit her last warnings to her relations to writing. After her death, he delayed in doing so, and one day, "the Spectre of his said Daughter did . . . plainly appear to him, being so near to him, that he plainly saw that she appeared with the same Clothes which she commonly wore before her Death. He also saw some Warts on one of her Feet, which were, in appearance, such as his Daughter had on hers." He did not have "the Power to speak to the Apparition, nor did that say any thing to him, but soon vanished out of his Sight," and that immediately "on the Sight of the Spectre his Breath and Strength did in a great measure fail him," remaining "weak, and uncapable of any Business," till he resolved, on the advice of some unnamed others, "that he had best fulfill the Will of his Daughter, by committing her Words to Writing as she had desired him to do."[31]

In fact, the daughter's last words had included a prayer for her relatives' salvation, and exhortation to right living, and a prophecy: "I would have you, my Father, remember one thing more: after I am dead you will quickly lose all your Estate, but if you worship and serve God as you ought to do, you will receive it again."[32] And this prediction came true in every particular, "for his Horses, Swine, and his other Cattle, all dy'd in a short time, [if I mistake not] within a Year; and whatever else he had, went unaccountably to Ruin, so that he became poor and miserable; but that in a few Years he again got things about him, so as to live comfortably, as he does to this Day."[33] Mayhew shied away from evaluating these remarkable events, writing only "I shall leave these strange Occurrences to the Thoughts of others, within spending my own Judgment on them; only I shall take liberty to say, that I hope the Maid to whom these Passages relate, was a truly pious person."[34]

This was a remarkable apparition in every respect. On the one hand, Pattompan's father, Josiah, was absolutely powerless in the face of the apparition (apparently suffering from the sleep paralysis that was thought to accompany such a visitor). But it was his neglect of duty that caused the visitation in the first place and which resulted, as the apparition warned him, in a temporary loss of worldly power: "after I am dead you will quickly lose all your Estate." But the visitation gave him a chance to mend his ways and to gain back his property, "if you worship and serve God as you ought to do." And this was a fulfillment, in any case, of his daughter's deathbed request that he would "commit to writing, for the Benefit of her Relations, some things which she then uttered."[35]

Elizabeth had been overheard in her last illness praying that God might extend his Mercy to her, and that "if he would graciously please so to do, she should be then willing to leave this World, and all her Enjoyments in it." She then made her request that her father write down her warnings, which, although he neglected it at first, he later did and passed them on to Mayhew, who published them in this narrative. Most notably, Elizabeth, after praying for her own soul and for that of her brethren, had asked that her father, in particular, would turn to God, and "call constantly upon him as long as you live, which, if you do, your God will shew a great Favour to you [or will greatly bless you] and you shall have great Joy, [or Comfort] but if you do not, you will be wretched and miserable for ever."[36]

Notable in a community suffering so much from poverty is the emphasis on the maintenance or loss of property, and the way Josiah's estate will come and go, and then come back again, with almost an Old Testament tone to the pronouncement: "I would have you, my Father, remember one thing more: after I am dead you will quickly lose all your Estate," and "he affirms that this came to pass according to that Prediction of hers; [etc.]"[37] There are echoes of the familiar tension between one's estate in this world and that spiritual estate so much more to be prized. Notable too was Elizabeth's attempt, in her last hours, to convert her father, and, in particular, to prevent his drinking, for drinking was a great affliction among the communities of Martha's Vineyard. The gripping apparition, which Pattompan had spoken about shortly after "to several Persons . . . as some of them do still testify," would quickly move, one senses, from dream into folklore, to be told and retold over the generations.[38] Yet in the initial telling, the apparition fitted so easily into English conventions that one suspects it was hard to discern where Josiah Pattompan's narrative ended and Mayhew's picked up.

Mayhew's book offers a collective portrait of a community in crisis, but also a community in which discussion of the fate of the Indian in New England colonial society remained a topic of great interest and considerable debate. Deathbed visions offered assurance that some could be among the saved—that

God would preserve even Indian Christians as his own. Warning dreams and related phenomena suggested that evils might overtake Native communities and that reform and repentance ought to be embraced by the survivors. One suspects that Mayhew's readers, both in England and New England, though perhaps spurred to give money to missionary efforts (the ostensible purpose of the volume), nevertheless took away a sense of Native communities as rapidly dwindling, close to extinction, and perhaps even providentially doomed to disappearance. But perhaps this would just be one more attempt to foreclose prematurely the ambivalent power embedded in these dream narratives. Native peoples doubtless had a different perspective, hearing again and again in different registers—strange lights, "melodious singing," or "bright shining persons"—the message "Wunnantinnea Kanaanut," "There is Favour now extended in Canaan."

Scholars have been able to cast off the assumption that Indians quickly disappeared from New England. They have been able as well to look for the ways in which Indians might have continued, reaffirmed, and reworked older traditions.[39] But too often, under pressure to dispel the notion that traditional cultures disappeared, those who have argued for Indian persistence have had to present their view as if it were a simple dichotomy—Indian disappearance or Indian continuance. Of course the truth of the matter is that Native peoples lived firmly within the stream of history, along with everyone else, and that their pursuit of traditions did not remove them from the complex worlds of the eighteenth, nineteenth, or twentieth centuries.

At the end of the seventeenth century, indigenous systems of dreaming, conjuring, and healing continued to exist, sometimes as alternatives to Christian practice, other times in tandem with it. Samuel Lee of Bristol, Rhode Island, reported the continued vibrancy of powwowing in this area of southern New England. Responding to queries from London physician Nehemiah Grew about the customs of local Indians, Lee wrote (of Native conjuring), "Being not acquainted with their waies: [I] onely heare, that conjuration is frequent among them. & then one appears like a rattlesnake & sometimes like a white-headed eagle."[40] He continues, in response to detailed questions about medications and medical practices, that the Indians "inquire of their oracle & if that saies they [the patient] shall dye, they use nothing [no medical intervention]," and just below, he describes the "oracle" as "being usually a rattlesnake, a crow or a hawke or &c."[41] Samson Occum reported on powwowing among the Montauk Indians on Long Island (where he was pastor for a time in the eighteenth century), including eyewitness descriptions from those who said that the pow-waws "get their art from dreams; and one has told me they get their art from the devil, but then part[l]y by dreams or night visions, and partly by the devil's immediate appearance to them by various shapes; sometimes in the shape of one creatures [*sic*], and sometimes in another, sometimes by a voice, &c."[42] These accounts match closely to descriptions of Indian *powwanomas* and the several reports of converted powwaws being much troubled by these "familiar spirits," some for years after their conversion to Christianity (see Chapter 2). Ezra Stiles, who talked with men and women in late eighteenth-century Connecticut, noted several examples of powwowing, conjuring, and Indian dances throughout the century, which suggests that the entire ritual complex, including dreaming, was still quite vibrant in many quarters.[43]

Native men and women would continue to bring important dream communications and dreamlike visions to the attention of various Englishmen, usually those well suited to play a role as cultural mediator. In sharing their dream reports, they would continue an intercultural discussion about the effects of colonialism in New England and about the role and the fate of Native peoples within later colonial society.

In April 1739, John Sergeant, the man sent to serve as missionary to the Mahican Indians in Stockbridge, noted in his diary that he had been absent from the prayer meeting on April 15, when an Algonquian newcomer, "a stranger" named Maumauntissekun, "from about 40 miles below" (meaning southward) had arrived. This man "came on purpose, as he said, to hear me preach, and to receive some instruction in the affairs of religion; he was gone before I returned, so that I had no opportunity [to] see him at that time." But Maumauntissekun—who must have cut a formidable figure, tattooed as he was with a snake on each cheek—"had some conversation with Mr. Woodbridge [Timothy Woodbridge, Sergeant's assistant], to whom he told a story which was somewhat odd, and which, he said, gave him a check in his former course of wicked life and made him seriously inquisitive after the way to please God."[44] Maumauntissekun's story was this:

> Being sent by some of his companions, designing a drunke frol-
> ick, to get some rum for that purpose, when he had obtained it,
> in his return he drank so freely of it, as to get drunk [himself];

and lying down to sleep, night came upon him; which proved so dark, that when he awaked, he was lost, & could not find the way to his companions, but presently heard a noise like the pumping of water, and saw a great number of Indians lying drunk and naked, and cold nasty water pumping on them, while they were not able to get out of the way, and were in great distress; and heard a voice, which said to him that he must take notice of & avoid such wickedness being admonish'd by such a sight of wretchedness. This vision (as he call'd it) or dream perhaps, continued for some time, with a strong light shining about him. Then he heard a noise like the blowing of a pair of bellows, which was follow'd with a violent blast of wind, which dispersed the Indians into the air. From that time he entertain'd serious thots of religion: and it made such an Impression on him, that he broke off from drinking, and had been drunk but one time since, which was about a year ago.[45]

Maumauntissekun returned to Stockbridge a few months later, on June 17, when Sergeant records that he came with "some strangers" for "the second time[,] on purpose, as he said[,] to inform himself in the affairs of Religion, and seemed to be very desirous of Instruction, and inclined to come & live with us for that purpose." Sergeant also noted that Maumauntissekun was known as "a man of some character among the Indians, of a sober and thotfull air." When Sergeant was able to speak with him the next day, the missionary "endeavour'd to shew him the necessity & importance of religion, & to encourage him with diligence & prayer to enquire after the truth. He seem'd to assent to & approve of what I said."

But did Maumauntissekun approve as much as Sergeant hoped? His dream vision told a tale of severe colonial incursion—in the destructive medium of "drinke," often the first European arrival on the frontier, other than disease, and certainly no less destructive—and he told his story in a thoroughly Native idiom, that of the vision. He politely, repeatedly, and somewhat urgently, sought to convey the story (and thus "perform" the dream in a social sense). He hoped to discuss the meaning of this event with someone he might think of as an English shaman, the missionary. His story of eventual removal by a "violent blast of wind" that "dispersed the Indians into the air" was already, in a way, in the process of happening in a rapidly colonizing New England.[46] Since his vision, he claimed to have nearly given up drinking altogether, except for isolated bingeing. The next year, in 1740, Maumauntissekun (now also known as Shabash) was one of two Mahicans who invited the German Moravian missionary, Christian Henry Rauch, to begin a mission community at Shekomeko, a town near present-day Salisbury, Massachusetts, and to the south and west of Stockbridge itself.[47] Perhaps with the Moravians—known for their pietist embrace of visions, Maumauntissekun found a type of Christianity more receptive to his visions.[48]

In 1761 Samson Occum, the converted Mohegan minister and missionary, wrote an account of the Montauk Indians on Long Island designed to convey their traditional practices and present state. The Montauk were culturally similar to the southern New England peoples, and Occum had lived among them since the late 1740s. He was married to Mary Fowler, daughter of one of the leading families. The narrative has several sections, covering marriage, family life, naming practices, burial customs, and the history of conversion. In a section on powwaws, he notes, "They say they get their art from dreams; and one has told me they get their art from the devil, but then part[l]y by dreams or night visions, and partly by the devil's immediate appearance to them by various shapes."[49]

Occum's account indicates that powwowing was still a vibrant tradition among the Montauk, as it was, indeed, among the Mohegan as well, based on complaints and narratives about them. A variety of accounts detail the continued use of traditional healing ceremonies, dances, and other activities—among the Mohegan in the 1730s, the Mashpee in the 1760s, and a variety of "frolics" across southeastern Massachusetts complained of by various missionaries, Indian and English, in the 1760s through the 1780s.[50] But as lively as things were, Bragdon notes that change was afoot as well: "Folk stories and memorates collected among New England's peoples in the nineteenth and twentieth centuries suggest that the old ways were understood to be forbidden or at least dangerous, that the Manitou that infused the world had become embodied in malevolent ghosts."[51]

The Native peoples who spoke about their dreams and visions with Christian missionaries were engaging in a critical conversation, a conversation in which Indian survival was very much at stake. In every encounter, Native people brought their practices of dreaming to life once again, trusting the dreams had meaning and that the knowledge obtained in them was of a higher and better order than ordinary. Missionaries, for their part, scrutinized the dreams as potential messages from the divine, taking time to hear and discuss the visions that came to them. In these encounters of the late seventeenth and early eighteenth centuries, we have a rapprochement of sorts between two very different cultures of dream belief and practice. English traditions (derived from centuries of western European Christian practice) and Algonquian ones (steeped in a larger Woodland respect for manitou) met in those discussions, sometimes talking together, more often, perhaps, speaking past each other. These were never equal conversations: the ritual practices of powwowing in which dream belief was embedded now had to be hidden or fundamentally reshaped, as genuine Christian conversion replaced indigenous animism. Poverty, disease, and social crisis left Native communities stricken, reeling, and often looking for guidance from any source. But as the visions suggest— especially that of Maumauntissekun—all was not lost. As Native apparitions flooded wigwams with a ghostly light or with eerie voices, the spark of tradition was requickened and divine power became a Native ally. The beauty of it all lay in the fact that English partners to these transactions often did not know that in having these conversations, they were, in some way, laying the groundwork for Native survival and resurgence over the next two centuries.

# Conclusion

In 1786, Samson Occum, the famous Mohegan minister, had a remarkable encounter with George Whitefield, renowned evangelist, in a memorable and detailed dream. As Occum recorded it, "I thought he was preaching as he use[d] to, when he was alive. I thought he was at a certain place where there was a great Number of Indians and Some White People—and I had been Preaching, and he came to me, and took hold of my wright [*sic*] Hand and he put his face to my face, and rub'd his face to mine and Said,—I am glad that you preach the Excellency of Jesus Christ yet." The dream continued as Whitefield said, "Go on and the Lord be with thee, we Shall now Soon done." Then a strange thing happened, as Whitefield "stretchd himself upon the ground flat on his face and reached his hands forward, and mad[e] a mark with his Hand, and Said I will out doe and over reach all Sinners, and I thought he Barked like a Dog, with a Thundering Voice." Occum was not sure what to make of this: "I thought Some People Laughd Some were pleased, and some were frighted. And after that he got up, Said to me I am going to Mr. Potters to preach and Said will you go[?], and I Said yes Sir—and as we were about to Sit [set] out I awoke, and behold it was a Dream—and this Drea'm' has put me much upon thinking of the End of my journey."[1]

Occum's dream seems a hopeful story. This visitation (Whitefield died in 1770) reached back to an earlier time in Occum's life, promising support. Whitefield "took hold of my wright Hand": ministers were given the "right hand of fellowship" from a mentoring minister when they were ordained; and Whitefield also offered comradeship ("will you go[?]"). The friendly tone is perhaps underscored in an implicit pun: the Mr. Potter mentioned in the dream was probably William Potter (1723–1814), who lived in South Kingstown,

Rhode Island, and was a "devoted follower of Jemima Wilkinson's Universal *Friends* movement" (emphasis mine).[2] And Occum—and the other Indians of New England—could certainly use a friend. Whitefield's other antics seem to have elicited a mixed response: amused, pleased and "frighted." While we cannot know why Occum dreamed of a barking evangelist, one who stretched out prostrate on the ground, as if in submission before a higher authority, and one who promised to contain and restrain sinners: "I will out doe and over reach all Sinners," conveyed a humble, yet powerful protection.

Dreams retained their ambivalent power for colonists all through the seventeenth century. When John Cotton Jr. and his wife, Joanna, endured an unexpected separation at the end of the seventeenth century, dreams spoke about the distance between them. Wrote Joanna in July 1699, "Was glad to hear [in a recent letter] of your welfare[;] the Lord continue it: sinc that [the aforesaid letter from John] a story is at Boston & all about the towns . . . that you were dead[;] it was talkt on 3 weaks or a month ago at Hingam." She continued, reassuring him, "You say you drempt I wear dead but yet the Lord strangly kepes me alive."[3] Since Cotton had left the colony for South Carolina in the wake of an adultery scandal, his long-suffering wife had good reasons to inform him of the gossip being spread about him; at the same time, she might have longed at times for a merciful God who would take her home to Him rather than "strangely" extending her life. John, having lost his wife, home, and life's work all in one blow, now found his dreams troubled by visions of his wife—here a condensed symbol of these several losses—being taken from him by death. Yet the patterns—prediction of death in dreams, or dreams of family members far distant—are familiar repetitions of the themes common in dreaming throughout the early modern period, differing not at all from those of contemporaries such as Samuel Sewall.

Dreaming would take on new life amid the awakenings of the 1730s and 1740s. English men and women would, throughout the rest of the century, once again ponder dreams for inspiration and practical guidance, as the work of Douglas Winiarski, Mechal Sobel, Carla Gerona, and many others makes clear.[4] Hannah Heaton, a farm woman of eighteenth-century Connecticut, preserved the earlier ambivalence of European dream theories in her belief that, although "'dreams & imaginations reuelations & impressions are a foundation of sand,' they could also 'do good when they driue or lead the soul to god & his

word.'"5 Rebecca Dickinson, a seamstress in western Massachusetts in the mid-
to late eighteenth century, frequently recorded her dreams as part of her practice of piety—and to deal with bitter disappointments, intense loneliness, and
other strong emotions—as reported by historian Marla Miller, who has worked
extensively with the diary.6

By the early nineteenth century, some remarkable individuals would keep
diaries exclusively devoted to their dreams, as, for example, did William Jenks.
For some, these were intended as devotional or personal reflections. Jenks's purpose, however, was not for inspiration but rather as a scientific exercise in preserving his night thoughts. As the probably insufferably priggish twenty-year-old
wrote in the entry for October 6, 1798, "It is not from a desire or expectation of
receiving *admonitions* of future events, or extraordinary *illuminations* from
Heaven . . . That I have resolved to keep some account & notice of my *dreams*."
Rather, Jenks assumed that dreams "frequently, if not mostly, arise from the natural state of the body, thus from *physical causes*, and that those dispositions, or
secret inclinations of the mind, which, while reason governs, are concealed,
then display themselves." Jenks complained that nighttime observations about
his dreams often "left me in the morning." Thus, he hoped by recording his
dreams to accomplish two things, first, "that we may by them discover our innate propensities, & frequently the real character," and second, to "preserve a
*continuity* of mental exertion. . . . For, it often happens, that when the mind has
been intensely employed on any favorite subject, its thoughts still, even in sleep,
pursue it, I have thought fit to observe & use them."7

It is this new approach that we see in Jenks's writing, which emphasized the
old naturalistic explanations for dream phenomena and a new emphasis on
rational observation that supported the notion of a post-Enlightenment "disenchantment" of the world. But the evidence from folklorists, ethnographers,
and local historians supports the idea that older traditions of dream belief and
folk practice continued unabated, and historians of religion have shown that
among more enthusiastic traditions, dream practices remained central to the
discernment of divine will.8 In Native communities across New England, practices of insightful dreaming continued to be a source of inspiration during the
nineteenth and twentieth centuries. Indeed, for many modern Americans,
dreams continue to be sources of truth, inspiration, and insight deeper than
that found in the everyday world.

\*       \*       \*

Exchanges between European and Indian peoples brought two very different cultures together. Historians have described the consequences of these encounters—events that had profound economic, political, military, demographic, and social effects. As the seventeenth century advanced, the Native peoples of New England experienced an ever-tightening colonialism with an increasingly limited range of possible responses. While the work of Christian missionaries has long been recognized as a central feature of these new challenges, the role of dreams, visions, and associated practices has often been overlooked in telling the stories of North American colonization.

The invisibility of dream belief and practice for both Europeans and Native Americans is perhaps understandable: historians have given relatively little sustained attention to dreams and visions, despite their importance to both groups often, perhaps, because of the puzzling images, vivid stories, and lively—sometimes strange—action of dream reports. Dreams were, nevertheless, an important source of knowledge for people of the seventeenth century, even if they were regarded with considerable suspicion by the radical reformation Protestants who made up most of New England's European colonial population. Steeped in a worldview that emphasized the centrality of the invisible world and constant scrutiny of the workings of providence, it should not be a surprise that New England's colonists sought to use dreams and visions in very particular, culturally prescribed ways. Nor should it be a surprise to us that, in their encounter with Native Americans, they were curious about the Indians' reported dreams and visions. They were alarmed, to be sure, at the thought that practices of dreaming were seamlessly interwoven with rituals that called on the Devil and his dark powers. But the first generations continued to scrutinize Native dreams, not only because these might have an important role in determining Algonquian action but also because they could perhaps be another means of discerning God's plan for the whole colonial enterprise.

The sources impose another level of invisibility on seventeenth-century dreams and dreaming. In general, in reporting their own dreams, colonists chose private forms of discourse—the cryptic shorthand of Michael Wigglesworth, the Latin of Samuel Sewall, or the scrawled notations of Peter Easton. Dreams were shared with spouses or close friends, but beyond that, such private, individualized dream reports rarely left the confines of intimate conversation. Dream lore, on the other hand, circulated far and wide, betraying an interest in such phenomena, but it was nearly always circulated in an anonymous format, or, if there were names attached, one could not be too sure of how reliable these reports might be. Even the very nature of an event could be called into question: what one person thought of as a "natural" nightmare was another's malevolent specter. Defining specific dreamlike experiences could often involve witnesses, judges, and the accused in a complex discussion. The context—who was the dreamer, what was her situation—was often the only thing distinguishing between a good dream and a bad one, or between a mere dream and a terrifying reality.

Because specific dreams (as opposed to more generalized wonder lore) were reported primarily in intimate settings, surviving dream reports are deeply skewed toward those dreamers with the skills of literacy. Some might argue that dream recording—and the personal reflection and self-definition that goes along with diary keeping—helped to develop a nascent sense of interiority: self-awareness or personal identity. Here, I think the evidence may be too thin to speculate. But what does come through are the ways in which dreams encoded emotionally powerful experience, often leaving the dreamer full of feeling, even if they were not sure how it connected to the dream's images. In addition, and because of their emotional power, dreams appear to have offered an important avenue for pious expression of a "manly restraint." Whether male or female, orthodox believers were supposed to exercise diligent caution and admirable suspicion about the nature of any particular dream event, just as Hannah Heaton tried to do in her eighteenth-century reports.

When we consider the experiences of the Indians, the problem of what is visible and what remains hidden multiplies rapidly. For one thing, representations of Indian experience are almost invariably told in the language of the colonizer. Translated into English, captured by unsympathetic pens, and framed within a powerful, almost overwhelming context drawn from biblical lore and Christian providentialism, the actual practices and beliefs of the Algonquian peoples across New England at the time of contact are virtually impossible to determine. The existence of separate waking and sleeping souls are described in early sources, but the framing discourse of English witch belief—the role of familiars, the specter who walks abroad at the Devil's urging—these cultural assumptions color the descriptions made by even the most diligent English observer. Later analyses based on anthropological fieldwork are, once again, made within various contexts—social Darwinism, structural-functional theory, cultural relativism, ethnolinguistic analysis—which themselves help to shape the resulting texts in mostly silent ways. The possibility of neutral description quickly disappears into the maw of culturally delimited representation.

Dreaming in colonial New England, then, has indeed been an invisible world, of which the historian can only paint a partial, necessarily patchy image. Yet something important was captured by the reported dreams and dreamlike phenomena of colonial New England, which at times functioned as a coherent intercultural conversation over right meanings and appropriate actions. These conversations have mostly gone unrecorded in the scholarly literature. In tracing the outlines of such interchanges, this book has attempted to open the door to new ways of conceptualizing the colonization of New England. Colonization both shaped and was shaped by dreaming and dream reporting, which reflected both cultural expectations and emotional responses to encounter, trauma, and radical cultural difference. This book has emphasized the centrality of the "invisible world"—an immanent world that colonists and Indians conceived somewhat differently but which both valued greatly. While dreams have gone largely unnoticed, to study them more closely is to value phenomena which, for the peoples of this world, were perhaps the most important communications of all.

# Abbreviations

| | |
|---|---|
| Beard, *Theatre* | Thomas Beard, *Theatre of Gods judgements: wherein is represented the admirable justice of God against all notorious sinners, great and small . . .*, 4th ed. (London: By Susan Islip for Mary Heron, [1648]). |
| Bible GV | Bible, Genevan Version (1560). |
| Bible KJV | Bible, King James Version (1611). |
| Church, *Diary* | Benjamin Church [ed. Thomas Church], *Diary of King Philip's War, 1675–1676*, ed. and intro. Alan and Mary Simpson (Chester, Conn.: Pequot Press, for the Little Compton Historical Society, 1975). |
| Cooper, *Mystery of Witchcraft* | Thomas Cooper, *The Mystery of Witchcraft. Discovering the Truth, Nature, Occasions, Growth and Power thereof. Together With the Detection and Punishment of the Same. As Also, The severall Stratagems of Sathan, ensnaring the poore Soule by this desperate practize of annoying the bodie with the Severall Uses thereof to the Church of Christ. Very necessary for the redeeming of these Atheisticall and secure times* (London: Printed by Nicholas Okes, 1617). |
| [Dane] "Declaration" | [John Dane], "A Declaration of Remarkabell Prouedenses in the Corse of my Lyfe," *New England Historical and Genealogical Register* 8 (1854): 147–56. |
| *Dreams of Daniel* | [Anonymous], *Dreams of Daniel: Here begynneth the dreames of Daniell. VVith the exposycions of the. xij. sygnes, deuyded by the. xij. monthes of the yeare. And also the destenyes both of man and woman borne in eche monthe of the yere. Very necessarrye to be knowen* ([London]: Imprynted by me Robert Wyer: dwellynge at the sygne of seynt Iohn Euangelyst, in seynt Martyns parysshe, besyde Charynge Crosse, [1556?]). |
| Easton, marginalia | Peter Easton, MS marginalia to Nathaniel Morton, *New England's Memoriall* (1669), Redwood Library, Newport, R.I. |

| | |
|---|---|
| Easton, MS diary | Peter Easton (1622–94), MS diary (1662–70), American Antiquarian Society, Worcester, Mass. |
| Foxe, *Actes* | John Foxe, *The Actes and Monuments of John Foxe*, ed. Josiah Pratt, 8 vols. (London: Religious Tract Society, n.d. [1877]). |
| [Gonzalo] *Divine Dreamer* | [Gonzalo], *The Divine Dreamer; or, A short treatise discovering the true effect and power of Dreames; Confirmed by the most learned and best approved Authors. Whereunto is annexed The Dreame of a young Gentleman, immediately before the death of the late Earle of Strafford. Printed in the yeare 1641*, unpaginated, unbound pamphlet, catalogue #53992, Huntington Library, San Marino, Calif. |
| Goodwin, *Mystery* | Philip Goodwin, *The Mystery of Dreames, Historically Discoursed; or a Treatise wherein is clearly Discovered, The secret yet certain Good or Evil, the inconsidered and yet assured Truth or Falsity, Virtue or Vanity, Misery or Mercy, of mens differing Dreames* . . . (London: Printed by A.M. for Francis Tyton, 1658). |
| Gookin, "Historical Collections" | Daniel Gookin, "Historical Collections of the Indians in New England," *Collections of the Massachusetts Historical Society* 1 (1792; rpt. 1968): 141–229. |
| Hubbard, *A Narrative* | William Hubbard, *A Narrative of the troubles with the Indians in New-England, from the first planting thereof in the year 1607 to this present year 1677. But chiefly of the late Troubles in the two last years, 1675 and 1676. To which is added a Discourse about the Warre with the Pequods, in the year 1637* (Boston: John Foster, 1677). |
| Mather, *Magnalia* | Cotton Mather, *Magnalia Christi Americana: or, The Ecclesiastical History of New-England, From its First Planting, in the Year 1620, Unto the Year of Our Lord 1698*. 7 vols. (London: for Thomas Parkhurst, 1702; rpt. 2 volumes, Hartford: Silas Andrus and Son, 1853), contrib. by Thomas Robbins and Lucius F. Robinson |
| C. Mather, *Diary* | [Cotton Mather], *Diary of Cotton Mather*, ed. and intro. Worthington Chauncy Ford, *Massachusetts Historical Society Collections*, 7th ser., 7, 8 (1911, 1912). |
| Mather, *Brief History* | Increase Mather, *A brief history of the warr with the Indians in New-England, (from June 24, 1675 when the first Englishman was murdered by the Indians, to August 12, 1676, when Philip alias Metacomet, the principal author and beginner of the warr, was slain.) Wherein the grounds, beginning, and progress of the warr, is summarily expressed. Together with a serious exhortation to the inhabitants of that land* (Boston: John Foster, 1676). |

| | |
|---|---|
| I. Mather, "Diary" | [Increase Mather], "Diary of Increase Mather," *Massachusetts Historical Society Proceedings*, 2nd ser., 13 (1899–1900). |
| Mather, *Illustrious Providences* | Increase Mather, *An Essay for the recording of illustrious Providences: Wherein an Account is given of many Remarkable and very Memorable Events, which have hapned this last Age; Especially in New-England* (Boston: Samuel Green for Joseph Browning, 1684). |
| Mayhew, *Indian Converts* | Experience Mayhew, *Indian Converts, or, some Accounts of the Lives and Dying Speeches of a considerable number of the Christianized Indians of Martha's Vineyard, in New England* (London: Samuel Gerrish, 1727). |
| *MHS Coll.* | *Collections of the Massachusetts Historical Society.* |
| *MHS Proc.* | *Proceedings of the Massachusetts Historical Society.* |
| *Salem Witch-Hunt* | *Records of the Salem Witch-Hunt*, gen. ed. Bernard Rosenthal (New York: Cambridge University Press, 2009). |
| Sewall, *Diary* | Samuel Sewall, *The Diary of Samuel Sewall, 1674–1729*, ed. M. Halsey Thomas, 2 vols. (New York: Farrar, Straus and Giroux, 1973). |
| Shepard, *Clear Sun-Shine* | Thomas Shepard, *The Clear Sun-Shine of the Gospel Breaking Forth upon the Indians in New-England. Or, An Historicall Narration of Gods Wonderfull Workings upon sundry of the Indians, both chief Governors and Common-people in bringing them to a willing and desired submission to the Ordinances of the Gospel; and framing their hearts to an earnest inquirie after the knowledge of God the Father, and of Jesus Christ, the Saviour of the World* (London: Printed by R. Cotes for John Bellamy, 1648). |
| [Shepard], *Day-Breaking* | [Thomas Shepard], *The Day-Breaking if Not the Sun-Rising of the Gospell with the Indians in New-England* (London: Richard Cotes for Fulk Clifton, 1647). |
| Taylor, "Diary" | Edward Taylor, "Diary of Edward Taylor [1668–71]," *Proceedings of the Massachusetts Historical Society*, 1st ser., 18 (1880–81): 4–18. |
| Whitfield, *Strength* | Henry Whitfield, *Strength out of Weakness; Or a Glorious Manifestation of the Further Progress of the Gospel amongst the Indians in New-England, Held Forth in Sundry Letters from divers Ministers and others to the Corporacion established by Parliament for promoting the Gospel among the Heathen in New-England* (London: By the Corporation, Printed by M. Simmons, 1652). |
| Wigglesworth, *Diary* | [Michael Wigglesworth], *The Diary of Michael Wigglesworth, 1653–1657: The Conscience of a Puritan*, ed. and intro. Edmund S. Morgan (1946; New York: Harper and Row, 1965). |

Williams, *Key*

Roger Williams, *A Key Into the Language of America*, ed. and intro. John J. Teunissen and Evelyn J. Hinz (1643; Detroit: Wayne State University Press, 1973).

Winslow, *Glorious Progress*

Edward Winslow, *The Glorious Progress of the Gospel, amongst the Indians in New England. Manifested by three Letters, under the Hand of that famous Instrument of the Lord Mr. John Eliot, And another from Mr. Thomas Mayhew, jun: both Preachers of the Word, as well to the English as Indians in New England, Wherein the riches of Gods Grace in the effectuall calling of many of them is cleared up: As also a manifestation of the hungring desires of many People in sundry parts of that Country after the more full Revelation of the Gospel of Jesus Christ, to the exceeding Consolation of every Christian Reader* (London: Printed for Hannah Allen, 1649).

Winthrop, *Journal*

[John Winthrop], *The Journal of John Winthrop, 1630–1649*, ed. Richard S. Dunn, James Savage, and Laetitia Yeandle (Cambridge, Mass.: Belknap Press of Harvard University Press, 1996).

# Notes

## Preface

1. Matt B. Jones, "The Early Massachusetts-Bay Colony Seals: With Bibliographical Notes Based upon Their Use in Printing," *Proceedings of the American Antiquarian Society* 44 (1934): 13.

2. Cathy Rex, "Indians and Images: The Massachusetts Bay Colony Seal, James Printer, and the Anxiety of Colonial Identity," American Quarterly 63:1 (2011): 64.

3. Bible, KJV, Acts 16:9–10. The seal invokes the wording of the King James Bible rather than the Geneva translation often more used by English and especially puritan readers until the middle of the seventeenth century: David S. Katz, God's Last Words: Reading the English Bible from the Reformation to Fundamentalism (New Haven: Yale University Press, 2004), 44. The Genevan version of Acts 16:9 reads: "Where a vision appeared to Paul in the night. There stood a man of Macedonia, and prayed him, saying, Come into Macedonia, and help us." Verse ten continues: "And after he had seen the vision, immediately we prepared to go into Macedonia, being assured that the Lord had called us to preach the Gospel unto them." Bible, GV, Acts 16:9–10.

4. Bible, GV, Acts 16:10, note j.

5. Bible, KJV, Acts 16:1–5.

6. Bible, KJV, Acts 16:20–40.

## Introduction

1. Samuel Sewall, *The Diary of Samuel Sewall, 1674–1729*, ed. M. Halsey Thomas, 2 vols. (New York: Farrar, Straus and Giroux, 1973), 2:1062–63 (September 10, 1728).

2. He retired July 29, 1728, and died January 1, 1729/30, a year and a half later: see "Chronology of Samuel Sewall," in Sewall, *Diary*, 1:xxvii–xxviii.

3. Cf. Sigmund Freud, *The Interpretation of Dreams*, trans. and ed. James Strachey, rpt. ed. (New York: Avon Books, 1965), 374–79. A third meaning of "watch" is in the disturbance that perhaps initiated the dream, the regular cry of "the Watch" or night watchman, which every city maintained.

4. Mary Baine Campbell, "The Inner Eye: Early Modern Dreaming and Disembodied Sight," in *Dreams, Dreamers, and Visions: The Early Modern Atlantic World*, ed. Ann Marie Plane and Leslie Tuttle (Philadelphia: University of Pennsylvania Press, 2013), 47.

5. Ibid., 41.

6. Sewall, *Diary*, 2:1062 (August 16, 1728). The "better world" he means is, of course, heaven.

7. I am grateful to H. A. (Hal) and Kathleen Drake for the Latin translation. This phrase was one that Sewall had composed by at least December 1709 and he frequently inscribed into books he would then give to friends. Sewall, *Diary*, 2:682 n. 14.

8. David D. Hall, *Worlds of Wonder, Days of Judgment: Popular Religious Belief in Early New England* (Cambridge, Mass.: Harvard University Press, 1989), 215–16, and the entire discussion of his "Mental World," 213–38.

9. Merle Curti, "The American Exploration of Dreams and Dreamers," *Journal of the History of Ideas* 27, no. 3 (1966): 392. He continued, "The general lack of scholarly concern with the dream in colonial thought is understandable when American writing of the XVIIth and XVIIIth centuries is examined. To be sure, the transfer of culture from the Old World included the Biblical view of the dream as a divine or devilish monitor of things unseen and otherwise unknown. The transfer also includes folklore notions about the premonitory character of the dream. But on the whole references to dreams are casual and derivative" (393). Curti's main interest in dreams was "whether discussions of the nocturnal dream hold any significant clues to American conceptions of human nature . . . and whether the dream has a meaningful place in American literature" (393).

10. Cf. Carla Gerona, *Night Journeys: The Power of Dreams in Transatlantic Quaker Culture* (Charlottesville: University of Virginia Press, 2004); and Mechal Sobel, *Teach Me Dreams: The Search for Self in the Revolutionary Era* (Princeton, N.J.: Princeton University Press, 2000).

11. For a review of the literatures of dreaming, both in the early modern period and among modern historians writing about the medieval and early modern periods, see Ann Marie Plane and Leslie Tuttle, "Introduction," in *Dreams, Dreamers, and Visions: The Early Modern Atlantic World*, ed. Plane and Tuttle (Philadelphia: University of Pennsylvania Press, 2013), 1–30.

12. See Steven F. Kruger, *Dreaming in the Middle Ages*, Cambridge Studies in Medieval Literature 14 (Cambridge: Cambridge University Press, 1992); Paul Edward Dutton, *The Politics of Dreaming in the Carolingian Empire*, Regents Studies in Medieval Culture (Lincoln: University of Nebraska Press, 1994); and Lisa M. Bitel, " 'In Visu Noctis': Dreams in European Hagiography and Histories, 450–900," *History of Religions* 31, no. 1 (1991): 39–59.

13. John Bunyan, *The Pilgrim's Progress*, intro. Roger Lundin (1678; rpt., New York: Signet Classic, 1994), xiii.

14. For the early modern period, see especially Carlo Ginzburg, *The Night Battles: Witchcraft and Agrarian Cults in the Sixteenth and Seventeenth Centuries*, trans. John and Anne C. Tedeschi (Baltimore: Johns Hopkins University Press, 1983); Carole Levin, *Dreaming the English Renaissance: Politics and Desire in Court and Culture* (New York: Palgrave Macmillan, 2008); and Richard L. Kagan, *Lucrecia's Dreams: Politics and Prophecy in Sixteenth-Century Spain* (Berkeley: University of California Press, 1990); Kagan offers a very helpful overview of early modern dream theory (36–43). Works on visionaries and accused witches also include much relevant material, including, for example, William A. Christian Jr., *Apparitions in Late Medieval and Renaissance Spain* (Princeton, N.J.: Princeton University Press, 1981); Lyndal Roper, *Oedipus and the Devil: Witchcraft, Sexuality, and Religion in Early Modern Europe* (London: Routledge, 1994), esp. ch. 10, and 226–48. In addition, the essays in Plane and Tuttle, eds., *Dreams, Dreamers, and Visions: The Early Modern Atlantic World*, especially Campbell's "The Inner Eye," link changes in European dream theory to the progress of colonialism in the Americas (33–48, esp. 40–48).

15. Cf. Neal Salisbury, *Manitou and Providence: Indians, Europeans, and the Making of New England, 1500–1643* (New York: Oxford University Press, 1982); see also Kathleen J. Bragdon, *Native People of Southern New England, 1500–1650* (Norman: University of Oklahoma Press, 1996),

and Kathleen J. Bragdon, *Native People of Southern New England, 1650–1775*, Civilization of the American Indian 221 (Norman: University of Oklahoma Press, 2009); for my earlier work on this history see Ann Marie Plane, *Colonial Intimacies: Indian Marriage in Early New England* (Ithaca: Cornell University Press, 2000), esp. ch. 2.

16. Cf. Lisa Brooks, *The Common Pot: The Recovery of Native Space in the Northeast*, Indigenous Americas (Minneapolis: University of Minneapolis Press, 2008); Amy E. Den Ouden, *Beyond Conquest: Native Peoples and the Struggle for History in New England* (Lincoln: University of Nebraska Press, 2005); Jean M. O'Brien, *Firsting and Lasting: Writing Indians Out of Existence in New England*, Indigenous Americas (Minneapolis: University of Minneapolis Press, 2010); and the influential early collection edited by Colin G. Calloway, *After King Philip's War: Presence and Persistence in Indian New England*, Reencounters with Colonialism: New Perspectives on the Americas (Hanover, N.H.: University Press of New England, 1997).

17. Barbara Tedlock, ed., *Dreaming: Anthropological and Psychological Interpretations* (Santa Fe: School of American Research Press, 1992), preface (ix–x, xiii–xiv), introduction (21–23).

18. Monique Scheer, "Are Emotions a Kind of Practice (and Is That What Makes Them Have a History)? A Bourdieuian Approach to Understanding Emotion," *History and Theory* 51, no. 2 (2012): 194.

19. Ibid., 195.

20. Cf. Alexandra Walsham, "The Reformation and 'The Disenchantment of the World' Reassessed," *Historical Journal* 51, no. 2 (2008): 497–528.

21. It is worth noting that this book, which attempts an analysis of these events, may itself constitute, due to its origins in limited sources, just the latest appropriation of an indigenous experience understood partially, at best.

22. Cf. Melissa Jayne Fawcett, *Medicine Trail: The Life and Lessons of Gladys Tantaquidgeon* (Tucson: University of Arizona Press, 2000), 53–54, 75, 135–36.

23. John Comaroff and Jean Comaroff, *Ethnography and the Historical Imagination*, Studies in the Ethnographic Imagination (Boulder, Colo.: Westview Press, 1992), 256–57.

24. Alan Macfarlane, *The Family Life of Ralph Josselin, a Seventeenth-Century Clergyman* (1970; rpt. New York: W. W. Norton, 1977), 183; Peter Burke, "L'histoire sociale des rêves," *Annales: Économies, Sociétés, Civilisations* 28 (1973): 333.

25. Cf. Peter N. Stearns and Carol Z. Stearns, ed., *Emotion and Social Change: Toward a New Psychohistory* (New York: Holmes and Meier, 1988), 3–4.

26. Psychohistory was most famously advocated by William L. Langer in "The Next Assignment," *American Historical Review* 63, no. 2 (1958): 283–304, but more modern approaches have obviated some of the early anachronisms. Thomas A. Kohut discusses the critiques of psychohistory and then argues that there is no need for a separate psychohistorical method, and that the psychological dimensions of historical problems need not be abandoned because some practitioners failed to live up to the accepted professional standards of the discipline. Kohut argues that a major error has been the conflation of contemporary theory with historical fact, an assumption of universal applicability of the theory, and a failure to "begin with his historical subject" (339). Further, Kohut avers, the work of the historian and the work of the clinical psychoanalyst are quite similar in that "both disciplines, to the extent that they seek to understand human feelings, thoughts, and actions," share a common methodology, "that is, knowing by empathic understanding" (344). Thus "this fundamental methodological unity makes clear that, in studying the past's psychological dimension, the historian can remain a historian; he can continue to use traditional historical methods and, in doing so, function in a way that is fundamentally compatible with the way in which the psychoanalyst functions as a clinician . . . [leading] to work that is both

psychologically sophisticated and historically significant" (347–48): Thomas A. Kohut, "Psychohistory as History," *American Historical Review* 91, no. 2 (1986): 336–54, esp. 336–37. See also Fred Weinstein, "Psychohistory and the Crisis of the Social Sciences," *History and Theory* 34, no. 4 (1995): 299–301.

27. See Barbara H. Rosenwein, "Problems and Methods in the History of Emotions," *Passions in Context: International Journal for the History and Theory of Emotions* 1 (2010): 10.

28. Sigmund Freud, *On Dreams*, trans. and ed. James Strachey, rpt. ed. (New York: W. W. Norton, 1952), 59.

29. Erik Homburger Erikson, "The Dream Specimen of Psychoanalysis," *Journal of the American Psychoanalytic Association* 2 (1954), rpt. in *Essential Papers on Dreams*, ed. Melvin R. Lansky (New York: New York University Press, 1992), see 146–47. For a useful review of anthropological approaches to dreams from Freud's early associates to the present, see also Jeannette Marie Mageo, "Theorizing Dreaming and the Self," in *Dreaming and the Self: New Perspectives on Subjectivity, Identity, and Emotion*, ed. Jeannette Marie Mageo, SUNY series in Dream Studies (Albany: State University of New York Press, 2003), 3–22.

30. See discussion in Douglas Hollan, "Selfscape Dreams," in Mageo, *Dreaming and the Self*, 64–65.

31. As James L. Fosshage writes, dreams "further the internal process of integration and organization of experiences and memories." Fosshage, "The Psychological Function of Dreams: A Revised Psychoanalytic Perspective," *Psychoanalysis and Contemporary Thought* 6 (1983): 641–69, rpt. in *Essential Papers on Dreams*, ed. Melvin R. Lansky (New York: New York University Press, 1992), 257.

32. Ernest Hartmann, *The Nature and Functions of Dreaming* (New York: Oxford University Press, 2011), 5.

33. For a statement in this direction, see W. Gordon Lawrence, "Won from the Void and Formless Infinite: Experiences of Social Dreaming," *Free Associations* 2, part 2, no. 22 (1991): 259–94.

34. Erikson, "The Dream Specimen," 146–47.

35. Ibid., 137.

36. For more on the early modern self, see, for example, John Jeffries Martin, *Myths of Renaissance Individualism* (New York: Palgrave Macmillan, 2004). I am grateful to my student Wendy Hurford for sharing this reference. The role of dream reporting in spiritual autobiography, and the way in which that plays into the formation of a modern individualist consciousness, are major themes of Mechal Sobel's *Teach Me Dreams*, cited above.

37. See Plane and Tuttle, "Introduction," in *Dreams, Dreamers, and Visions*, 14.

## Chapter 1. English Dream Belief and Practice in the Tudor-Stuart World

1. [John Winthrop], *The Journal of John Winthrop, 1630–1649*, ed. Richard S. Dunn, James Savage, and Laetitia Yeandle (Cambridge, Mass.: Belknap Press of Harvard University Press, 1996), 111.

2. Ibid. His father wrote proudly, "& so beinge received into the congregation upon good proofe of his understandinge in the things of God, he went on cheerfully in a Christian course."

3. Ibid.

4. Ibid., 112; Keith Thomas, *Religion and the Decline of Magic: Studies in Popular Beliefs in Sixteenth- and Seventeenth-Century England* (London: Weidenfeld and Nicolson, 1971), 128.

5. Winthrop, *Journal*, 112.

6. One significance of blue ribbons may be found in Numbers 15:37–40: "And the Lord spake unto Moses, saying [v. 38] Speake unto the children of Israel, and byd them that thei make them fringes upon the borders of their garments, throughout their generations, and put upon the fringes of the borders a rybande of blewe silke. [v. 39] And he shal have the fringes, that when ye loke upon them, ye may remember all the commandements of the Lord, & do them. & that ye seke not after your owne heart, nor after your owne eies, after the which ye go a whoring. [v. 40] That ye may remember and do all my commandements, and be holy unto your God." Bible GV. I am grateful to Warren Hofstra of Shenandoah University for noting the reference.

7. Winthrop, *Journal*, 111.

8. David D. Hall, *Worlds of Wonder, Days of Judgment: Popular Religious Belief in Early New England* (Cambridge, Mass.: Harvard University Press, 1989), 71, and ch. 2.

9. An orthodox son of New England, Increase Mather, noted near the century's close that a chief objection to the "enthusiasms" of Quakerism lay in its denial of scripture as the "final rule" of all conduct: Increase Mather, *An Essay for the recording of illustrious providences: Wherein an Account is given of many Remarkable and very Memorable Events, which have hapned this last Age; Especially in New-England* (Boston: Samuel Green for Joseph Browning, 1684), 348–49.

10. The quote is from Experience Mayhew, *Indian Converts, or, some Accounts of the Lives and Dying Speeches of a considerable number of the Christianized Indians of Martha's Vineyard, in New England* (London: Samuel Gerrish, 1727), 148.

11. Winthrop, *Journal*, 111, 112.

12. Hall, *Worlds of Wonder*, 71–72.

13. John Winthrop, "A Modell of Christian Charity," *MHS Coll.*, 3rd ser., 1 (1838): 33–35, 44–48.

14. Cf. Susan Parman, *Dream and Culture: An Anthropological Study of the Western Intellectual Tradition* (New York: Praeger, 1991), esp. 3–16.

15. Maria V. Jordán, "El buen dormir: Francisco de Monzón y el sueño en el siglo xvi," *Cuadernos de Historia Moderna* (Universidad Complutense, Madrid) 26 (2001): 169–84. I am grateful to Maria V. Jordán for the English translation.

16. See Steven F. Kruger, *Dreaming in the Middle Ages*, Cambridge Studies in Medieval Literature 14 (Cambridge: Cambridge University Press, 1992), 6, and see also 17–34 on dreams as "middle" or "double" phenomena. See also A. Roger Ekirch, *At Day's Close: Night in Times Past* (New York: W. W. Norton, 2005), esp. 311–23.

17. For case studies of church trials of visionaries, see Richard L. Kagan, *Lucrecia's Dreams: Politics and Prophecy in Sixteenth-Century Spain* (Berkeley: University of California Press, 1990); Carlo Ginzberg, *The Night Battles: Witchcraft and Agrarian Cults in the Sixteenth and Seventeenth Centuries*, trans. John and Anne Tedeschi (Baltimore: Johns Hopkins University Press, 1983); and Sara Tilghman Nalle, *Mad for God: Bartolomé Sánchez, the Secret Messiah of Cardenete* (Charlottesville: University Press of Virginia, 2001).

18. Diane Watt, "Barton, Elizabeth (c. 1506–1534)," *Oxford Dictionary of National Biography* (Oxford University Press), online ed., January 2008, http://www.oxforddnb.com/view/article/1598.

19. Thomas Beard, *Theatre of Gods judgements: wherein is represented the admirable justice of God against all notorious sinners, great and small . . .*, 4th ed. (London: By Susan Islip for Mary Heron, [1648]), 71; see also Kagan, *Lucrecia's Dreams*, and María V. Jordán, "Competition and Confirmation in the Iberian Prophetic Community: The 1589 Invasion of Portugal in the Dreams of Lucrecia de León," in *Dreams, Dreamers, and Visions: The Early Modern Atlantic World*, ed. Ann Marie Plane and Leslie Tuttle (Philadelphia: University of Pennsylvania Press, 2013), 72–87. Diane Watt notes that the authorities hoped to nip in the bud any circulation of Barton's prophecies via

the printing press. The indictments issued against Barton also "called upon the public to surrender any books, scrolls or other writings about the revelations and miracles attributed to Barton and her adherents, on pain of imprisonment and the imposition of a fine." Watt, "Barton, Elizabeth."

20. Beard, *Theatre*, 70–71.

21. Ibid, 71.

22. Ibid. For date of death, see Watt, "Barton, Elizabeth."

23. Francis J. Bremer, *John Winthrop: America's Forgotten Founding Father* (New York: Oxford University Press, 2003), 35. Bremer notes, "His assistance to Foxe would be a matter of pride to William's brother Adam and Adam's son John, who would carry the tale with him to New England and pass it on to his own children."

24. John Foxe, *The Actes and Monuments of John Foxe*, ed. Josiah Pratt, 8 vols. (London: Religious Tract Society, [1877]), 2:52.

25. Cf. Jordán, "El buen dormir."

26. Foxe, *Actes*, 2:52.

27. Gervase Holles, *Memorials of the Holles Family, 1493–1656*, ed. A. C. Wood, Camden Third Series 55 (London: Camden Society, 1937), 231; also cited in Thomas, *Religion*, 128.

28. Foxe, *Actes*, 8:456.

29. Ibid.

30. Ibid.

31. Thomas, *Religion*, 128, and 128–30. See also Carole Levin, *Dreaming the English Renaissance: Politics and Desire in Court and Culture* (New York: Palgrave Macmillan, 2008), e.g., 6–7.

32. Thomas, *Religion*, 129.

33. Cf. Ann Marie Plane and Leslie Tuttle, "Introduction," in Plane and Tuttle, *Dreams, Dreamers, and Visions*, 9–15.

34. Ekirch, *At Day's Close*, 313–14, 316–17, 321, quotation 312.

35. Thomas Cooper, *The Mystery of Witchcraft. Discovering the Truth, Nature, Occasions, Growth and Power thereof. Together With the Detection and Punishment of the Same. As Also, The severall Stratagems of Sathan, ensnaring the poore Soule by this desperate practize of annoying the bodie with the Severall Uses thereof to the Church of Christ. Very necessary for the redeeming of these Atheisticall and secure times* (London: Printed by Nicholas Okes, 1617), 145–46.

36. Ibid., 145.

37. One seventeenth-century dream dictionary referenced Hippocrates and Galen and offered similar links between humors, illness, and particular types of dream imagery; for example, "Hee that dreameth he seeth smoake or mists, or profound darknesse, is much disposed to melancholy sicknesses." See [Gonzalo], *The Divine Dreamer; or, A short treatise discovering the true effect and power of Dreames; Confirmed by the most learned and best approved Authors. Whereunto is annexed The Dreame of a young Gentleman, immediately before the death of the late Earle of Strafford. Printed in the yeare 1641*, unpaginated, unbound pamphlet, catalogue #53992, Huntington Library, San Marino, Calif., [9].

38. Cooper, *Mystery of Witchcraft*, 145.

39. Ibid., quotation 148–49. The Genevan version of 2 Timothy 3:17 reads: "That the man of God may be absolute, being made perfite [perfect] unto all good workes." The verse immediately preceding emphasizes the teaching of the scripture as perfect and sufficient in itself. Thomas Beard echoed Cooper's depiction of "these latter days," noting an increasing "disorder and corruption of manners," which is "because the world every day groweth worse and worse, according to the saying of our Saviour and Redeemer (Christ Iesus, the Sonne of God) That *in the latter dayes* (which are these wherein we live) *Iniquity shall be increased.*" Beard, *Theatre*, 3.

40. See Henry M. Dexter, "Elder Brewster's Library," *MHS Proc.*, 2nd ser., 5 (1889–90): 37–85; Franklin B. Dexter, "Early Private Libraries in New England," *Proceedings of the American Antiquarian Society*, n.s., 18 (1907): 135–47; Samuel Eliot Morison, *The Puritan Pronaos: Studies in the Intellectual Life of New England in the Seventeenth Century* (New York: New York University Press, 1936), esp. 130–47, "Libraries, Private and Public"; Charles F. Robinson and Robin Robinson, "Three Early Massachusetts Libraries," *Publications of the Colonial Society of Massachusetts, Transactions* 28 (1930–33): 107–75; David D. Hall makes it clear that, although there were both profane and classical texts in New England libraries, the book market "aligned itself with godliness and orthodoxy" for most of the 1600s "because to do otherwise was to risk the intervention of the civil government." David D. Hall, "Readers and Writers in Early New England," in *A History of the Book in America*, vol. 1, *The Colonial Book in the Atlantic World*, ed. Hugh Amory and David D. Hall (Chapel Hill: University of North Carolina Press for the American Antiquarian Society, 2007), 127–28. Hall also notes that the clergy offered consistent and vigorous defense of " 'learnedness,' " quoting midcentury divines who claimed "that 'Extraordinarie Revelations are now ceased,' [and categorizing] the prophecies voiced by lay people as delusions created by the Devil." Those who disagreed were accused "of being 'ignorant and unlettered' " (140). Morison argues that the book lists he examined prove that ministers were important to the practice of medicine as well as religion (Morison, *Puritan Pronaos*, 136), and the work of Walter W. Woodward suggests that alternative routes to knowledge—including resort to magic and induced trance states favored by Tudor-Stuart alchemists—were also a part of the repertoire of certain highly trained individuals, such as John Winthrop Jr. and Gershom Bulkeley. Cf. Walter W. Woodward, *Prospero's America: John Winthrop, Jr., Alchemy, and the Creation of New England Culture, 1606–1676* (Chapel Hill: For the Omohundro Institute of Early American History and Culture by the University of North Carolina Press, 2010), esp. 16–20, 215–19, and 243–50; for a list of Winthrop's books, see "Catalogue of the Winthrop Library" [presented by Francis B. Winthrop], in *Alphabetical and Analytical Catalogue of the New York Society Library with the Charter, By-Laws &c. of the Institution* (New York: R. Craighead, 1850), 491–505.

41. Cf. Janine Rivière, " 'Filthy Dreamers and Scurrilous Dreams': The Politics of Dreams in Seventeenth-Century England," *Proceedings of the University of Queensland History Research Group* 12 (2001): 15–16.

42. Alan Macfarlane, *The Family Life of Ralph Josselin, a Seventeenth-Century Clergyman: An Essay in Historical Anthropology* (New York: W. W. Norton, 1970), 184–85.

43. Philip Goodwin, *The Mystery of Dreames, Historically Discoursed . . .* (London: Printed by A.M. for Francis Tyton, 1658). Goodwin does not appear to have been owned or read in New England (see above, n. 40), and therefore must be treated as a source that was shaped by the same influences as shaped the views of New England divines. Hall notes that New England's "learned culture" was shaped fundamentally "by scholastic and humanist ways of thinking" transferred largely intact from England, facilitated by the fact that "a hundred or so of the founding generation had attended one of the English universities, especially Emmanuel College, Cambridge." Hall, "Readers and Writers," 131. Goodwin graduated St. John's College, Cambridge, in 1627 and was ordained at Peterborough. In 1630 he advanced to MA, by 1633 he was curate at All Saints' in Hertford, and fifteen years later he was appointed vicar at Watford in Hertfordshire by Parliament (1645; later ejected for nonconformity with the Restoration, in 1661). He was the author of four published works: see H. R. French, "Goodwin, Philip (d. 1667)," *Oxford Dictionary of National Biography* (Oxford University Press, 2004), online ed., January 2008, http://www.oxforddnb.com/view/article/10995. For an extended discussion of Goodwin, see Janine Rivière, "Dreams in Early Modern England: Frameworks of Interpretation," Ph.D. thesis (University of Toronto, Toronto,

Canada, 2013), ch. 3, esp. 120–22. I am grateful to Dr. Rivière for her helpful communications and generous collegiality regarding Goodwin's career and English dream beliefs in general.

44. Goodwin, *Mystery*, 268–69; Hebrews 1:1–2 reads: "At sondrie times & in divers maners God spake in the olde time to our fathers by the Prophetes: In these last dayes he hathe spoken unto us by his Sonne, whome he hathe made heir of all things, by whome also he made the worldes." Bible GV.

45. Goodwin, *Mystery*, 268–69. Joel 2:28 reads: "And it shall come to pass afterward, that I will pour out my spirit upon all flesh; and your sons and your daughters shall prophesy, your old men shall dream dreams, your young men shall see visions." Bible KJV. Acts 2:17 offers almost exactly the same language: "And it shall come to pass in the last days, saith God, I will pour out of my Spirit upon all flesh: and your sons and your daughters shall prophesy, and your young men shall see visions, and your old men shall dream dreams."

46. Goodwin, *Mystery*, unpaginated epistle dedicatory.

47. Richard Baxter, *Works*, vol. 556, xii, 500; quoted in Geoffrey F. Nuttall, *The Holy Spirit in Puritan Faith and Experience* (Oxford: Basil Blackwell, 1946), 56.

48. Nuttall, *The Holy Spirit*, 56–57.

49. Kruger, *Dreaming in the Middle Ages*, ch. 3, esp. 40–41, 64–65.

50. David D. Hall traces a picture of general consensus, with little differentiation between lay and clergy in fascination with "wonder lore" (see his *Worlds of Wonder*), while Richard Godbeer paints a more conflict-laced picture of actual magical practice, suggesting a deeper rift between laity and clergy over matters of magical practice, but still a very broad acceptance of white magic among ordinary New England colonists. Richard Godbeer, *The Devil's Dominion: Magic and Religion in Early New England* (New York: Cambridge University Press, 1992), 5–6; see especially his analysis of Keith Thomas's dichotomizing discussion of the relation between religion and magic.

51. The quote continues: "[That] he may not like Isaac, abide beguiled with Kid for Venison, Gen. 18:32." Goodwin, *Mystery*, unpaginated epistle dedicatory.

52. Ibid., unpaginated epistle dedicatory (b).

53. Beard, *Theatre*, 18, citing Daniel 5. This book makes clear that Belshazzar, like Nebuchadnezzar, could not interpret his dreams without the help of Daniel, a particularly gifted visionary. On Beard among New England readers, see Hall, *Worlds of Wonder*, 73.

54. Bible GV.

55. Goodwin, *Mystery*, unpaginated epistle dedicatory.

56. Goodwin cited one further example from scripture, the dream of Pontius Pilate's wife as found in Matthew 27:19. Ibid.

57. See, for example, [Gonzalo] *Divine Dreamer*, 10–16.

58. Goodwin, *Mystery*, unpaginated epistle dedicatory. The story of Augustus's physician is retold in a seventeenth-century dream dictionary, [Gonzalo] *Divine Dreamer*, 11–12: an angel appears "in the form of the goddesse Pallas to Antonius (Physitian to Augustus)," telling him that although the emperor was ill and thought he might remain in his tent during the battle against Brutus and Cassius, that he must be present; and sure enough, "It came to passe that the enemies souldiers [won] the tents" and would doubtless have slain Augustus "if hee had beene present there; So by this dreame he prevented his death, wonne the day, and remained sole Monarch of the Roman Empire: under his Reigne was borne the Redeemer of the World." The story of Calpurnia is also retold in the same work. The author notes of Julius: "He instead of converting of it [her dream] to his benefit; dispised the dreame, and went to the Senate house, the day following where the dreame sorted to wofull effect." [Gonzalo] *Divine Dreamer*, 15.

59. Goodwin, *Mystery*, unpaginated epistle dedicatory.

60. Goodwin, *Mystery*, 6–7: "The Dreame is swift and goes away with a quick foot, or as upon the wing rather. *The wicked shall fly away as a Dreame*, Job 20. 8. The Ancients hence phancied, that a Dreame had wings like a Bird of the aire."

61. Goodwin, *Mystery*, 39–40; see also Parman, *Dream and Culture*, 22, on this tradition.

62. Beard, *Theatre*, 39.

63. On Foxe being well known in New England, see Hall, *Worlds of Wonder*, 50–51.

64. Foxe, *Actes*, 7:146, 706–7. Philpot (and, through him, Foxe as well) took pains to make clear that although a dream was not a replacement for understanding "learned out of God's word," in scripture, nevertheless, he thought this dream "not to have come of the illusion of the senses, because it brought with it so much spiritual joy, . . . [therefore] I take it to be of the working of God's Spirit." Philpot went on to offer a detailed interpretation of the dream, in which the city was "the glorious church of Christ, and the appearance of it in the sky, signifieth the heavenly state thereof, whose conversation is in heaven." The four quadrants of the dream city represented the unity of "the church here militant" with "the primitive church throughout the four parts of the world." And his call to others in the dream "to behold this wonderful city, I construe it by [be] the will of God this vision to have come upon me musing on your letter, to the end, that under this figure I might have occasion to move you with many others, to behold the primitive church in all your opinions concerning faith." As he tried to call to others to enjoy this sight, "by and by, to my great grief, it vaded [faded] away."

65. Foxe, *Actes*, 8:454–55.

66. Such a dream dictionary would probably have been regarded with suspicion by disciplined Protestants. The exact quotation is as follows: "To have a longe bearde, betokeneth strength. / To se[e] a berde, betokeneth harme." [Anonymous], *Dreams of Daniel: Here begynneth the dreames of Daniell. VVith the exposycions of the. xij. sygnes, deuyded by the. xij. monthes of the yeare. And also the destenyes both of man and woman borne in eche monthe of the yere. Very necessarrye to be knowen* ([London]: Imprynted by me Robert Wyer: dwellynge at the sygne of seynt Iohn Euange-lyst, in seynt Martyns parysshe, besyde Charynge Crosse, [1556?]), unpaginated.

67. Foxe, *Actes*, 8:454–55. The *Oxford English Dictionary* includes two relevant definitions for fire-pan: "1. A pan or receptacle for holding or carrying fire, e.g. a brazier, a chafing dish, a portable grate. 2. A pan for heating anything over a fire. *Obs.*" *Oxford English Dictionary* online, s.v. "fire-pan," accessed April 21, 2008, http://www.oed.com. But here, it doubtless signifies the coming death by burning that Mearing, Rough, and Symson would face. For the relationship between Rough and Mearing, see Richard L. Greaves, "Rough, John (c. 1508–1557)," *Oxford Dictionary of National Biography* (Oxford University Press, 2004), online ed. http://www.oxforddnb.com/view/article/24167.

68. Foxe, *Actes*, 8:457.

69. Thomas, *Religion*, 131.

70. Charles Carlton notes of William Laud's early seventeenth-century dream reports: "Not once does he attribute his nocturnal experiences to physical stimuli, such as over-eating." Charles Carlton, "The Dream Life of Archbishop Laud, *History Today* 36, no. 12 (1986): 14. Rivière notes the frequent resort to dreams as a determination of disease or cure: see "Dreams in Early Modern England."

71. Janine Rivière, "Demons of Desire or Symptoms of Disease? Medical Theories and Popular Experiences of the 'Nightmare' in Premodern England," in Plane and Tuttle, *Dreams, Dreamers, and Visions*, 49–71. Mather, *Illustrious Providences*, 340–45, includes a lengthy discussion of the afflictions of Thomas Harris, a Quaker on Long Island, and his reappearance after death to townsfolk in the shape of an apparition.

72. Alan Macfarlane suggested four categories of recorded dreams in his study of Ralph

Josselin: "Religious," "Political," "Religio-Political," and "Personal." Macfarlane, *Family Life*, 183–84. These are unsatisfying, however, as they capture nothing beyond the level of what a modern psychoanalyst would know as "manifest content" and do not derive from categories inherent in early modern traditions, either of learned discussion of dreams or from more common folk practices.

73. Cf. Hall, *Worlds of Wonder*, 86–89.

74. [Adam Winthrop], "Diary of Adam Winthrop," in *Life and Letters of John Winthrop*, ed. Robert C. Winthrop, 2 vols. (Boston: Ticknor and Fields, 1864), 1:439 (December 5, 1621).

75. Even Foxe himself was known to have predicted the fall of the oppressive Queen Mary, although his knowledge came from divine inspiration reached while preaching a sermon rather than from a dream per se. Foxe "preached a sermon in exile in which he announced, by miraculous prescience, that the time had at last come for the return to England, though the news of Queen Mary's death on the previous day had not yet reached him." As late as 1634, Foxe's granddaughter "claimed that there was an old man still alive who had been present on that notable occasion." Thomas, *Religion*, 131–32.

76. See Mary Baine Campbell, "The Inner Eye: Early Modern Dreaming and Disembodied Sight," in Plane and Tuttle, *Dreams, Dreamers, and Visions*, 33–34.

77. [Joseph Hall], *The Shaking of the Olive-Tree. The Remaining Works of that Incomparable Prelate Joseph Hall, D. D. Late Lord Bishop of Norwich. With Some Specialties of Divine Providence in his life, noted by his own hand. Together with his Hard Measure, written also by Himself* (London: printed by J. Cadwel, 1660), 2–3.

78. Ibid., 3. See also Thomas, *Religion*, 129 n. 4.

79. [Hall], *Shaking*, 3. Gilby was a prominent associate of the Earl of Huntingdon and a major contributor to the Genevan translation of the Bible. Claire Cross, "Gilby, Anthony (c. 1510–1585)," *Oxford Dictionary of National Biography* (Oxford University Press, 2004), online ed., http://www .oxforddnb.com/view/article/10709.

80. [Hall], *Shaking*, 3.

81. Fynes Moryson, *An itinerary vvritten by Fynes Moryson Gent . . . containing his ten yeeres trauell through the tvvelue dominions of Germany, Bohmerland, Sweitzerland, Netherland, Denmarke, Poland, Jtaly, Turky, France, England, Scotland, and Ireland. Diuided into III parts . . .* (1617). [Early English Books Online, STC (2nd ed.) 18205, 19–20, Accessed July 7, 2009]. I am grateful to William Rudder Jr. of Plimoth Plantation, Plymouth, Massachusetts, for bringing this reference to my attention. The full passage reads: "Whilst I liued at Prage, and one night had set vp very late drinking at a feast, early in the morning the Sunne beames glancing on my face, as I lay in bed, I dreamed that a shadow passing by, told me that my father was dead, at which awaking all in a sweat, and affected with this dreame, I rose and wrote the day and houre, and all circumstances thereof in a paper booke, which Booke with many other things I put into a barrel, and sent it from Prage to Stode, thence to be conuaied into England. And now being at Nurnberg, a Merchant of a noble family, well acquainted with me and my friends, arriued there, who told me that my Father died some two moneths past, I list not write any lies, but that which I write is as true as strange. When I returned into England some foure yeeres after, I would not open the barrell I sent from Prage, nor looke on the paper Booke in which I had written this dreame, till I had called my sisters and some friends to be witnesses, where my selfe and they were astonished to see my written dreame answere the very day of my Fathers death.

"I may lawfully sweare, that which my kinsmen haue heard witnessed by my brother Henry whilst he liued, that in my youth at Cambridge I had the like dreame of my Mothers death, where my brother Henry lying with me, early in the morning I dreamed that my mother passed by with a sad countenance, and told me that shee could not come to my commencement; I being within fiue moneths to proceed Master of Arts, and shee hauing promised at that time to come to Cambridge: And when I related this dreame to my brother, both of vs awaking together in a sweat, he protested to me that he had dreamed the very same, and when wee had not the least knowledge of our Mothers sickenesse, neither in our youthfull affections were any whit affected with the strangenesse of this dreame, yet the next Carrier brought vs word of our mothers death."

82. Macfarlane, *Family Life*, 183, 187; the word "replacement" comes from Macfarlane's text.

83. Macfarlane, *Family Life*, 184 (quoting from Josselin's diary [January 5, 1679]). Later in life, a dream of Josselin's predicted the death of his son-in-law: 184, 187.

84. Holles, *Memorials*, 231.

85. Ibid.

86. Ibid.

87. The quotation comes on the heels of his report of a second predictive dream in 1643: He "dreampt that [some]one came to me and tolde me my son was dead; after which I wakened with a great passion and palpitation of my heart. Nor could I rest after it, but arose and wrote letters to my wife, charging hir upon the receipt of them to send a messenger away to me to let me know how my childe did." But as it happened, this dream foretold news that Holles's nephew, who was like a son to him, had died the very day before (189). Holles speculated, "though it proved not my dreame exactly true, yet relatively it did. . . . I deny not but amongst the variety of dreames sometimes they may casually sort with the present accidents, yet I doubt not at all (notwithstanding Hob[b]s his new and atheisticall philosophy) but when there is between two an harmony in their affections, there is likewise betweene their soules an acquaintance and sometimes an intelligence." Holles, *Memorials*, 190.

88. Edward Burghall, "Providence Improved," ed. James Hall, *The Record Society for the Publication of Original Documents relating to Lancashire and Cheshire* 19 (1889): 4. See also Thomas, *Religion*, 129.

89. [John Dane], "A Declaration of Remarkabell Prouedenses in the Corse of my Lyfe," *New England Historical and Genealogical Register* 8 (1854): 149.

90. Patricia Crawford, "Women's Dreams in Seventeenth-Century England," *History Workshop Journal* 49 (Spring 2000): 129–49, rpt. in *Dreams and History: The Interpretation of Dreams from Ancient Greece to Modern Psychoanalysis*, 91–103, ed. Daniel Pick and Lyndal Roper (New York: Routledge, 2004), 97.

91. Foxe, *Actes*, 2:52.

92. [Cresacre More], D.O.M.S. *The life and death of Sir Thomas Moore Lord high Chancellour of England. Written by M.T.M. and dedicated to the Queens most gracious Majestie* ([Douai: Printed by B. Belliere, 1631?]), 15–16.

93. Lucy Hutchinson, *Memoirs of the life of Colonel Hutchinson*, ed. and intro. James Sutherland, with the fragment of an autobiography of Mrs. Hutchinson (New York: Oxford University Press, 1973), 287–88.

94. John Dane recalled that when he was decided on emigration, he traveled home to speak with his parents, but, he wrote, "My fatther and my motther showd themselfs unwilling." Sitting by a table where there was a Bible, Dane "hastily toke up" the book, "and tould my fatther if whare I opend the bybell thare i met with anie thing eyther to incuredg or discouredg that should settell me." On opening the book, "The first I cast my eys on was: [']Cum out from among them, touch no unclene thing, and I will be your god and you shall be my pepell.[']" Thus, Dane had settled this family dispute: "My fatther and motther never more aposd me, but furderd me in the thing; and hasted after me as sone as thay could." Dane, "Declaration," 154. See also Godbeer, *Devil's Dominion*, 52.

95. Winthrop, *Journal*, 72.

96. Ibid., 135.

97. Edward Taylor, "Diary of Edward Taylor [1668–71]," *Proceedings of the Massachusetts Historical Society*, 1st ser., 18 (1880–81): 12 (June 19, 1668).

98. John 4:9. The second major narrative of John 4 is the story of the ruler of Cana in Galilee, who asks Jesus to cure his son. Jesus says unto him, "Except ye see signes and wonders, ye will not believe," a potent warning to be cautious in one's reliance on dreams. John 4:48 (Bible GV).

99. Taylor, "Diary," 12 (June 26, 1668).

100. Winthrop, *Journal*, 112.

101. *Dreams of Daniel*, unpaginated.

102. [Alice Thornton], "The Autobiography of Mrs. Alice Thornton," ed. C. Jackson, *Publications of the Surtees Society* 62 (1873): 111–12. Revelation 2:10 (Bible GV): "Feare none of those things, which though shalt suffer: beholde, it shall come to passe, that the devil shal cast some of you into prison, that ye may be tried, and ye shal have tribulation ten dayes: be thou faithful unto the death, and I wil give thee the crowne of life."

103. [Thornton], "Autobiography," 112.

104. Goodwin, *Mystery*, 83.

105. Winthrop, *Journal*, 72.

106. Ibid., 173.

107. Winthrop, *Journal*, 241. See also Michael P. Winship, *The Times and Trials of Anne Hutchinson: Puritans Divided* (Lawrence: University Press of Kansas, 2005), 17–20, and also Michael P. Winship, *Seers of God: Puritan Providentialism in the Restoration and Early Enlightenment* (Baltimore: Johns Hopkins University Press, 1996), ch. 1, esp. 17–18: Hutchinson's error did not lead to greater caution with regard to providential signs; when Thomas Hooker's family was discussing Hutchinson's sins, they interpreted the occurrence of a minor earthquake as diabolical commentary on the woman herself (18).

108. Thomas Tryon, *Pythagoras his mystick philosophy reviv'd; or, The mystery of dreams unfolded. Wherein the causes, natures, and uses, of nocturnal representations, and the communications both of good and evil angels, and also departed souls, to mankind, are theosophically unfolded; that is, according to the word of God, and the harmony of created beings. To which is added, a discourse of the causes, natures, and cure of phrensie, madness, or distraction. By Tho. Tryon, student in physick, and author of The way to long life, health, and happiness* (London: for Thomas Salusbury, 1691), 3. This is a second edition of a work Tryon originally published (under the pseudonym Philtheos Phyliologue) as *A Treatise of Dreams and Visions, Wherein the Causes Natures and Uses of Nocturnal Representations, and the Communications both of Good and Evil Angels, as also departed Souls, to Mankinde are Theosophically Unfolded; that is, according to the word of God, and the Harmony of Created Beings, Night unto night sheweth Wisdom, Psal. 19. 2. To which is added, a Discourse of the Causes, Natures, and Cure of Phrensie, Madness, or Distraction* (London: s.n., 1689).

109. Thomas Hobbes, *Leviathan, or, the Matter, Forme, and Power of a Common-Wealth ecclesiasticall and civill* (London [Holland]: Printed for Andrew Ckooke [sic], 1651); Henry More, *The Immortality of the Soul, so farre forth as it is demonstrable from the knowledge of nature and the light of reason* (London: Printed by J. Flesher, 1659). Cf. Sarah Rivett, *The Science of the Soul in Colonial New England* (Chapel Hill: University of North Carolina Press for the Omohundro Institute of Early American History and Culture, 2011). I am indebted to Sarah Rivett for initially pointing me toward the More work.

110. Tryon, *Pythagoras*, 6.

111. Ibid., 6–7.

112. Ibid., 7.

113. Ibid., 7, 9.

# Chapter 2. Representation of Indigenous Dreaming at Contact and Beyond

1. Roger Williams, *A Key Into the Language of America*, ed. and intro. John J. Teunissen and Evelyn J. Hinz (1643; Detroit: Wayne State University Press, 1973), 108.

2. Ibid. The full text reads: "I once travailed to an Iland of the wildest in our parts, where in the night an Indian (as he said) had a vision or dream of the Sun (whom they worship for a God) darting a Beame into his Breast, which he conceived to be the Messenger of his Death: this poore Native call'd his Friends and neighbours, and prepared some little refreshing for them, but himselfe was kept waking and Fasting in great Humiliations and Invocations for 10. Dayes and nights: I was alone (having travailed from my Barke, the wind being contrary) and little could I speake to them to their understandings, especially because of the change of their Dialect, or manner of Speech, from our neighbours: yet so much (through the help of God) did I speake, of the *True* and *living only Wise God*, of the Creation: of Man, and his *fall* from God, &c. that at parting many burst forth, *Oh when will you come againe, to bring us some more newes of this God?*" It seems unlikely that Williams remained in the village for a full ten days, and therefore the reading I have made implies that he arrived midway through, where he was told "(as he said)" about the dream or vision and observed the ritual in which the dreamer fasted while his household "prepared some little refreshing" for "his Friends and neighbours."

3. Ibid.

4. The quotation is from Thomas Mayhew Jr. to Mr. John [*sic*] Whitfield, Minister in Winchester, letter, October 16, 1651, in Henry Whitfield, *Strength out of Weakness; Or a Glorious Manifestation of the Further Progress of the Gospel amongst the Indians in New-England, Held Forth in Sundry Letters from divers Ministers and others to the Corporacion established by Parliament for promoting the Gospel among the Heathen in New-England* (London: By the Corporation, Printed by M. Simmons, 1652), 24.

5. See Frank G. Speck, "Penobscot Shamanism," *Memoirs of the American Anthropological Association* 6 (October–December 1919): 268. Speck lists the root words as *Ki•-* "going about," *-gwaso* "dream," and *-i•no* "person" (268 n. 2). On another point of translation, Annette Kolodny notes that "recent studies of the Penobscot language suggest a more nuanced range of meanings that [those] offered by Speck," suggesting that his etymology might need refinement; see her introductory essay in Joseph Nicolar, *The Life and Traditions of the Red Man*, ed., annot., and intro. Annette Kolodny (1893; Durham, N.C.: Duke University Press, 2007), 47. I am grateful to Lisa Brooks for bringing Nicolar's *Red Man* and Kolodny's edition of his work to my attention.

6. See Speck, "Penobscot Shamanism," 268–73, quotation 269. Speck lists the root words as *gwi•láo* "to search for," and *-wab-* "to see" (269 n. 1). Several references to dreams, both used alone and in combination with other more direct forms of divination (such as scapulamancy) for hunting are to be found in the Frank G. Speck Papers, MS Coll. 126 Subcollection I, throughout, but see for example, miscellaneous notes on divination, within Series I–II (4B5e) Religion–e. Miscellaneous notes on Montagnais-Naskapi Religion, 1929 (Freeman Guide 2308), American Philosophical Society, Philadelphia, Pennsylvania.

7. Chrestien Le Clercq, *New Relation of Gaspesia, with the Customs and Religion of the Gaspesian Indians*, ed. and trans. William F. Ganong (n.d.; rpt., Toronto: Champlain Society, 1910), 172–73, (online edition, accessed July 9, 2009, "Early Encounters In North America: Peoples, Cultures and the Environment," 216). http://www.alexanderstreet2.com.proxy.library.ucsb.edu:2048/EENALive/. Cf. W. Gordon Lawrence, "Won from the void and formless infinite: Experiences of Social Dreaming," *Free Associations* 2, no. 2 (1991): 259–94, esp. 263–64, 278–80. Lawrence

discusses the tendency of psychoanalysis to overemphasize the "individual dream" and thereby miss seeing the social dimensions of dreams (as have many small-scale societies), or, in his phrase, following the analyst Wilfrid R. Bion, the way that some dreams "belong to the group" (263). I am grateful to M. Gerard Fromm for directing me to this article.

8. Kathleen J. Bragdon, *The Native People of Southern New England, 1650–1775*, Civilization of the American Indian Series 259 (Norman: University of Oklahoma Press, 2009), 36.

9. William S. Simmons, *Spirit of the New England Tribes: Indian History and Folklore, 1620–1984* (Hanover, N.H.: University Press of New England, 1986), 65–72.

10. Josiah Jeremy (Mi'kmaq), "The Dream of the White Robe and the Floating Island," in Silas Tertius Rand, *Legends of the Micmacs*, rpt. ed. (1894; New York: Johnson Reprint Corp., 1971), 225. I am indebted to the reference and quotation of this story in Colin G. Calloway, ed., *The World Turned Upside Down: Indian Voices from Early America* (New York: Bedford Books of St. Martin's Press, 1994), 33–34. For a similar story from a seventeenth-century source but without the predictive dream, see William Wood, *New England's Prospect*, ed. and intro. Alden T. Vaughan (Amherst: University of Massachusetts Press, 1977), 95–96: "They took the first ship they saw for a walking island, the mast to be a tree, the sail white clouds, and the discharging of ordnance for lightning and thunder, which did much trouble them, but this thunder being over, and this moving-island steadied with an anchor, they manned out their canoes to go and pick strawberries there."

11. Rand, *Legends of the Micmacs*, 225.

12. Ibid., 225–26.

13. Ibid., 226.

14. Ibid.

15. See the discussion of Waban's rise to power at Natick, a newly formed "Praying Town," Francis Jennings, *The Invasion of America: Indians, Colonialism, and the Cant of Conquest* (New York: Norton, 1975), 239–41. For another New England example, see Experience Mayhew's discussion of Hiacoomes, the first convert on Martha's Vineyard: "His Descent was but mean, his Speech but slow, and his Countenance not very promising. He was therefore by the Indian Sachims, and others of their principal Men, looked on as but a mean Person, scarce worthy of their Notice or Regard." Experience Mayhew, *Indian Converts, or, some Accounts of the Lives and Dying Speeches of a considerable number of the Christianized Indians of Martha's Vineyard, in New England* (London: Samuel Gerrish, 1727), 1–2.

16. Nicolar, *Red Man*, 164–65; quotation is Kolodny's gloss, 54–55; on the ship as swan or "K'chi-wump-toqueh," see 55–56.

17. Nicolar, *Red Man*, 165; see also 55.

18. Thomas Shepard, *The Clear Sun-Shine of the Gospel Breaking Forth upon the Indians in New-England* . . . (London: Printed by R. Cotes for John Bellamy, 1648), 10.

19. Ibid. I discussed this dream in the context of resistance to missionaries in chapter 2 of my earlier book *Colonial Intimacies: Indian Marriage in Early New England* (Ithaca, N.Y.: Cornell University Press, 2000), 45–46.

20. Shepard, *Clear Sun-Shine*, 10.

21. The first official voyages by Giovanni da Verrazano in the southern parts and Jacques Cartier in the north occurred in the 1520s and 1530s. European fishermen visited the coastal regions seasonally perhaps some decades earlier than that.

22. Neal Salisbury, *Manitou and Providence: Indians, Europeans, and the Making of New England, 1500–1643* (New York: Oxford University Press, 1982), ch. 7.

23. Shepard, *Clear Sun-Shine*, 9.

24. Ibid. For a wider review, see James P. Ronda, "'We Are Well As We Are': An Indian

Critique of Seventeenth-Century Christian Missions," *William and Mary Quarterly*, 3rd ser., 34, no. 1 (1977): 66–82, esp. 68.

25. Le Clercq, *New Relation of Gaspesia*, 172–73.

26. Ibid., 174.

27. Ibid., 172–73.

28. Ibid., 174.

29. Ibid., 172.

30. Ibid., 216.

31. Ibid., 216. Indeed, he cautioned, "No one must come here in hopes of suffering martyrdom . . . for we are not in a country where savages put Christians to death on account of their religion. They leave every one in his own belief" (221). In fact, Indians were incapable of killing someone due to religious beliefs alone. Instead, he noted, "They kill people only in private quarrels, from intoxication, brutality, vengeance, a dream or extravagant vision" (222).

32. Ibid., 174. This story of the cross was recorded in another version, "Monseigneur de Saint Valier's well-known book, *Estat present de l'Eglise*" (1688), 35, as recorded in the editor's notes to the 1910 volume. Quoting Saint Valier: "If one trusts in the matter to one of the oldest men who was still living a few years ago, one will find without doubt something most remarkable in that which it has been possible to learn from him. This man, aged a hundred or a hundred and twenty years, [was] questioned one day by M. de Fronsac, son of M. Denis, [and] said that he had seen the first ship from Europe which had landed in their country; that before its arrival they had already among them the usage of the Cross; that this usage had not been brought to them by strangers; and that everything he knew about it he had learned by tradition from his ancestors." Ibid., 189, and 189 n. 237.

33. This is just one example of many instances in which Indians vigorously rejected Christian teachings, whether Catholic or Protestant: "These men and women [thoughtful Indian critics] reacted emphatically against the Christian theological ideas of sin, guilt, heaven, hell and baptism." In Ronda, "'We Are Well As We Are,'" 68.

34. Samuel de Champlain, *The Voyages of the Sieur de Champlain of Saintonge, Captain in the Ordinary for the King in the Navy* [1613] vol. 2, book, 2, trans. J. Squair, in *The Works of Samuel de Champlain*, ed. Henry Percival Biggar, et al. (Toronto: Champlain Society, 1922–35; Toronto: University of Toronto Press, 1971), 44–51; I am indebted to the work of Gayle K. Brunelle, *Samuel de Champlain, Founder of New France: A Brief History with Documents* (New York: Bedford/St. Martin's Press, 2012), 79.

35. Ibid.

36. Champlain, *The Voyages*, in Biggar, *Works of Samuel de Champlain*, 82–101, reprinted in Brunelle, *Samuel de Champlain*, 85.

37. Ibid.

38. As noted in a forthcoming article cited by permission of its author, Champlain both resists and embraces Native exhortations about dreaming, and, to his own surprise, is "soon flirting with the prophetic potential of his own dreams." Drew Lopenzina, "Le Jeune Dreams of Moose: Altered States Among the Montagnais in the *Jesuit Relation* of 1634," *Early American Studies* (forthcoming).

39. John Eliot to Edward Winslow, letter, February 2, 1648/9, in Edward Winslow, *The Glorious Progress of the Gospel, amongst the Indians in New England . . .* (London: Printed for Hannah Allen, 1649), 20. A marginal note references Ecclesiastes 5:7, "If in a countrey thou seest the oppression of the poore, and the defrauding of iudgement and iustice, be not astonished at the matter: for he that is higher then the highest, regardeth, and there be higher than they." Other passages of

the same chapter are more relevant, such as 5:6, "For in the multitude of dreames, & vanities are also manie wordes: but feare thou God." Bible GV.

40. John Eliot to Edward Winslow, November 12, 1648, 14.

41. J.D., appendix, in Winslow, *Glorious Progress*, 25.

42. Bragdon, *Native People of Southern New England, 1500–1650*, The Civilization of the American Indian Series 221 (Norman: University of Oklahoma Press, 1996), 190–91; Simmons, *Spirit of the New England Tribes*, 44–45.

43. Williams, *Key*, 193.

44. John Eliot to Edward Winslow, November 12, 1648, 12.

45. Bragdon, *Native People . . . 1500–1650*, 191.

46. Ibid.

47. Williams, *Key*, 190.

48. Bragdon, *Native People . . . 1500–1650*, 192.

49. Ibid., 193.

50. Ibid., 184, 190–191.

51. Williams, *Key*, 108. A similar concern about and ritual management of dream materials occurred among the Iroquois: see Anthony F. C. Wallace, "Dreams and Wishes of the Soul: A Type of Psychoanalytic Theory among the Seventeenth Century Iroquois," *American Anthropologist* 60 (1958): 244–45.

52. Williams, *Key*, 107. Williams here links this practice to "David's zealous heart to the true and living God: "At midnight I will rise &c. I prevented the dawning of the day, &c., *Psal* 119 &c." (107); see Psalm 119, verse 62, "At midnight I will rise to give thankes unto thee, because of they righteous judgements," and Psalm 119, verses 147–48: "I prevented the morning light, & cryed: for I waited on thy worde. / Mine eyes prevent the night watches to meditate in they worde." Bible GV.

53. Cf. Gilbert Herdt, "Selfhood and Discourse in Sambia Dream Sharing," in *Dreaming: Anthropological and Psychological Interpretations*, ed. Barbara Tedlock (Santa Fe: School of American Research Press, 1992), 55–85,esp. 59–63, on the complex cultural rules that govern how, when, and to whom particular kinds of dreams may be discussed.

54. Speck, "Penobscot Shamanism," 268.

55. Gladys Tantaquidgeon, "Mohegan Medicinal Practices, Weather-Lore, and Superstition," in Frank G. Speck, *Native Tribes and Dialects of Connecticut: A Mohegan-Pequot Diary, Forty-Third Annual Report of the Bureau of American Ethnology*, 1925–26 (Washington, D.C.: United States Government Printing Office, 1928), 264–76. Tantaquidgeon notes, "The practitioners [of herbal medicine] were mostly old women, although sorcerers (moigu' wag) employed herb cures in addition to their magical practices" (264). See also Gladys Tantaquidgeon, *Folk Medicine of the Delaware and Related Algonkian Indians*, rpt. ed. (1942; Harrisburg: Pennsylvania Historical and Museum Commission, 1977).

56. Bragdon, *Native People . . . 1500–1650*, 200.

57. Ibid., 201.

58. Ibid.

59. Speck, "Penobscot Shamanism," 246. This description is consistent with the narratives of living medicine persons; for example, see Gerald Mohatt and Joseph Eagle Elk, *The Price of a Gift: A Lakota Healer's Story* (Lincoln: University of Nebraska Press, 2000).

60. Bragdon, *Native People . . . 1500–1650*, 203.

61. Ibid.

62. Nicolar, *Red Man*, 164; see also 164 ed. note: "In certain dream states, Penobscot shamans were said to be capable of out-of-body travel."

63. Bragdon, *Native People . . . 1500–1650*, 204.

64. Champlain, *The Voyages*, in Biggar, *Works of Samuel de Champlain*, 44–51, reprinted in Brunelle, *Samuel de Champlain*, 78.

65. Ibid., 78.

66. Bragdon, *Native People . . . 1500–1650*, 188.

67. Ibid., 189.

68. Wood, *New England's Prospect*, 58–59.

69. Williams, *Key*, 189.

70. Ibid., 190, 191.

71. Mayhew, *Indian Converts*, 77–78, quotation 78. The problem with manitou for the English was explained to the Indians as "worshipping of false Gods, and adhering to Pawwaws or Wizards, and giving that Honour to Creatures that was due to Jehovah only." Ibid., 9.

72. Simmons, *Spirit of the New England Tribes*, 37–38.

73. Bragdon, *Native People . . . 1500–1650*, 190.

74. Williams, *Key*, 192.

75. Bragdon, *Native People . . . 1500–1650*, 190.

76. Ronda, "'We Are Well As We Are,'" 77–78.

77. Ibid., 77–78.

78. Williams, *Key*, 192. Ephesians 5:11 reads: "And have no fellowship with the unfruitful workes of darkenes, but even reprove them rather." Bible GV.

79. Wood, *New England's Prospect*, 102.

80. [Thomas Shepard], *The Day-Breaking if Not the Sun-Rising of the Gospell with the Indians in New-England* (London: Richard Cotes for Fulk Clifton, 1647), 21.

81. Ibid.

82. Daniel Gookin, "Historical Collections of the Indians in New England," *Collections of the Massachusetts Historical Society* 1 (1792; rpt., 1968), 154.

83. Simmons, *Spirit of the New England Tribes*, 37–38. See also Frank Shuffelton, "Indian Devils and Pilgrim Fathers: Squanto, Hobomok, and the English Conception of Indian Religion," *New England Quarterly* 49, no. 1 (1976): 108–16, esp. 112, 116.

84. [Shepard], *Day-Breaking*, 21–22.

85. Ibid. Eliot could not resist making a further dig at shamans, who were, in his opinion, not only witches but also cheats: he notes that should the patient not recover, sometimes his "friends" would take vengeance on the shaman, "especially if they could not get their mony againe out of their hands, which they receive afterhand for their care."

86. Speck, "Penobscot Shamanism," 242–43, quotation 243.

87. Simmons, *Spirit of the New England Tribes*, 53. The quotation is Edward Johnson, *Johnson's Wonder Working Providence, 1628–1651*, rpt. ed. (1654; New York: Charles Scribner's Sons, 1910), 14, quoted in Simmons, *Spirit of the New England Tribes*, 53.

88. Speck, "Penobscot Shamanism," 269–72, quotation 269.

89. Williams, *Key*, 192.

90. Gookin, "Historical Collections," 154.

91. Wood, *New England's Prospect*, 101.

92. Simmons, *Spirit of the New England Tribes*, 51.

93. Ibid., 50–51.

94. Thomas Mayhew Jr. to Mr. John Whitfield, October 16, 1651, in Whitfield, *Strength out of Weakness*, 24.

95. Bragdon, *Native People . . . 1500–1650*, 204.

96. Thomas Mayhew Jr. to Mr. John Whitfield, October 16, 1651, 25. The quote continues: "It was therefore the more to be acknowledged the work of God, that he should forsake this way, his friends, his gain, to follow the Lord, whose wayes are so despisable in the eyes of devilish minded men."

97. Edward Winslow, *Good News from New England, or a true Relation of things very remarkable at the Plantation of Plimoth in New England*, rpt. ed. (1624; Bedford, Mass.: Applewood Books, n.d.), 59. Winslow identifies three groups who could see Hobbamock: "One, I confess I neither know by name nor office directly; of these they have few, but esteem highly of them, and think that no weapon can kill them"; the other two groups were powwaws and pnieses (spiritually powerful counselors to the sachems) (59).

98. Thomas Mayhew Jr. to Mr. John Whitfield, October 16, 1651, 24. Bragdon notes that the crow is associated with Kiehtan (Cautantowwit). Bragdon, *Native People . . . 1500–1650*, 188.

99. Mayhew, *Indian Converts*, 7.

100. Speck, "Penobscot Shamanism," 247, 265.

101. "Conclusions and Orders made and agreed upon by divers Sachims and other principall men amongst the Indians at Concord, in the end of the eleventh moneth, An[no]. 1646," in Shepard, *Clear Sun-Shine*, 4. And Gookin reports that powwowing was prohibited in "English jurisdictions" by a fine of five pounds each to both the shaman and the "procurer," and twenty pence from every person who was present. Gookin, "Historical Collections," 154.

102. John Eliot to Thomas Shepard, letter, September 24, 1647, in Shepard, *Clear Sun-Shine*, 28. Yet he notes that some were concerned about how to heal the sick if they had given up powwowing, "for they have no skill in Physick, though some of them understand the virtues of sundry things [i.e., plants], yet the state of mans body, and skill to apply them they have not: but all the refuge they have and relie upon in time of sicknesse is their *Powwaws*, who by antick, foolish and irrationall conceits delude the poore people" (25).

103. Ibid., 28.

104. Shepard, *Clear Sun-Shine*, 32. The quote continues, "but in it you may see the guilt of the man, & that Satan is but a coward in his Lyons skin even upon his own dunghill, as also the hatred and enmity against the Word which is in some, which argues that the attention which others give to it, is a power of God, and not merely to flatter and get favour with the English" (32–33).

105. Mayhew, *Indian Converts*, 2–3.

106. Matthew Mayhew, *A Brief Narrative of the Success which the Gospel Hath Had Among the Indians* (Boston: B. Green, 1694), 15, see also Simmons, *Spirit of the New England Tribes*, 53.

107. *MHS Proc.*, 10 (1867–69): 393, cited in [Roger Williams], *The Correspondence of Roger Williams*, ed. Glenn W. LaFantasie, 2 vols. (Providence, R.I.: For the Rhode Island Historical Society by University Press of New England, 1988), 1:110 n. 5. Edward Winslow probably did not realize the ways in which Pokanoket Natives were treating him as a powwow after his successful "cure" of the sachem Massasoit in 1623. Winslow, *Good News*, 33–38, esp. when Massasoit requests that Winslow spend the morning "in going from one to another amongst those that were sick in the town, requesting me to wash their mouths also, and give to each of them some of the same I gave him, saying they were good folk" (35), and when Conbatant (Corbitant) asked, if he were "dangerously sick" like Massasoit and he were to send to Plymouth for "*maskiet*, that is physic, whether then Mr. Governor would send it; and if he would, whether I would come therewith to him" (38).

108. Simmons, *Spirit of the New England Tribes*, 73.

109. Gookin, "Historical Collections," 154.

110. Mayhew, *Indian Converts*, 44–45. Having asked this god for mercy, she "dedicated this Son of hers to the service of that God who had thus preserved his Life." Very early in his life she

"informed" him and "did, as far as she could, educate him accordingly" and he did, indeed, grow to be a very important Indian minister, in a manner similar to that reported in the dreams of pregnant and parturient women in English tradition (see Chapter 1).

111. Mayhew, *Indian Converts*, 44. The mother is named in her biography (135) and the meaning of the name is given as "a humble, or lowly Woman" (137).

112. Ibid., 44–45.

113. Ibid., 136.

114. Cf. Gregory Evans Dowd, *A Spirited Resistance: The North American Indian Struggle for Unity, 1745–1815*, Johns Hopkins University Studies in Historical and Political Science, 109th ser., 4 (Baltimore: Johns Hopkins University Press, 1992); the classic study is Anthony F. C. Wallace, *The Death and Rebirth of the Seneca* (New York: Alfred A. Knopf, 1970).

115. See Winslow, *Good News*, 40–52. For a full account of the events, see Salisbury, *Manitou and Providence*, 125–40.

116. Thomas Morton, *New English Canaan, or New Canaan containing an abstract of New England composed in three bookes: the first booke setting forth the originall of the natives, their manners and customes, together with their tractable nature and love towards the english: the second booke setting forth the naturall indowments of the countrie, and what staple commodities it yeeldeth: the third booke setting forth what people are planted there, their prosperity, what remarkable accidents have happened since the first planting of it, together with their tenents, and practice of their church* ([London]: Printed for Charles Greene, 1632), 106. This incident and source is also referenced by Simmons, *Spirit of the New England Tribes*, 248.

117. Ibid., 107.

118. Ibid.

119. Ibid.

120. Ibid., 108.

121. The events include scouting parties that took corn and opened a grave at "Cornhill" on Cape Cod, and then were harassed at "First Encounter" beach in 1620, with a battle that took place between the Plymouth men and the Indians near Wessagusset in March 1623, the result of a conflict between the men of Wessagusset and the Massachusett Indians nearby: see William Bradford, *Of Plymouth Plantation*, ed. and intro. Samuel Eliot Morison, rpt. ed. (1952; New York: Alfred A. Knopf, 1996), 69–70 (Bradford mentions Indian houses and corn but no graves); *Mourt's Relation: A Journal of the Pilgrims at Plymouth*, intro. Dwight B. Heath, rpt. ed. (1622; Bedford, Mass.: Applewood Books, 1963); this account mentions taking seed corn, opening graves, and looking in Indian houses (26–29), and the site of conflict (35–36); see also Winslow, *Good News*, for an account of the battle after Wituwamet is slain, in which one of the enemies is shot in the arm (49).

122. But see the account in Mayhew, *Indian Converts*, 241, discussed here in Chapter 6; see also discussion in Chapter 5 of the ghost of murder victim Rebecca Cornell who visited her brother.

123. Thus, in June 1690, Samuel Lee of Bristol, Rhode Island, responded to queries from London physician Nehemiah Grew about the customs of local Indians. Lee wrote (in response to a question about Native conjuring), "Being not acquainted with their waies: [I] onely heare, that conjuration is frequent among them. & then one appears like a rattlesnake & sometimes like a white-headed eagle." George Lyman Kittredge, ed., *Letters of Samuel Lee and Samuel Sewall relating to New England and the Indians*, rpt. of the Colonial Society of Massachussetts Publications, vol. 14 (Cambridge, Mass.: John Wilson and Son, 1912), 149. He continues, in response to detailed questions about medications and medical practices, that the Indians "inquire of their oracle & if that saies they [the patient] shall dye, they use nothing [no medical intervention]," and just below, he describes the "oracle" as "being usually a rattlesnake, a crow or a hawke or &c." (151). Lee credits

"Mr Arnold a practitioner in Physick of good request in Rhode Island, who hath conversed much with the Indians" (151).

124. Gladys Tantaquidgeon, "Notes on the Gay Head Indians of Massachusetts," *Indian Notes* 7, no. 1 (1930): 1–26, quotation in Simmons, *Spirit of the New England Tribes*, 104.

125. Simmons, *Spirit of the New England Tribes*, 104.

126. Speck, "Penobscot Shamanism," 268–72, quotation 270. The story concerns the grand-mother of Speck's informant Newell Lion.

127. Tantaquidgeon, "Mohegan Medicinal Practices," 274.

128. Melissa Jayne Fawcett, *Medicine Trail: The Life and Lessons of Gladys Tantaquidgeon* (Tucson: University of Arizona Press, 2000), 53–54, on Tantaquidgeon's dream belief.

129. Williams, *Key*, 108.

130. Glenn W. LaFantasie, "Expectations of Indian Conversions 1637/38," 141–44, in *The Correspondence of Roger Williams*, 1:142. LaFantasie summarizes Roger Williams, *Christenings make not Christians* (1645), *Complete Writings*, 7:35–39.

131. Roger Williams, *George Fox Digg'd out of his Burrowes* (1676), *Complete Writings*, 5:447, quoted in LaFantasie, *The Correspondence of Roger Williams*, 1:143.

# Chapter 3. Lived Religion and Embedded Emotion in Midcentury Dream Reporting

1. Janine Rivière, "Dreams in Early Modern England: Frameworks of Interpretation," Ph.D. dissertation (University of Toronto, 2013), 64.

2. Philip Goodwin, *The Mystery of Dreames, Historically Discoursed . . .* (London: Printed by A.M. for Francis Tyton, 1658), 169–70.

3. Ibid., unpaginated introduction. Goodwin lists the known divine dreams in scripture: "But plain proofs we have from holy Scripture of Gods undoubted hand in divers Dreames: Gen. 20. 3. Gen. 40. 5. Gen 41. 7. Judg. 7. 13. I King 3. 5. Dan 2. 1. Dan 7. 1. Math 2. 19, &c. . . . Dreames Divine may yet remain."

4. Personal communications with David D. Hall, October 10, 2012, and Mark Peterson, September 8, 2012. Men who reported dreams are John Winthrop, John Hull, Michael Wigglesworth, Peter Easton, John Dane, Thomas Minor, Increase Mather, Cotton Mather, Samuel Sewall, John Briggs, and Edward Taylor. Of these, three (Hull, Dane, and Increase Mather) recorded others' dreams but not their own; Cotton Mather recorded both his own and those of others. See texts cited throughout the chapter. No seventeenth-century New England women kept diaries. A few women's dreams were reported in records generated by men. Doubtless additional dream reports remain hidden in letters, personal narratives, or other sources that may yet come to light, especially once scholars have a historiographic frame within which to lodge dream reports and their significance.

5. Anne S. Lombard, *Making Manhood: Growing Up Male in Colonial New England* (Cambridge, Mass.: Harvard University Press, 2003), 15; Lisa Wilson, *Ye Heart of a Man: The Domestic Life of Men in Colonial New England* (New Haven, Conn.: Yale University Press, 1999).

6. Sewall, *Diary*, 1:12, 518, and 592 (July 31, 1675, February 13, 1705, and April 2, 1708).

7. Sewall, *Diary*, 1:25 (October 16, 1676).

8. Goodwin, *Mystery*, 78–79.

9. Ibid., 79.

10. Ibid., 118. Goodwin wrote in the context of midcentury upheavals, particularly the chaotic challenges offered by Baptists, Quakers, and many others. Moderation in dreaming mirrored his

middle-of-the-road puritan stance. Ironically, with the Restoration, he would be viewed as too radical and was expelled from his post.

11. Ibid., 233–34.

12. Ibid.

13. Reference comes in relation to a dream report: Sewall, *Diary*, 2:1062–63 (September 10, 1728).

14. But see Amory's discussion of market limits for Wigglesworth's *Day of Doom*. Hugh Amory, "Printing and Book Selling in New England, 1638–1713," in *The Colonial Book in the Atlantic World*, ed. Hugh Amory and David D. Hall, A History of the Book in America 1 (Chapel Hill: University of North Carolina Press for the American Antiquarian Society, 2007), 106–8.

15. [Michael Wigglesworth], *The Diary of Michael Wigglesworth, 1653–1657: The Conscience of a Puritan*, ed. and intro. Edmund S. Morgan (1946; New York: Harper and Row, 1965), introduction.

16. Richard Godbeer, "Wigglesworth, Michael (b. 1631; d. 1705) minister," 277–79 in *Encyclopedia of Lesbian, Gay, Bisexual, and Transgender History in America*, ed. Marc Stein, 3 vols. (New York: Charles Scribner's Sons/Thomson Gale, 2003), 3:277–78.

17. Goodwin, *Mystery*, 94–96.

18. Ibid., 122, 126.

19. Ibid., 122.

20. Wigglesworth, *Diary*, 5 (February 17, 1652/3); other examples include p. 6 (February 25/26, 1652/3); p. 50 (October 18, 1653); a general mention of multiple instances, p.78 (February 15, 1653/4); nocturnal emission "without any dream that I knew of," p. 80 (February 22, 1653/4).

21. We must note the ambiguous syntax here: "vengeance *of* himself," rather than the more conventional "vengeance *on* himself." The latter phrase would have been fairly clear—he had a desire to harm himself as punishment for his filthy dreams. But the former phrase, which he actually uses, has two meanings: he might take something *of* himself, as in *from* himself, again as punishment. Or, he might have intended (consciously or not) to say that he wished to take vengeance *for* himself; we will see later that he did feel, in another realm, that he had been victimized by his father.

22. Wigglesworth, *Diary*, 78–87 (February 15, 1653/4, through July 1655).

23. Ibid., 93 (September 16, 1655).

24. In the later eighteenth century, William Jenks kept a similar record, but these are apparently singular instances: William Jenks, "Somnia" (1798), MS diary, William Jenks Papers, Massachusetts Historical Society, Boston, Mass., Box 2, Folder marked 1798. I am grateful to John Demos for recalling this diary and for his persistence in directing me to its correct location.

25. Wigglesworth, *Diary*, 50 (October 15, 1653).

26. Ibid., 14 (After March 23, 1653).

27. Ibid.

28. Ibid., 50 (October 15, 1653).

29. Ibid., 50 (October 18, 1653).

30. Wigglesworth, *Diary*, 51 (October 24, 1653); as to popularity, cf. Ronald A. Bosco, ed. and intro., *The Poems of Michael Wigglesworth* (Lanham, Md.: University Press of America, 1989), x: "The Bible and the *Bay Psalm Book* were the only serious rivals to Wigglesworth's *The Day of Doom*, which during the poet's life went through three known American editions (in 1662, 1666, and 1701), two supposed but unverified American editions (in 1663 or 1664 and in 1683), and three known but unauthorized English editions (in 1666, 1673, and 1687)."

31. Cf. Charles L. Cohen, "Conversion among Puritans and Amerindians: A Theological and

Cultural Perspective," in *Puritanism: Transatlantic Perspectives on a Seventeenth-Century Anglo-American Faith*, ed. Francis J. Bremer (Boston: Massachusetts Historical Society, 1993).

32. Wigglesworth, *Diary*, 57 (December? 1653).

33. Ibid.

34. Richard Crowder, *No Featherbed to Heaven: A Biography of Michael Wigglesworth, 1631–1705* (East Lansing: Michigan State University Press, 1962), 107.

35. Ibid., 160. For another interpretation agreeing that Wigglesworth "was able to translate a private nightmare into Colonial America's best-selling poem," see Jeffrey A. Hammond, *Sinful Self, Saintly Self: The Puritan Experience of Poetry* (Athens: University of Georgia Press, 1993), 40.

36. "Ill, depressed, lonely, and subject to fits of doubt and anxiety over his own spiritual condition, Wigglesworth was unable to discharge the principal responsibilities of his ministry between the late 1650s and the mid-1680s." Bosco, *Poems of Michael Wigglesworth*, xix.

37. Cotton Mather, *Magnalia Christi Americana* (1702; rpt. Hartford: Silas Andrus and Son, 1853), 1:486.

38. Wigglesworth, *Diary*, introduction.

39. Ibid.

40. Indeed, in a famous work of social history, Philip J. Greven Jr. gave us an inkling of the awkward dependence imposed by older fathers on young and middle-aged adult men in one seventeenth-century New England town. It is a short step from his description of economic dependency to infer that some might have felt profound psychological domination as well. Wigglesworth's frank revelation of his animosity toward his father lends concrete proof that at least some resentment did boil over. See Greven, *Four Generations: Population, Land, and Family in Colonial Andover, Massachusetts* (Ithaca, N.Y.: Cornell University Press, 1970), ch. 6, esp. 171–72.

41. John Demos makes this point about the obligations of superiors to inferiors in his book, *A Little Commonwealth*, in which he also argues that anger generated inside New England households had to be displaced and projected outward in this society which so emphasized subordination and obedience. My argument here largely corroborates his: John Demos, *A Little Commonwealth: Family Life in Plymouth Colony* (New York: Oxford University Press, 1970), 135–138.

42. Wigglesworth, *Diary*, 14 (after March 23, 1653).

43. Cf. Theodore Nadelson, "Victim, Victimizer: Interaction in the Psychotherapy of Borderline Patients," *International Journal of Psychoanalytic Psychotherapy* 2, no. 5 (1976): 115–29.

44. Wigglesworth, *Diary*, 14 (after March 23, 1653).

45. Wigglesworth, *Diary*, 51 (October 24, 1653).

46. I am grateful to H. A. Drake and Kathleen Drake for this and other translations throughout; the phrase can also be rendered as "home of the saints," since *beatus* (blessed) came to mean saints generally.

47. Sewall, *Diary*, 1:12; the *Oxford English Dictionary* offers several meanings for *vile* in this period; Sewall appears to use one of the lesser known: "Of things: Of little worth or account; mean or paltry in respect of value; held in no esteem or regard." The word carries within it all the others, which include several versions of its modern meaning, including base, bestial, lowborn, and, when applied to animals, dangerous or destructive. *Oxford English Dictionary* online, s.v. "vile," accessed August 16, 2012, http://www.oed.com.

48. Sewall, *Diary*, 1:12.

49. Sigmund Freud, *The Interpretation of Dreams*, trans. and ed. James Strachey, rpt. ed. (New York: Avon Books, 1965), 390, see also 272–73, 399–401, 403–6, and 419–20 for the varieties of staircase dreams, including the feeling of flying down the staircase, and the role of the "case" or vagina in which the climbing is taking place.

50. Thomas Hill, *The moste pleasuante arte of the interpretacion of dreames* (London: by Thomas Marshe, 1576), Oi(r), cited in Rivière, "Dreams in Early Modern England," 99–100. John Bunyan, *The Pilgrim's Progress*, intro. Roger Lundin, rpt. ed. (1678; New York: Signet Classic, 1994).

51. *Oxford English Dictionary Online*, s.v.v. *"ramshackled," "ramshackle,"* accessed February 17, 2013, http://www.oed.com.

52. I am grateful to John Muller and other members of the Williams College–Austen Riggs psychoanalytic study group meeting, December 6, 2010, for this insight.

53. Sewall had been elected a member of the Court of Assistants, and as such became both a magistrate and an overseer of Harvard College.

54. Merle Curti, "The American Exploration of Dreams and Dreamers," *Journal of the History of Ideas* 27, no. 3 (1966): 395; the dream report is found in Sewall, *Diary*, 1:561, entry for January 26, 1706/7: "I dream'd last night that I was chosen Lord Maior of London; which much perplex'd me: a strange absurd Dream!"

55. Both the sumptuary laws and the apology are from Perry Miller, "Solomon Stoddard, 1643–1729," *Harvard Theological Review* 34, no. 4 (1941): 281–82.

56. Sewall, *Diary*, 1:518–19, entry for February 13, 1705.

57. [Cotton Mather], "Diary of Cotton Mather," ed. and intro. Worthington Chauncy Ford, *Massachusetts Historical Society Collections*, 7th ser., 7, 8 (1911, 1912), 86, 87 n. 2 (Latin translation per Wendell, *Cotton Mather*, 64, as cited).

58. The verse, in Mather's rendering, continues: "Thus was hee fair in his Greatness in the Length of his Branches, for his Root was by the great Waters. Nor was any Tree in the Garden of God like unto him in his Beauty. I have made him fair by the multitude of his Branches so that all the Trees of Eden, that were in the Garden of God envied him."

59. C. Mather, "Diary," 86, 87 n. 2.

60. Each of these three men was just launched into adulthood. The early twenties were, in fact, a notable life stage for young men in this society—a time when they might first petition and be recognized as "freemen" of the colony. Achieving political personhood usually preceded the ability to enter in to other marks of male adult status, including, perhaps most importantly, marriage. Across the seventeenth century, New England men's average age at first marriage typically hovered between twenty-four and twenty-six, slightly lower than but still comparable to what it had been in England. See data compiled for the region in Greven, *Four Generations*, 35–37.

61. Cf. David D. Hall, *Worlds of Wonder, Days of Judgment: Popular Religious Belief in Early New England* (Cambridge, Mass.: Harvard University Press, 1989), 83–85.

62. [John Hull], "The Diaries of John Hull, Mint-master and Treasurer of the Colony of Massachusetts Bay, from the original manuscript in the collection of the American Antiquarian Society," *Transactions and Collections of the American Antiquarian Society* 3 (1857): 220, entry for November 22, 1665.

63. Increase Mather, *An Essay for the recording of illustrious providences: Wherein an Account is given of many Remarkable and very Memorable Events, which have hapned this last Age; Especially in New-England* (Boston: Samuel Green for Joseph Browning, 1684), ch. 3, 72–99, esp. 76–78.

64. Ibid., 76.

65. Hull, "Diaries," 216–17 (April 12–29, 1665).

66. Mather, *Illustrious Providences*, 340–41.

67. Ibid., 347.

68. Harriette Merrifield Forbes, *New England Diaries, 1602–1800: A Descriptive Catalogue of Diaries, Orderly Books and Sea Journals* (1923; New York: Russell and Russell, 1967), 90–91. The compiled manuscript diary, along with the almanacs (catalogued separately), is Peter Easton

(1622–94), MS diary (1662–70), American Antiquarian Society, Worcester, Mass. This perhaps explains why few colonial historians have used Easton's writings, even though their existence has been widely known since the 1920s.

69. Cf. Carla Gerona, *Night Journeys: The Power of Dreams in Transatlantic Quaker Culture* (Charlottesville: University of Virginia Press, 2004). See also Phyllis Mack, *Visionary Women: Ecstatic Prophecy in Seventeenth-Century England* (Berkeley: University of California Press, 1992).

70. Carla Gardina Pestana, *Quakers and Baptists in Colonial Massachusetts* (Cambridge: Cambridge University Press, 1991), 12–13.

71. Easton, MS diary, 7.

72. Easton, MS diary, 5–6. The phrase repeats again, p. 7 (reverse side), following the dream report.

73. Immediately below the dream report are some lines of alphabet in a child's hand. Sandwiched in between is the following line: "The position of the heavens at the time of iesus Christ the sun [son] david and the sunn [son] iacub [Jacob]." Is it merely a coincidence that he mentions Jacob, the famous dreamer and dream interpreter from Exodus?

74. Easton, MS diary, 20.

75. Ibid. I am grateful to Bertram Lippincott III of the Newport Historical Society for his assistance in identifying the connection between Barker and Easton. After the death of Barker's father aboard ship, his paternal aunt took him in. Marrying Nicholas Easton, she became stepmother to Peter and John, and James became a cousin of sorts. See also Robert Charles Anderson, *The Great Migration Begins: Immigrants to New England, 1620–1633*, 3 vols. (Boston: New England Historic Genealogical Society, 1995), vol. 1 (A–F), "Thomas Beecher," 146. See also Robert Charles Anderson, George F. Sanborn Jr., and Melinde Lutz Sanborn, *The Great Migration: Immigrants to New England, 1634–1635*, 5 vols. (Boston: New England Historic Genealogical Society, 2001), vol. 2 (C–F), "Nicholas Easton," 400, for the detail that she married Easton by 1637 and died February 20, 1665.

76. Easton, MS diary, 20.

77. [Anonymous], *Dreams of Daniel . . .* ([London]: Imprynted by me Robert Wyer . . . , [1556?]), unpaginated.

78. Cf. Richard Godbeer, " 'Love Raptures': Marital, Romantic and Erotic Images of Jesus Christ in Puritan New England, 1670–1730," *New England Quarterly* 68, no. 3 (1995): 355–84, esp. 368, 368 n. 37.

79. John Morill, "Oliver Cromwell (1599–1658)," *Oxford Dictionary of National Biography* (Oxford University Press, 2004), online ed., May 2008, http://www.oxforddnb.com/view/article/6765. Cromwell's body in death has an interesting history. Incompetently embalmed, the real body was secretly buried and an effigy displayed in state with a death mask, scepter, orb and crown, first at Somerset House and later processed through the streets to Westminster Abbey where it rested in the Chapel of Henry VII. After the Restoration, the Convention Parliament decreed that he and other Puritan leaders "suffer the fate of traitors," to be administered on the twelfth anniversary of the death of Charles I, January 30, 1661: "A body purporting to be Cromwell's was hanged in its cerecloth for several hours, then decapitated. The body was put into a lime-pit below the gallows and the head, impaled on a spike, was exposed at the south end of Westminster Hall for nearly two decades before being rescued during the exclusion crisis." Several family stories suggest alternative fates for the body, which was allegedly switched: "One tradition has the skull rescued from Westminster Hall in or about 1688 and surviving with a fairly complete itinerary—as a fairground exhibit, or one brought out at dinner parties in great houses—until it was acquired by Cromwell's descendants and by them donated to Sidney Sussex, Cromwell's college in Cambridge, where it was interred in an unmarked grave in 1960."

80. Another period reference related to these dream images involves generation, generativity, and connections across the generations of a family or a movement. Goodwin, writing in 1658, cited Daniel chapters 4, 5 and 6, to reference Nebuchadnezzar's dream as told to Daniel: "I saw a Tree, the Boughs strong, the Leaves faire, the height great, and behold one from Heaven came and cryed, Hew down the Tree, cut off the Branches, &c." Nebuchadnezzar's dream foretold his own expulsion from power, until he acknowledged God's higher dominion. Goodwin, *Mystery*, 209.

81. This instance of the proverb is found in a diary entry commenting on the 1704 attack on Deerfield, Massachusetts, in which the chastening hand of God brought shocking devastation to those who seemed to be a community of upstanding Christian believers. [Marshall, John], "John Marshall's Diary," ed. Charles F. Adams Jr., *MHS Proc.*, 2nd ser., 1 (1884–85): 148–164, and 2nd ser., 14 (1900–1901): 29.

82. Easton, MS diary, 20.

83. Ibid.

84. Ibid., 20 (reverse), 21.

85. Ibid. The passage continues: "The first thought was how I should pay F Grindly the 70 ll for Jefferies[?] and cotterells medows than began my great sickness which continued still[.] then about my childr[en] then about my own condition and at last it came all to paine."

86. See, for example, the controversy that rent the Newport Quaker meeting into two separate ones, dividing Peter and his widowed stepmother, Ann Easton Bull, who attended the one, from his brother, Governor John Easton, who hosted the other, a rift that extended for a period of many years. Friend's Records Monthly Meetings, 1676–1707, MS notebook, Newport Historical Society (Newport, R. I.). Trouble began almost immediately after Nicholas Easton's death in 1675 and centered on controversy over a bequest, but it quickly expanded to encompass a variety of issues. An entry from 1681 is typical: "An [Ann] Bull Came to this meeting & friends very tenderly sought her to Bee Reconsiled But Could Not Heele the sauer of her spirit in that wch unites into Christ & also found that she had contrived & provided one (peter Easton) & hee did privily wright down what [illegible] in this meeting whilst in dealing with her; wch act is for Judgment & Condemnation &c & it is the uneanemos [unanimous] sence & Judgement of this meeting that her speirit was very hard & wronge & gave friends noe satisfaction" (April 21, 1681), 19.

87 Easton, MS diary, 28. On eagles see *Wikipedia*, s.v. "Lectern" last modified October 20, 2013, http://en.wikipedia.org/wiki/Eagle_lectern.

88. *Dreams of Daniel*, n.p. An earlier meaning, in which an eagle's appearance in a dream signified the impending death of the dreamer, seems not as central here but may have formed a background meaning: Hill, "*The moste pleasuante arte*," Mv(v), cited in Rivière, *Dreams in Early Modern England*, 99.

89. A nearly identical list of events appears in the diary itself, entered in 1669, see p. 24 (reverse).

90. Nicholas served as president of the colony in 1650, 1651, and 1654, as deputy governor in 1666–71, and as governor in 1672–74; Peter was active in town and colony affairs, serving as general treasurer in 1672–77 and attorney general in 1674–76. John Easton served as governor of the colony as well. See Rosemary Canfield, *Some Rhode Island Descendants of Nicholas Easton* (Pacific Grove, Calif.: [by the author], 1995), 2–3. See also John Easton, *A Narrative of the Causes which led to Philip's Indian War, of 1675 and 1676, with other documents concerning this Event in the Office of the Secretary of State of New York*, ed. and intro. Franklin B. Hough (Albany, N.Y.: J. Munsell, 1856).

91. Massachusetts General Court, May 17, 1638, cited in Joseph Dow, *History of the Town of Hampton, New Hampshire from its settlement in 1638 to the autumn of 1892* (Salem, Mass.: L. E. Dow, 1893), 7–9, esp. 8.

92. Peter Easton, MS marginalia in Nathaniel Morton, *New England's Memoriall* (1669) (Redwood Library, Newport, R.I.), 112. This house was on Farewell Street near Broad and burned in 1641, according to Canfield, *Some Rhode Island Descendants*, 1.

93. [John Winthrop], *The Journal of John Winthrop, 1630–1649*, ed. Richard S. Dunn, James Savage, and Laetitia Yeandle (Cambridge, Mass.: Belknap Press of Harvard University Press, 1996), 363–64. Winthrop earlier referred to Nicholas Easton, who "taught that fits and graces were that antichrist mentioned [in] Thess., and that which withheld, etc., was the preaching of the law," 274, and n. 98; n. 99 specifies the passage as 2 Thess. 2:3–12.

94. Winthrop, *Journal*, 364.

95. Easton, marginalia, 111–12.

96. There is a possible additional opposition between the story of Nicholas Easton and his sons (1634–43) versus the emergent narrative of Peter Easton's own family, in the person of his new wife and son. Peter married Ann Coggeshall in 1643. Canfield, *Some Rhode Island Descendants*, 2.

97. Easton, marginalia, 114.

98. Ibid., 115, 120, 121, 122, 123, 129.

99. Ibid., 120, 121.

100. Ibid., 124.

101. Ibid., 176; Easton also noted a providential event associated with his purchase in the New Country (apparently the Narragansett purchase): "The blazing star was seen in winter 1664 before I went to the New Country in yeare 1665 three or fower months[?] it was se[seen?] in the Evening." Easton, MS diary, 11.

102. Easton, marginalia, 139, 141, 143. James Nayler was an early Quaker associate of George Fox and a proselytizer persecuted by the Puritan authorities in England. Cf. Leo Damrosch, *The Sorrows of the Quaker Jesus: James Nayler and the Puritan Crackdown on the Free Spirit* (Cambridge, Mass.: Harvard University Press, 1996).

103. Easton, marginalia, 144.

104. Ibid., 151.

105. Easton, *A Narrative*, 30–31.

106. Easton, marginalia, 139, 155.

107. See a similar argument in my essay, "Indian and English Dreams: Colonial Hierarchy, and Manly Restraint in Seventeenth-Century New England," in *New Men: Manliness in Early America*, ed. Thomas A. Foster (New York: New York University Press, 2011), 31–47.

## Chapter 4. Dreams and Visions in King Philip's War

1. See Jill Lepore, *The Name of War: King Philip's War and the Origins of American Identity* (New York: Alfred A. Knopf, 1998), 11, and ch. 2, esp. 65, 66.

2. Increase Mather, *A brief history of the warr with the Indians in New-England, (from June 24, 1675 when the first English-man was murdered by the Indians, to August 12, 1676, when Philip alias Metacomet, the principal author and beginner of the warr, was slain.) Wherein the grounds, beginning, and progress of the warr, is summarily expressed. Together with a serious exhortation to the inhabitants of that land* (Boston: John Foster, 1676), unpaginated preface. Mather notes that he had received a narrative, "said to be written by a Merchant in Boston," and began to consider writing a history. "Whilst I was doing this, there came to my hands another Narrative of this Warr, written by a Quaker in Road-Island [John Easton], who pretends to know the Truth of things; but that Narrative being fraught with worse things then meer Mistakes, I was thereby quickned to expedite what I had in hand."

3. Ibid., 49.

4. William S. Simmons, *Spirit of the New England Tribes: Indian History and Folklore, 1620–1984* (Hanover, N.H.: University Press of New England, 1986), 51. Lepore asks if the war was a holy war, and, "if so, whose?" Lepore, *The Name of War*, 99.

5. Mary Rowlandson, *The Sovereignty and Goodness of God, together with the Faithfulness of His Promises Displayed: Being a Narrative of the Captivity and Restoration of Mrs. Mary Rowlandson [1682] and Related Documents*, ed. and intro. Neal Salisbury (Boston: Bedford Books, 1997), 100–101; see also Benjamin Church [ed. Thomas Church], *Diary of King Philip's War, 1675–1676*, ed. and intro. Alan and Mary Simpson (Chester, Conn.: Pequot Press, for the Little Compton Historical Society, 1975), 69–70, on Awashonks's dance, and p. 73 on Philip's dance. Captive Quentin Stockwell witnessed a remarkable ceremony before the Hatfield attack: Increase Mather, *An Essay for the recording of illustrious providences: Wherein an Account is given of many Remarkable and very Memorable Events, which have hapned this last Age; Especially in New-England* (Boston: Samuel Green for Joseph Browning, 1684), 57.

6. Ezra Stiles, *Extracts from the Itineraries and Other Miscellanies of Ezra Stiles, D.D., LL.D., 1755–1794*, ed. Franklin B. Dexter (New Haven, Conn.: Yale University Press, 1916), 232.

7. William Hubbard, *Present State*, 1:283–85, cited in R. Todd Romero, *Making War and Minting Christians: Masculinity, Religion, and Colonialism in Early New England* (Amherst: University of Massachusetts Press, 2011), 166–67.

8. See Frank G. Speck, "Penobscot Shamanism," *Memoirs of the American Anthropological Association* 6 (October–December 1919): 268–73.

9. Lion Gardener, "Leift Lio Gardener his relation of the Pequot Warres," *Collections of the Massachusetts Historical Society*, 3rd ser., 3 (1833): 154–55; see also Neal Salisbury, *Manitou and Providence: Indians, Europeans, and the Making of New England, 1500–1643* (New York: Oxford University Press, 1982), 231.

10. While well known in his day, Squando's story has received scant scholarly attention. I am particularly grateful to Walter W. Woodward for initially bringing it to my attention. See also Ann Marie Plane, "'God hath left our Nation to them to destroy': Visionaries, Revenge, and Traumatic Reenactment on the Maine Frontier in King Philip's War, 1675–1677," in *European and American Borderlands: An Innovative Approach*, ed. John W. I. Lee and Michael North (Lincoln: University of Nebraska Press, forthcoming).

11. Squando's story unfolds in three period histories, Mather's *Brief History*, 13, as well as his 1684 *Illustrious Providences*, 359–361; and William Hubbard, *A Narrative of the troubles with the Indians in New-England, from the first planting thereof in the year 1607 to this present year 1677. But chiefly of the late Troubles in the two last years, 1675 and 1676. To which is added a Discourse about the Warre with the Pequods, in the year 1637* (Boston: John Foster, 1677), esp. postscript, 29, 48–49, 61, and in "Francis Card, his Declaration of their Beginning, August the fourteenth [1676]" in Hubbard, *A Narrative*, postscript, 62, 67, and throughout. Squando's death is also noted in [Increase Mather], "Diary of Increase Mather," *Massachusetts Historical Society Proceedings*, 2nd ser., 13 (1899–1900), 409, in an entry for the year 1682. Squando's story is retold once more in Cotton Mather's *Magnalia Christi Americana*, 7 vols. (London: for Thomas Parkhurst, 1702), 3: 99 (rpt. ed. 1853 I: 566–67), though Squando's name does not appear.

12. Cf. Anthony F. C. Wallace, *The Death and Rebirth of the Seneca* (New York: Vintage Books, [1972]), and Gregory Evans Dowd, *A Spirited Resistance: The North American Indian Struggle for Unity, 1745–1815*, Johns Hopkins University Studies in Historical and Political Science, 109th ser., vol. 4 (Baltimore: Johns Hopkins University Press, 1992).

13. Lepore, *The Name of War*, 99.

14. Hubbard, *A Narrative*, 29.

15. Ibid., 2, 29.

16. Rowlandson, *Sovereignty*, 73; "heart-sinking tryals" is Mather's phrase, 67.

17. Rowlandson, *Sovereignty*, 67.

18. Lepore, *The Name of War*, x.

19. Defining Squando as motivated by implacable anger and vengeful barbarity, Euro-American authors displaced their own desires for vengeance (and, presumably, any nascent sense of guilt) onto their adversary: cf. the general discussion of psychodynamic theory of racism in Lourdes Mattei, "Coloring Development: Race and Culture in Psychodynamic Theories," in *Inside Out and Outside In: Psychodynamic Clinical Theory and Psychopathology in Contemporary Multicultural Contexts*, ed. Joan Berzoff, Laura Melano Flanagan, and Patricia Hertz, 2nd ed. (New York: Jason Aronson, 2008), 256–58.

20. David D. Hall, *Worlds of Wonder, Days of Judgment: Popular Religious Belief in Early New England* (Cambridge, Mass.: Harvard University Press, 1989), 77–79.

21. I am grateful to Lisa Brooks for providing me with her research notes documenting the career of Atecouando, also known as Squando, in eighteenth-century records. Brooks bases her linkage of the two names on the definitive statement by P.-André Sévigny, in *Les Abénaquis: Habitat et migrations (17e et 18e siècles)* (Montreal: Éditions Bellarmin, 1976), 153–54, citing a document from 1715 by Père Aubry, the Jesuit missionary, who references "the one named Athurnando (alias Squando), one of the principal chiefs of this nation who has lived for eight years at St. Francis."

22. Gordon M. Day, a respected scholar of Abenaki language and ethnohistory, identifies Atecouando as fl. 1701–26 when the sachem represented the Pigwackets in treaty negotiations, but making his earliest known appearance in the records as a Pennacook "working for war in the uneasy summer of 1688 which preceded the outbreak of King William's War," and appearing again on November 29, 1690, when he "witnessed the truce and exchange of prisoners made between the Abenakis and the English 'upon the water in canoes' at Sagadahoc, at the mouth of the Kennebec River, Maine." Gordon M. Day, "Atecouando (fl. 1710–26)," in *Dictionary of Canadian Biography*, vol. 2 (University of Toronto/Université Laval, 2003⊠), accessed January 21, 2013, http://www.biographi.ca/en/bio/atecouando_1710_26_2E.html. Pigwacket/Pequawket, now Fryeburg, Maine, is located inland on the Saco River. Perhaps Squando withdrew inland after King Philip's War, or perhaps he was always paramount sachem based at Pigwacket but also identified with Saco. See also Emerson W. Baker, who notes that Squando was the principal Saco River sachem of the 1660s and 1670s, based on deeds and other documents, and notes that "the sachem's religious activism might be reflected in his name." Baker notes that Squando last appears in the deed and treaty records in 1678 when he signs the Treaty of Casco Bay in April of that year, and hypothesizes that perhaps he took the new name of Netambomet, "the name of the sachem of the Saco in the 1680s: "Finding the Almouchiquois: Native American Families, Territories, and Land Sales in Southern Maine," *Ethnohistory* 51, no. 1 (2004): 87–88. And see also Colin G. Calloway, who notes the dramatic dispersals of Indian populations following King Philip's War, following Harald E. L. Prins, to identify Adeawando as a Pennacook who lived at Pigwacket before moving to St. Francis mission in New France: *The Western Abenakis of Vermont, 1600–1800: War, Migration, and the Survival of an Indian People* (Norman: University of Oklahoma Press, 1990), 275 n. 34, 277 n. 58, see also 100.

23. Joshua Scottow, "Letter to Increase Mather, 30th [Octo]ber [1683]," *MHS Coll.*, 4th ser., 8 (1868): 631–32; I. Mather, "Diary," 409 (undated entry, 1682).

24. Samuel Sewall did document a suicide by hanging by Isaac Nehemiah (a Natick Indian) in October 1715, describing the means in detail (Nehemiah hanged himself with his own "girdle," being "3 foot and 4 inches long, buckle and all." But this was a much later context with a significantly acculturated community; cf. Samuel Sewall, *The Diary of Samuel Sewall, 1674-1729*, ed.

M. Halsey Thomas, 2 vols. (New York: Farrar, Straus and Giroux, 1973), 2:801–2 (October 12, 1715). Samson Occum suggested that poisoning was a more regular danger, though he does not speak about suicide specifically. Samson Occum, "Account of the Montauk Indians on Long Island (1761)," in *The Collected Writings of Samson Occum, Mohegan: Leadership and Literature in Eighteenth-Century Native America*, ed. Joanna Brooks, with a foreword by Robert Warrior (New York: Oxford University Press, 2006), 49. Lee reported of southern New England that "they have many poysons & are expert in their use. The women often pyson themselves & children: if their husbands will not owne them." George Lyman Kittredge, ed., *Letters of Samuel Lee and Samuel Sewall relating to New England and the Indians*, rpt. of Colonial Society of Massachusetts Publications, vol. 14 (Cambridge, Mass.: John Wilson and Son, 1912), June 25, 1690, 150. However, the Rev. Ezra Stiles noted in the late eighteenth century: "N. B. Tho' Suicide frequent among the English, never among Indians." *Literary Diary of Ezra Stiles*, ed. Dexter, iii 348, entry for March 16, 1789, cited in Kittredge, *Letters of Samuel Lee*, n. 1.

25. Cf. Gerry Mohatt and Joseph Eagle Elk, *The Price of a Gift: A Lakota Healer's Story* (Lincoln: University of Nebraska Press, 2000).

26. Mather, *Brief History*, 13.

27. Mather, *Illustrious Providences*, 360–61.

28. Ibid., 361.

29. Ibid.

30. Hubbard, *A Narrative*, appendix, 48.

31. Ibid. The italicized reference is to 2 Corinthians 11:14, in which Paul writes from Macedonia on the dangers of false prophets: "For such false apostles are deceitful workers, and transform themselves into the Apostles of Christ. / And no marvel: for Satan himself is transformed into an Angel of light." Bible GV.

32. Hubbard, *Narrative*, appendix, 48. The reference is to James 3:11, in a passage speaking about the good and evil that reside side by side in man, particularly in speech and feeling: "Doeth a fountain send forth at one place sweet *water* and bitter?" But it is overlaid with other meanings, including the link of God's law to sweet waters found in Exodus 15:23–25, "And when they came to Marah, they colde not drinke of the waters of Marah, for they were bitter. . . . Then the people murmured against Moses, saying, What shal we drinke? And he cryed unto the Lord, & the Lord shewed him a tre[e], which when he had cast into the waters, the waters were swete: there he made them an ordinance & a lawe, and there he proved them." Bible GV.

33. Jane Monnig Atkinson, "Shamanisms Today," *Annual Review of Anthropology* 21 (1992): 309. See also Janice Boddy, "Spirit Possession Revisited: Beyond Instrumentality," *Annual Review of Anthropology* 23 (1994): 407–34.

34. Hubbard, *A Narrative*, appendix, 61.

35. The most famous of these is Passaconaway. See William Wood, *New England's Prospect*, ed. and intro. Alden T. Vaughan (Amherst: University of Massachusetts Press, 1977), 101–2.

36. Kathleen J. Bragdon, *Native People of Southern New England, 1500–1650* (Norman: University of Oklahoma Press, 1996), 190, 202, on shamans taking the names of powerful manitous.

37. Day, "Atecouando."

38. See the dream of a Cape Cod powwaw and the Martha's Vineyard case in which the spirit of a drowned Englishman apparently tormented an Indian woman, Chapter 2.

39. Mather, *Brief History*, 45. Fitch's efforts were successful, and "the Heathen were affected therewith, acknowledging that the God whom we serve is a great God, and there is none like unto him."

40. Mather, *Illustrious Providences*, 48. Elsewhere he notes that the English have such good

success in God answering English prayers to send rain, that "the Heathen, now for more than twenty years, upon occasion of want of Rain, will speak to us to call upon the Name of the Lord our God" (363).

41. Hubbard, *A Narrative*, appendix, 48.

42. Ibid., appendix, 81–82.

43. Ibid., appendix, 70–71. The reference is to 1 Samuel 28:3–20, in which Saul asks a witch to raise the prophet Samuel from the dead because God will no longer speak to Saul, "by Prophetes nether by dreames" (28:15); Samuel predicts Saul's death and the destruction of his people. Marginal note "f" makes clear that the "Samuel" that arose was actually Satan, "who to blinde his eyes toke upon him the forme of Samuel, as he can do of an Angel of light." Bible GV.

44. Mather, *Brief History*, 13.

45. Hubbard, *A Narrative*, postscript, 29.

46. According to Mather, this story was first told in April 1676, as the Maine Indians began to ask for a truce, when an English man explained that there was some justification for their having taken revenge on the English. Mather, *Brief History*, 28.

47. Hubbard, *A Narrative*, postscript, 29; see also Samuel G. Drake, with H. L. Williams, *The Aboriginal Races of North America*, 15th ed. (New York: Hurst and Co., 1880), 286.

48. Mather, *Brief History*, 28.

49. On incompatibility, see William Cronon, *Changes in the Land: Indians, Colonists, and the Ecology of New England* (New York: Hill and Wang, 1982); and, for a slightly more nuanced view and specific discussion of King Philip's War, see Virginia DeJohn Anderson, *Creatures of Empire: How Domestic Animals Transformed Early America* (New York: Oxford University Press, 2004), 230–37. Interestingly, during the war in Maine, Indians sought to thresh English grain for their own use and pressed English boats into service to transport themselves around the coast. The constant complaint was that the English failed to sell powder and shot to the Indians (because of the hostilities) and so their hunting was disrupted and many went hungry in the wintertime. Hubbard, *A Narrative*, appendix; see, for example, threshing (50), English captive threshing for the Indians (60), John Abbott, forced to transport Indian war party in Mr. Fryer's ketch (65).

50. Hubbard, *A Narrative*, 10. Wamsitta (Philip's brother) inherited the sachemship in 1660 at the death of Massasoit their father, and "hee being desirouse, according to the custome of the natives, to change his name, that the Court would confer an English name upon him, which accordingly they did, and therefore ordered, that for the future hee shalbee called by the name of Allexander Pokanokett; and desireing the same in the behalfe of his brother, they have named him Philip." David Pulsifer, ed., *Records of the Colony of New Plymouth in New England* (Boston: William White, 1861; repr. New York: AMS Press, 1968), 3:192, cited in Lepore, *Name of War*, 251–52 n. 26. The request for an English name would have fulfilled the Native custom of taking a new name when assuming a new role, but it also would have been seen as a gratifying ratification (and submission) of Indian custom to English courts of law. The choice appears to have referenced Alexander the Great of Macedon (fl. 356–323 BCE), and his brother Philip III Arrhidaeus (fl. 323–317 BCE). The exact significance of choosing these names is unclear, though they link Native Americans to a noble "ethnic" and pagan history and perhaps also were intended by the English as an absurdity in much the way that slave names were used: naming the local Indian chieftain after one of the world's greatest military conquerers. The names also link the Wampanoag sachemdom to Macedon, perhaps, as Lepore suggests (xvi) intending this as an addition reference to the Macedonian plea for Christian missionization, although the events recorded in Acts 16 took place some three centuries later.

51. Hubbard, *A Narrative*, 10–11.

52. Ibid., 10.

53. Ibid., 11.

54. Ibid., appendix, 11.

55. Ibid., 12. See also Lepore, *The Name of War*, xvii, on the disagreement between Hubbard and Mather on this score.

56. Hubbard, *A Narrative*, 63.

57. Ibid., 13.

58. Matthew 12:34 (Bible GV).

59. Lepore, *The Name of War*, 118; she writes: "If the English had examined Algonquian actions not as signs from God but as signs from Indians, they might have seen a great deal about Algonquian motives." The present volume, of course, explains why they did not.

60. Church, *Diary*, 92.

61. Ibid.

62. Lepore, *The Name of War*, 118. The reference is to Psalm 124, verses 3, 6.

63. Ibid. The reference is to Numbers 24:8.

64. I. Mather, "Diary," 353 (October 7, 1675). Indeed, throughout the conflict, Mather remained frustrated: the "Magistrates have no Heart to doe wt they might in order to Reformation. Esply the Governor. Nor will they call upon the churches to renew their covt wth God" (359 [January 28, 1675/6]). In February 1675/6 he preached sermons against drunkenness that the governor and council demanded he retract (he refused, 358), and in March he chastised his congregation for their faults, reading the laws to them regarding too much luxury in dress, as well as those prohibiting drinking and loitering (359 [March 4, 1675/6]).

65. I. Mather, "Diary," 359 (February 28, 1675/6).

66. Hubbard, *A Narrative*, 17–18.

67. Mather, *Brief History*, 34. He notes that this occurred on June 15, 1676.

68. Ibid.

69. I. Mather, "Diary," 403 (May 15, 1676).

70. Hubbard, *A Narrative*, 18.

71. Mather, *Brief History*, 34.

72. Ibid., 35.

73. Mather, *Brief History*, 34: An earthquake is sometimes accompanied by a loud bang, much like a gun or explosion, as the author can attest from her personal experience of an earthquake in Massachusetts.

74. Charles E. Clark, *The Eastern Frontier: The Settlement of Northern New England, 1610–1763* (Hanover, N.H.: University Press of New England, 1970), 65–67.

75. Hubbard, *A Narrative*, appendix, 29. In addition to the violence against Squando's family, Hubbard also talks about conflicts over alcohol sales, as well as the violence done by Indians to their own families in the midst of drinking sprees: appendix, 77.

76. Cf. Mary Beth Norton, *In the Devil's Snare: The Salem Witchcraft Crisis of 1692* (New York: Alfred A. Knopf, 2002), 82–83, on the 1689 torture and killing of Major Richard Waldron in retaliation for "Waldron's perfidy in the mid-1670s" during the war (83). The assaults, ambushes, and massacres of the war meet the definition of type 1 trauma, following the typology proposed by Lenore Terr, in which a defined catastrophic event (as opposed to chronic, repetitive trauma) "shatters the survivor's sense of invulnerability to harm, rendering him acutely vulnerable to stressors." Lenore Terr, "Childhood Trauma: An Outline and Overview," *American Journal of Orthopsychiatry* 148 (1999): 10–20, cited in Kathryn Basham, "Trauma Theories," in *Inside Out and Outside In: Psychodynamic Clinical Theory and Psychopathology in Contemporary Multicultural Contexts*, ed. Joan Berzoff,

Laura Melano Flanagan, and Patricia Hertz, 2nd ed. (New York: Jason Aronson, 2008), 415–16. The quotation is from Basham, "Trauma Theories," referring to the definition offered by C. Figley (415).

77. On the trauma of captivity, see Kathryn Zabelle Derounian, "Puritan Orthodoxy and the 'Survivor Syndrome' in Mary Rowlandson's Indian Captivity Narrative," *Early American Literature* 22, no. 1 (1987): 83.

78. The best general history of the war, though sorely outdated, is still Douglas E. Leach, *Flint-lock and Tomahawk: New England in King Philip's War* (New York: Macmillan, 1958); updated histories can be found in James David Drake, *King Philip's War: Civil War in New England, 1675–1676* (Amherst: University of Massachusetts Press, 1999), and Daniel R. Mandell, *King Philip's War: Colonial Expansion, Native Resistance, and the End of Indian Sovereignty* (Baltimore: Johns Hopkins University Press, 2010).

79. The estimates come from Nathaniel Saltonstall and Samuel Symonds, cited in Lepore, *The Name of War*, 71 and 77, respectively.

80. Lepore, *The Name of War*, xii.

81. Hubbard, *A Narrative*, appendix, 43. The quote continues: "All the rest of the inhabitants of Kennibeck River, Shipscot River, Sagade-hock, Damaniscottee, fearing to be served in the same kind, fled to the Islands of Cape bonawagan and Damerils Cove."

82. Ibid., appendix, 46.

83. Ibid., appendix, 62.

84. Ibid., appendix, 48.

85. Ibid.

86. Ibid.

87. Massachusetts Archives vol. 30, doc. 206b, reprinted in *Early American Indian Documents: Treaties and Laws, 1607–1789*, ser. ed. Alden T. Vaughan, vol. 20, *New England Treaties, North and West, 1650–1776*, ed. Daniel R. Mandell (Washington, D.C.: University Publications of America, 2004), 20–21.

88. Hubbard, *A Narrative*, appendix, 16, who comments on Squando's actions: "a strange mixture of mercy and Cruelty." See also George Folsom, *A History of Saco and Biddeford*, facsimile edition (1830; Somersworth, N.H.: New Hampshire Publishing Co., 1975), 157–58, on 1723 deposition.

89. Hubbard, *A Narrative*, appendix, 80.

90. Ibid., appendix, 71–72.

91. Ibid.

92. Ibid., appendix, 80–81.

93. Ibid., 71–72.

94. Bible GV. A second frame of reference is also apparent in the early accounts, and that is the trope of the "inraged Barbarian" of the ancient world. Mather, *Brief History*, 13. Once provoked, "these *Pagans* in the *West*," would prove, "as one says of the *Mahometans* in the *East*, like a *nest of Hornets*, that if any one of them chance to be provoked, they will be *all about his Ears* that comes near them." Hubbard, *A Narrative*, 13 (italic in original).

95. Mather, *Brief History*, 38.

96. Hubbard, *Narrative*, 54 ("Barbarous . . ."), 59 ("Salvage . . ."), 13 ("a nest . . . ;" "this subtle . . .").

97. Ibid., 63.

98. Mather, *Illustrious Providences*, 361.

99. Ibid.

100. Joshua Scottow, "Letter to Increase Mather, 30th [Octo]ber [1683]," *MHS Coll.*, 4th ser., 8 (1868): 631–32.

101. I. Mather, "Diary," 409.

102. Scottow, "Letter to Increase Mather," 631.

103. C. Mather, *Magnalia*, 3:199 (1853 rpt. 1:566–67).

104. Ibid., 632.

105. Mather, *Illustrious Providences*, 359.

106. Ibid.

107. Mather, *Brief History*, 46.

108. Ibid.

109. Church, *Diary*, 150.

110. Ibid., 153.

111. Mather, *Brief History*, 46.

112. The dream is told in Judges 7:13.

113. The entire story is found in Judges 7:9–25.

114. Church, *Diary*, 153.

115. Mather, *Brief History*, 47. The full passage of Isaiah 33:1 (Bible KJV) reads: "Woe to thee that spoilest, and thou *wast* not spoiled; and dealest treacherously, and they dealt not treacherously with thee! when thou shalt cease to spoil, thou shalt be spoiled; *and* when thou shalt make an end to deal treacherously, they shall deal treacherously with thee." ("Spoil" is used in the sense of plundering or looting.)

116. Mather, *Brief History*, 47.

117. Church, *Diary*, 154.

118. Ibid., 156.

119. Ibid., 156.

120. Ibid., 156.

121. Mather, *Brief History*, 47.

122. Ibid. Agag was executed and cut into pieces by Samuel, in 1 Samuel 15:33.

123. Mather, *Brief History*, 47.

124. Church, *Diary*, 170.

125. Ibid., 173.

126. Ibid.

127. Ibid.

128. Hubbard, *A Narrative*, 107.

129. I. Mather, "Diary," 409 (dated 1681).

130. Several histories of colonial New England have suggested the wide-ranging impact of wartime trauma, including Lepore's *The Name of War*, Norton's *In the Devil's Snare*, and John Demos, *The Unredeemed Captive: A Family Story from Early America* (New York: Alfred A. Knopf, 1994). Historians of the region have begun to explore unresolved trauma's lingering social effects, whether in posttraumatic events like the Salem witchcraft crisis, or in the ethnocentrism and racist rhetoric that infuses most English accounts of the war. Societies can take up a "defensive traumatic silence" in the wake of shattering events, and, if unaddressed, the unresolved trauma can be passed on to subsequent generations "not only through the actual [explicitly told] memories or stories of parents . . . but also through the traces of affect [emotional response], particularly affect that remains unintegrated and unassimilable." Quotation from Gabriele Schwab, *Haunting Legacies: Violent Histories and Transgenerational Trauma* (New York: Columbia University Press, 2010), 13, 14.

## Chapter 5. Emotion, Embodiment, and Context

1. As is well known, the entire Salem crisis eventually turned on whether observers believed that the witch must cooperate in order for her specter to "walk abroad." Once an argument was made that the Devil could take the shape of an innocent person without their consent, the cases of witchcraft—many of which hinged solely on spectral testimony—fell apart. See Bernard Rosenthal, "General Introduction," in *Records of the Salem Witch-Hunt*, gen. ed. Bernard Rosenthal (New York: Cambridge University Press, 2009), 24.

2. William Stacy, Deposition, doc. 231 (May 30, 1692), in *Salem Witch-Hunt*, 331.

3. Ibid. Several strange occurrences happened in the years after (as Stacy phrased it, he had "mett with severall other of her Pranks," too many to take the time to tell). But by far the worst of these, and one Stacy laid at Bishop's door, was the sudden death of his daughter Priscilla, "aboute two years agoe; the Child was a likely Thriueing Child. And suddenly Screaked out and soe contin-ued in an vnvsuall Manner for aboute a fortnight & soe dyed in that lamentable manner." Stacy thought Bishop had been "Instrumentall" in the death.

4. Bridget Bishop, Examination (Cheever), doc. 63 (April 19, 1692), in *Salem Witch-Hunt*, 183.

5. Bridget Bishop, Examination (Parris), doc. 64 (April 19, 1692), in *Salem Witch-Hunt*, 185.

6. Bridget Bishop, Examination (Cheever), doc. 63 (April 19, 1692), in *Salem Witch-Hunt*, 184.

7. Mary Warren, Deposition, doc. 258 (June 1, 1692), in *Salem Witch-Hunt*, 353.

8. Abigail Hobbs, Deposition, doc. 255 (June 1, 1692), in *Salem Witch-Hunt*, 350.

9. Sarah Churchill, Deposition, doc. 258 (June 1, 1692), in *Salem Witch-Hunt*, 353.

10. Indictments, docs. 273–76 (April 19, 1692), in *Salem Witch-Hunt*, 364–67. An editor's note indicates that a fifth indictment is missing, "presumably it was for afflicting Mary Walcott" (doc. 275), p. 366; Warrant for execution, doc. 313 (June 8, 1692, with the Officer's return dated June 10, 1692), in *Salem Witch-Hunt*, 394–95.

11. John Cook, Testimony, doc. 277; John Louder, Testimony, doc. 278; Richard Coman, Testi-mony, doc. 282 (all dated June 2, 1692), in *Salem Witch-Hunt*, 367–69, 372. Also used at trial was William Stacy, Testimony, doc. 231 (May 30, 1692), 332; see editor's note; the deposition of Samuel Gray was never used at trial. Other neighbors complained about bewitchments of children or live-stock: Samuel and Sarah Shattuck testified to the bewitchment of their eldest son, and John and Rebecca Bly to the bewitchment of a sow they purchased from the Bishops. Samuel Shattuck and Sarah Shattuck, Deposition, doc. 279; John Bly Sr. and Rebecca Bly, Deposition, doc. 281; Susannah Shelden, doc. 283 (all dated June 2, 1692), in *Salem Witch-Hunt*, 369–73.

12. John Bly Sr. and William Bly, Testimony, doc. 280 (June 2, 1692), in *Salem Witch-Hunt*, 371.

13. Mary Beth Norton, *In the Devil's Snare: The Salem Witchcraft Crisis of 1692* (New York: Alfred A. Knopf, 2002), 213–15, 291; Bernard Rosenthal, "General Introduction," in *Salem Witch-Hunt*, 24.

14. Janine Rivière, "Demons of Desire or Symptoms of Disease? Medical Theories and Popular Experiences of the 'Nightmare' in Premodern England," in *Dreams, Dreamers, and Visions: The Early Modern Atlantic World*, ed. Ann Marie Plane and Leslie Tuttle (Philadelphia: University of Pennsylvania Press, 2013), 49–50.

15. Richard Coman, Testimony, doc. 282 (June 2, 1692), in *Salem Witch-Hunt*, 372.

16. Janine Rivière, "Dreams in Early Modern England: Frameworks of Interpretation," Ph.D. dissertation (University of Toronto, Toronto, Canada, 2013), 22.

17. Rivière, "Dreams in Early Modern England," 27–29.

18. [Thomas Tryon], *Pythagoras his mystick philosophy reviv'd; or, The mystery of dreams un-folded* (London: for Thomas Salusbury at the Sign of the Temple near Temple-Bar in Fleet Street, 1691), 24–25.

19. Ibid.

20. Rivière, "Demons of Desire," 50.

21. Ibid.

22. Increase Mather, *An Essay for the recording of illustrious providences*... (Boston: Samuel Green for Joseph Browning, 1684), 175–76.

23. Ibid., 178–79. Mather cites "Sennertus in Pract. Med L. 6 Part 9 cap. 5," which is almost assuredly Daniel Sennert's 1646 *Practicae Medicinae*, the sixth book of which appeared in English translation in 1662. Daniel Sennertus, N. Culpeper, and Abdiah Cole, *The sixth book of Practical physick Of occult or hidden diseases; in nine parts*... (London: Peter Cole, 1662).

24. Mather, *Illustrious Providences*, 178–79.

25. Ibid., 177–78. The full quote about sexual congress with the incubus or succubus reads: "What Fables are there concerning Incubi and Succubae, and of Men begotten by Daemons? No doubt but the Devil may delude the fancy that one of his Vassals shall think (as the Witch at Hartford did) that he has carnal and cursed Communion with them, beyond what is real. Nor is it impossible for him to assume a dead Body, or to form a lifeless one out of the Elements, and therewith to make his Witches become guilty of Sodomy. Austin [St. Augustine] saith, they are impudent who deny this. But to imagine that Spirits shall really generate Bodies, is irrational" (175–76).

26. Barbara Tedlock, "Dreaming and Dream Research," in *Dreaming: Anthropological and Psychological Perspectives*, ed. Barbara Tedlock (Santa Fe: School of American Research Press, 1992), 17–18. Such delusions also occur in the hypnopompic state. Rivière, "Demons of Desire," 49.

27. Rivière, "Demons of Desire," 50. See also Owen Davies, "The Nightmare Experience, Sleep Paralysis, and Witchcraft Accusations," *Folklore* 114 (2003): 181–203; and Willem de Blécourt, "Bedding the Nightmare: Somatic Experience and Narrative Meaning in Dutch and Flemish Legend Texts," *Folklore* 114 (2003): 227–45, both cited in Rivière, "Demons of Desire," 261 n. 5. See also Rosenthal, "General Introduction," in *Salem Witch-Hunt*, 27, 27 n. 72, which attributes a very few such events to sleep paralysis.

28. William Stacy, Deposition, doc. 231 (May 30, 1692), in *Salem Witch-Hunt*, 331.

29. John Cook, Testimony, doc. 277 (June 2, 1692), in *Salem Witch-Hunt*, 367.

30. Joseph Safford, Deposition, doc. 243 (June 30, 1692), in *Salem Witch-Hunt*, 342.

31. John Louder, Testimony, doc. 278 (June 2, 1692), in *Salem Witch-Hunt*, 368.

32. Ibid.

33. Samuell Gray, Deposition, doc. 230 (May 30, 1692), in *Salem Witch-Hunt*, 330, and according to Robert Calef's later account as cited by Rosenthal, "Gray made a deathbed confession that his testimony . . . was groundless." Ibid., 330, editor's note.

34. Richard Coman, Testimony, doc. 282 (June 2, 1692), *Salem Witch-Hunt*, 372.

35. John Briggs, Testimony (February 20, 1672/3), Records of the General Court of Trials, 1671–1704, Newport Court, Book A, October 1673 (Rhode Island Supreme Court Judicial Records Center, Pawtucket, R.I.), also cited and discussed in Elaine Forman Crane, *Killed Strangely: The Death of Rebecca Cornell* (Ithaca, N.Y.: Cornell University Press, 2002), 19.

36. Crane, *Killed Strangely*, 21.

37. Ibid., 19–20.

38. Ibid., 21.

39. Mather, *Illustrious Providences*, unpaginated preface, 8.

40. Ibid., unpaginated preface, 2–3. Following the horrific spectacle, "The Dr . . . quickly grew Melancholly, and would[,] rising at Midnight[,] repair to the Graves and monuments at Eaton Colledge; saying, that he and his must shortly take up their habitation among the Dead. The Relater of this Story (a Person of great integrity) had it from Dr. Frith's Son, who also added,

My Fathers Vision is already Executed upon all the Family but my self, my time is next, and near at hand."

41. Ibid., unpaginated introduction, 3–4.

42. Ibid., unpaginated introduction, 9–10.

43. Ibid., 142–55 (Morse); 198 (Cole); 196 (Knapp).

44. Ibid., 338.

45. Ibid., 345–46.

46. Ibid., 279.

47. Ibid., 240–41. Mather cited the story as appearing in Glanvill's Collections, 189, 192.

48. Ibid., 241.

49. Ibid., 134. Mather cites Mr. Ambrose, *Treatise of Angels*, 265; and Mr. Clark, vol. 1, 512, which is Samuel Clarke, *A Mirrour or Looking Glasse both for Saints, and Sinners, Held forth in about two thousand Examples* (London: 1654), which was nicknamed Clarke's Examples, and went through five editions between 1648 and 1671. See David D. Hall, *Worlds of Wonder, Days of Judgment: Popular Religious Belief in Early New England* (Cambridge, Mass.: Harvard University Press, 1989), 73 and 271, n. 7.

50. [Manasseh Minor], *The Diary of Manasseh Minor, Stonington, Connecticut, 1696–1720*, ed. and published by Frank Denison Miner with Miner (n.p.: privately published, 1915), 11–12.

51. [Thomas Minor], *The Diary of Thomas Minor, Stonington, Connecticut, 1653–1684*, ed. Sidney H. Miner and George D. Stanton Jr. (New London, Conn.: Day Publishing Co., 1899), 192 (August 1662). The instance is recorded twice, in the body of the diary in chronological order: Wednesday August 20, 1662: "I & my wife both dreamed." Thomas Minor diary, August 20, 1662, 51, and again in random notes at the end, where the fuller report of content begins, "Agust [*sic*] 1662. I & my wife dreamed at one time" (192). I am grateful to Donald Larson for sharing his transcription from the original held in the Connecticut State Library, and for his thoughtful commentary that refined and corrected my initial reading of the source.

52. The *Oxford English Dictionary* indicates that the word had the same double meaning in Minor's period as it does in our own. *Oxford English Dictionary* online, s.v. "bitch," accessed May 15, 2009, http://dictionary.oed.com.

53. John Demos, *A Little Commonwealth: Family Life in Plymouth Colony* (New York: Oxford University Press, 1970).

54. For the timeline of her illness, see entries in [Cotton Mather], *Diary of Cotton Mather*, ed. and intro. Worthington Chauncy Ford, *Massachusetts Historical Society Collections*, 7th ser., 7, 8 (1911, 1912), 430, 437.

55. C. Mather, *Diary*, 7: 444 (October 22, 1702): "And unto my Surprise, the very first Verse that at the opening of the Book, my Eye was carried unto, was that: Psal. 105. 37 / *And there was not among their Tribes, / A Feeble Person told.* / Lord, thought I! This won't be fulfill'd until the Resurrection of the Dead."

56. Ibid.

57. Ibid., 7: 444–445. The anxious husband reports, "After this, my dear Consort continued much refresh'd and yet feeble. We had great Hopes of her becoming a strong Person again, and yet great Fears, lest some further latent Mischief within her, prove after all too hard for her" (444).

58. Ibid., 7: 448–449.

59. The specter had so frightened a pregnant Abigail Mather that, when their son suffered from a bowel obstruction and died, they attributed the cause of his infirmity to the injury received by his mother while he was still in her womb. Of the 1693 event, Cotton Mather wrote, "I had great Reason to suspect a Witchcraft, in this praeternaturall Accident." C. Mather, *Diary*, 7:164 (after April 1, 1693).

60. Mather, *Illustrious Providences*, 272.

61. Ibid., 205–6.

62. Ibid., 206–7.

63. Ibid., 207.

64. Ibid., 207–8.

65. Ibid., 208.

66. Ibid., 208, 210.

67. Susannah Shelden v. Elizabeth Colson and John Willard (doc.) (May 18, 1692), in *Salem Witch-Hunt*, 293–94.

68. Mather continued to wrestle with the impact of these losses. He composed an epigram for his wife; he preached on the death of Ezekiel's wife; members of the congregation and other friends helped to build a tomb for his six lost family members; he meditated on the "benefits" of his wife's death, which included preserving him from disease and her from the painful knowledge of a sibling's death. C. Mather, *Diary*, 7: 450 (epigram, sermon, tomb); 452–53 (benefits); 456 (publication of *Meat out of the Eater*).

69. Hall, *Worlds of Wonder*, quotation 108–9, and 277, n. 112, citing Cotton Mather, *Magnalia Christi Americana* (London, 1702; rpt. Hartford, Conn.: Silas Andrus and Son, 1853), 1:295. Mather hedges a bit, saying that when Cotton lay on his deathbed, his church asked him to recommend a successor; he named Mr. Norton: "That which gave encouragement unto this business, was not a dream of Mr. Cotton's, though it was indeed a strange thing, that Mr. Cotton in his illness, being solicitous what counsel to give unto his church, he dreamed that he saw Mr. Norton riding unto Boston, to succeed him, upon a white horse, in circumstances that were exactly afterwards accomplished" (1:294-95).

70. Mather, *Magnalia*, 1:486.

71. Hall, *Worlds of Wonder*, quotation 108–9, and 277 n. 112, citing Mather, *Magnalia*, 1:544.

72. Kohut spoke about the lifelong "needs of man for sustenance of his self in . . . three areas (i.e., his need to experience mirroring and acceptance; his need to experience merger with greatness, strength, and calmness; and his need to experience the presence of essential alikeness) from the moment of birth to the moment of death." Such needs could be met not by real people, but through "cultural selfobject"—activities, creativity, music, and art and other "hallucinatory creations" (76). If deprived of access to such sustaining selfobject experience, the individual would experience rupture and a sense of disequilibrium. Heinz Kohut, *How Does Analysis Cure?* rpt. ed. (Chicago: University of Chicago Press, 1984): ch. 10, 76, quotation 194.

73. Samuel Sewall, *The Diary of Samuel Sewall, 1674–1729*, ed. M. Halsey Thomas, 2 vols. (New York: Farrar, Straus and Giroux, 1973), 2:653–54 (February 9, 1710/11). John Leverett was a judge of the Superior Court and became the first secular president of Harvard in 1708, serving until 1724. Harvard University Web site, "John Leverett," http://www.harvard.edu/history/presidents/leverett (accessed July 7, 2013).

74. Sewall, *Diary*, 1:65 (June 3, 1685).

75. Ibid., 1:219 (June 16, 1689).

76. Ibid., 1:219 (June 20, 1689).

77. Sewall was already dreaming of his wife shortly after his departure and of having trouble reaching her, when he "dream'd much of my wife last night. She gave me a piece of Cake for Hannah Hett, was in plain dress and white Apron. Methoughts [she] was brought to bed [had given birth], and through inadvertency was got up into the uppermost Gallery, so that I knew not how to get down to hold up the Child." Sewall, *Diary*, 1:186 (December 18, 1688).

78. Preparations included obtaining a power of attorney to be able to conduct business in New

England. Sewall, *Diary*, 1:219 (June 13, 1689). The editor's identification of William Adams as the "Mr. Adams" of these dreams is made in the index entry, 2:1131, and additional information about Adams, who lived in Dedham and died August 16, 1685, is found in 2:1057 n. 9. Sewall outlived all his classmates from 1671.

79. Hull had died October 1, 1683. Sewall, *Diary*, 1:xxiv.

80. Ibid. 1:328 (March 18, 1695).

81. Ibid. 1:592 (April 2, 1708).

82. Ibid. 1:90 (December 26, 1685); see also the previous entries on 89–90.

83. Ibid. 2:1057 n. 9.

84. Harvard University Web site, "Charles Chauncy," http://www.harvard.edu/history/presidents/ chauncy (accessed July 7, 2013). Sewall took his degree in August 1671, and Chauncy died February 29, 1671/2. Sewall, *Diary*, 1:xxiii. Increase Mather quoted in Cotton Mather, *Magnalia Christi Americana*, 2:14, 14 n.

85. Sewall, *Diary*, 1:326 (January 5, 1695). The information on Urian Oakes comes from "Urian Oakes," http://www.harvard.edu/history/presidents/oakes (accessed July 7, 2013).

86. Mather remembered Oakes as "the excellent Pastor of the Church at Cambridge" and made a play on his name (as an oak tree) to conjure up an image of students gathered round, "as a rendezvous of happy Druids, under the influences of so rare a President: But alas! Our joy must be short lived; for, on July 25, 1681, the stroak of a sudden death fell'd the tree." Mather, *Magnalia Christi Americana*, 2:16.

87. Sewall, *Diary*, 1:326 (January 5, 1695).

88. Ibid., 1:187 (December 30, 1688).

89. Ibid.

90. Ibid., 1:184 (editor's note above November 22, 1688).

91. Roger Thompson, "Daniel Gookin (bap. 1612, d. 1687)," *Oxford Dictionary of National Biography* (Oxford University Press, 2004), online ed., http://www.oxforddnb.com/view/article/11005. For the Oakes reference, see n. 81 above.

92. Sarah Good, Sarah Osburn, and Tituba, Examinations (Cheever), doc. 3 (March 1, 1692), in *Salem Witch-Hunt*, 127.

93. Norton, *In the Devil's Snare*, 27.

94. Sarah Good, Sarah Osburn, and Tituba, Examinations (Cheever), doc. 3 (March 1, 1692), in *Salem Witch-Hunt*, 128.

95. Ibid.

96. Sewall, *Diary*, 1:544.

97. Cf. [John Marshall], "John Marshall's Diary," ed. Charles F. Adams Jr., *MHS Proc.*, 2nd ser., 1 (1884–85): 148–64, esp. 157–61; see also [Joseph Green], "Diary of Rev. Joseph Green, of Salem Village," ed. S. P. Fowler, *Essex Institute Historical Collections* 8, no. 1 (1866): 215–24, esp. 222–23, and vol. 10 (2nd ser., vol. 2) (1870): 73–104, esp. 74–101.

98. Marshall, "Diary," 159 (July 1707).

99. Cf. John Demos, *The Unredeemed Captive: A Family Story from Early America* (New York: Alfred A. Knopf, 1994), 134, 137.

## Chapter 6. Native Dream Reporting as Cultural Resistance

1. Experience Mayhew, *Indian Converts, or, some Accounts of the Lives and Dying Speeches of a considerable number of the Christianized Indians of Martha's Vineyard, in New England* (London: Samuel Gerrish, 1727), 146.

2. Ibid., 147.

3. Ibid., 147–48.

4. Ibid., 148.

5. David D. Hall, *Worlds of Wonder, Days of Judgment: Popular Religious Belief in Early New England* (Cambridge, Mass.: Harvard University Press, 1989), 243–45, quotations 243, 244.

6. See, for example, Daniel R. Mandell, *Behind the Frontier: Indians in Eighteenth-Century Eastern Massachusetts* (Lincoln: University of Nebraska Press, 1996).

7. For the eighteenth century, see Carla Gerona, *Night Journeys: The Power of Dreams in Transatlantic Quaker Culture* (Charlottesville: University of Virginia Press, 2004); Mechal Sobel, *Teach Me Dreams: The Search for Self in the Revolutionary Era* (Princeton, N.J.: Princeton University Press, 2000); and Phyllis Mack, *Heart Religion in the British Enlightenment: Gender and Emotion in Early Methodism* (Cambridge: Cambridge University Press, 2008). For later periods, see, for example, the work of Susan Juster, *Doomsayers: Anglo-American Prophecy in the Age of Revolution* (Philadelphia: University of Pennsylvania Press, 2003); Ann Kirschner, "'God Visited My Slumber': The Intersection of Dreams, Religion, and Society in America, 1770–1830" (Ph.D. dissertation, University of Delaware, 2004), or work in progress on nineteenth- and twentieth-century visionaries in the United States by Ann Taves, Department of Religious Studies, University of California, Santa Barbara (personal communication).

8. Kathleen J. Bragdon, *Native People of Southern New England, 1650–1775* (Norman: University of Oklahoma Press, 2009).

9. See Erik R. Seeman, "Reading Indians' Deathbed Scenes: Ethnohistorical and Representational Approaches," *Journal of American History* 88, no. 1 (2001): 17–47, esp. 21–23; Hall, *Worlds of Wonder*, 56–57.

10. Bragdon, *Native People . . . 1650–1775*, 25, 65.

11. Mayhew, *Indian Converts*, x, and "An Attestation by the United Ministers of Boston," in ibid., xvii.

12. Barbara Tedlock, "Zuni and Quiché Dream Sharing and Interpreting," in *Dreaming: Anthropological and Psychological Interpretations*, edited by Barbara Tedlock (New York: Cambridge University Press, 1987), 116–23.

13. During the Ononharoia or "Feast of Fools," "men and women ran madly from cabin to cabin, acting out their dreams in charades and demanding the dream be guessed and satisfied." Anthony F. C. Wallace, "Dreams and Wishes of the Soul: A Type of Psychoanalytic Theory Among the Seventeenth Century Iroquois," *American Anthropologist*, n.s., 60, no. 2 (1958): 240. Iroquoian theory posited that each dream expressed a wish or Ondinnonk ("secret desire of the soul") and held that the best thing to do with these wishes was to satisfy them, either literally or through symbolic actions (237–38).

14. [Thomas Shepard], *The Day-Breaking if Not the Sun-Rising of the Gospell with the Indians in New-England* (London: Richard Cotes for Fulk Clifton, 1647), 18; Edward Winslow, *The Glorious Progress of the Gospel, amongst the Indians in New England* (London: for Hannah Allen, 1649), 25.

15. David D. Hall, "Introduction," in *A History of the Book in America*, vol. 1, *The Colonial Book in the Atlantic World*, ed. Hugh Amory and David D. Hall (Chapel Hill: University of North Carolina Press for the American Antiquarian Society, 2007), 19.

16. See Mechal Sobel, "The Revolution in Inner Selves: Black and White Inner Aliens," in *Through a Glass Darkly: Reflections on Personal Identity in Early America*, ed. Ronald Hoffman, Mechal Sobel, and Fredrika J. Teute (Chapel Hill: University of North Carolina Press, for the Omohundro Institute of Early American History and Culture, 1997), 166, 170–77, quotation 188: and, she argues, frequently symbolized through racially "other" figures.

17. William Kellaway, *The New England Company, 1649–1776: Missionary Society to the American Indians* (New York: Barnes and Noble, 1961), 240–41.

18. Ann Marie Plane, *Colonial Intimacies: Indian Marriage in Early New England* (Ithaca, N.Y.: Cornell University Press, 2000), ch. 2.

19. Mayhew, *Indian Converts*, 33.

20. Ibid., 150.

21. Ibid., 160.

22. Ibid., 201.

23. Ibid., 221.

24. Ibid., 262–63.

25. Ibid., 164.

26. Ibid., 51.

27. Ibid., 55–56.

28. Ibid., 58–59.

29. William S. Simmons, *Spirit of the New England Tribes: Indian History and Folklore, 1620–1984* (Hanover, N.H.: University Press of New England, 1986), 257–70, esp. 262–63.

30. Mayhew, *Indian Converts*, 232.

31. Ibid., 238, 240–41.

32. Ibid., 240–41.

33. Ibid., 241.

34. Ibid., 242.

35. Ibid., 240, 241.

36. Ibid.

37. Ibid., 241.

38. Ibid.

39. Douglas L. Winiarski, "Native American Popular Religion in New England's Old Colony, 1670–1770," *Religion and American Culture: A Journal of Interpretation* 15, no. 2 (2005): 147–86.

40. George Lyman Kittredge, ed., *Letters of Samuel Lee and Samuel Sewall relating to New England and the Indians*, rpt. of *Colonial Society of Massachussetts Publications*, vol. 14 (Cambridge, Mass.: John Wilson and Son, 1912), 149.

41. Kittredge, *Letters of Samuel Lee*, 151.

42. Samson Occum, "Account of the Montauk Indians, on Long Island (1761)," in *The Collected Writings of Samson Occum, Mohegan: Leadership and Literature in Eighteenth-Century America*, ed. Joanna Brooks (New York: Oxford University Press, 2006), 49. He also heard from those who had been poisoned and were in great pain, "and when a powwaw takes out the poison they have found immediate relief"; see also Bragdon, *Native People . . . 1650–1775*, 5–6, on continued mobility, powwowing, and other traditional practices.

43. [Ezra Stiles], *Extracts from the Itineraries and other Miscellanies of Ezra Stiles, D.D., LL. D., 1755–1794, with a select list from his correspondence*, ed. Franklin B. Dexter (New Haven, Conn.: Yale University Press, 1916), 142–43 (powwowing for rain in Rhode Island, around 1680 or 1690); 401 (report of Indian "sacrifice" around 1720 or 1725 in Newtown or Ripton, Connecticut); 409 (report of Indian powwow at Mohegan around 1718); 413 (sacrifice of fawn near Saybrook, Connecticut).

44. MS copy of excerpt, "Journal of John Sergeant, April 1, 1739–March 30, 1740," original in Ezra Stiles Collection, Yale University, Beinecke Rare Books Library; copy in collection of Stockbridge Archives and Museum, Stockbridge Public Library, Stockbridge, Mass. For the tattoos, see Patrick Frazier, *The Mohicans of Stockbridge* (Lincoln: University of Nebraska Press, 1992), 60.

45. "Journal of John Sergeant," 1–2.

46. Ibid.

47. Frazier, *The Mohicans of Stockbridge*, 60–63; Maumauntissekun's binges included one, as Rauch would learn firsthand, during this 1740 visit to New York City; see also Shirley W. Dunn, *The Mohican World, 1680–1750* (Fleischmanns, N.Y.: Purple Mountain Press, 2000), 228.

48. Jane T. Merritt, *At the Crossroads: Indians and Empires on a Mid-Atlantic Frontier, 1700–1763* (Chapel Hill: University of North Carolina Press for the Omohundro Institute of Early American History and Culture, 2003), ch. 3, esp. 109–11.

49. Occum, "Account of the Montauk Indians," 49.

50. Bragdon, *Native People . . . 1650–1775*, 44–48.

51. Ibid., 219–20.

# Conclusion

1. Samson Occum, "Journal 15: Jan. 23, 1786–April 26, 1786," in *The Collected Writings of Samson Occum, Mohegan: Leadership and Literature in Eighteenth-Century America*, ed. Joanna Brooks (New York: Oxford University Press, 2006), 334.

2. Ibid., 422, editor's note.

3. Joanna Rosseter Cotton to John Cotton Jr. (July 13, 1699), *The Correspondence of John Cotton, Junior*, ed. Sheila McIntyre and Len Travers (Boston: Colonial Society of Massachusetts, 2009), 585.

4. Cf. Douglas L. Winiarski, "Souls Filled with Ravishing Transport: Heavenly Visions and the Radical Awakening in New England," *William and Mary Quarterly*, 3rd ser., 61, no. 1 (2004): 3–46; Carla Gerona, *Night Journeys: The Power of Dreams in Transatlantic Quaker Culture* (Charlottesville: University of Virginia Press, 2004); Mechal Sobel, *Teach Me Dreams: The Search for Self in the Revolutionary Era* (Princeton, N.J.: Princeton University Press, 2000).

5. Hannah Heaton, "Experiences or Spiritual Exercises," ms. diary cited in Barbara E. Lacey, "The World of Hannah Heaton: The Autobiography of an Eighteenth-Century Connecticut Farm Woman," *William and Mary Quarterly*, 3rd ser., 45, no. 2 (1988): 286 (orig. pagination 97, 284).

6. Marla R. Miller, "'My Part Alone': The World of Rebecca Dickinson, 1787–1802," *New England Quarterly* 71, no. 3 (1998): 341–77.

7. "Somnia" notebook kept by William Jenks, September 15, 1798, William Jenks Papers, Massachusetts Historical Society (Boston, Mass.), MS N-1494, Box 2, loose MS, 1797–1803: folder marked "1798." I am grateful to John Demos for his steadfast efforts in helping me to locate this document.

8. William S. Simmons, *Spirit of the New England Tribes: Indian History and Folklore, 1620–1984* (Hanover, N.H.: University Press of New England, 1986); Susan Juster, *Doomsayers: Anglo-American Prophecy in the Age of Revolution* (Philadelphia: University of Pennsylvania Press, 2003); and Ann Taves, *Fits, Trances, and Visions: Experiencing Religion and Explaining Experience from Wesley to James* (Princeton, N.J.: Princeton University Press, 1999).

# Index

# *Acknowledgments*

Just as I was finishing the manuscript for this book, I had a vivid dream—a nightmare, really. While there were many intricacies, the dream boiled down to this central element: I was in a car in rural Indiana, late (as usual) and racing to meet a professional colleague who was waiting for me at the airport some distance away. With the dashboard light warning me that I was running on empty, I fueled up at a gas station located, miraculously, in a tiny hamlet on my backcountry route. As I pulled out of the station—now later than ever—I pressed on the gas to accelerate out of town. Reaching the speed limit (well, truth be told, a bit above the speed limit), I noticed a strange pair of arms, dangling over the steering wheel and turning it away from where I wanted to go. Simultaneously, another hand operated a mechanism that was applying the brakes. I yelled at my passenger to stop interfering, but realized that the arms were not his; in fact, if they were anyone's, these bodiless hands were, somehow, mine.

The dream encapsulates many of the feelings I had toward the end of the project—being late for a deadline (trying to meet a "Plane," no less!); "running on empty" and racing to finish so I would not be further behind than I was already, yet not quite wanting to let go of my project, which I was enjoying at last. The setting, Indiana, conveys the happy double entendre of being both a real place (I have family there) and my field of research (the "Indiana," or Indian-colonial relations, of early New England). And the dream also speaks to an author's sense of solitary responsibility—at times a burden—for keeping the car on the road and moving forward, despite the many forces that might slow it down or drag it off the road altogether. With waking reflection, I came to believe that the dream also spoke to the ways in which I myself—neither my companion nor my professional obligations—might be getting in the way of finishing this project: wanting to speed up and "get there," of course, but also wanting to "put on the brakes" and slow the process down. Of course the dream has many other meanings, but it would be a rare analyst who would share every layer of her own dream in public.

It is a cliché that scholarship, however solitary it may feel, is always born out of a rich community of friends and colleagues. But the cliché is indeed apt in this case, and it is a particular pleasure, as at the end of any long project, to give thanks where it is due and to offer heartfelt gratitude to the many who helped along its way—those who helped to press the gas when needed as well as those who applied the brakes, forcing me to rethink conclusions or reshape my approach.

*Dreams and the Invisible World in Colonial New England* was born as an article more years ago than I care to remember. Although it was never published as such, I became convinced by initial research that there was more than enough untapped material for a book. Back when it was only a gleam in my mind's eye, there were already many midwives who can now, at last, be thanked.

I am grateful for the early support of the Robert J. Stoller Foundation for Psychoanalysis and Culture (Los Angeles, California), which provided me with a funded research mentorship under the direction of the experienced psychoanalyst Gerald Aronson. My meetings with Dr. Aronson were always challenging, informative, and lively. Other analysts who provided crucial support during these years include James E. Bews, Bettina Soestwohner, and Allen E. Bishop, and my treasured friends Maggie Magee and Diana C. Miller. Colleagues, classmates, and supervisors at the Institute of Contemporary Psychoanalysis in Los Angeles, including William Coburn, Lucyann Carlton, Estelle Shane, Susan Mendenhall, and, in particular, Bernard Brickman, were also essential mentors, friends, and supporters. Jessica Lehman lent her expertise and good cheer in partnering with me to lead a case conference on dreams. Members of my ICP postgraduate study group have also been a source of comfort, challenge, and inspiration. I benefited greatly from an internship in 2001 and 2002 at the New Beginnings Counseling Center in Santa Barbara, and I remember the interns, staff, and supervisors with gratitude. Some of these— Miranda Field, Christine Lewis, Angelica Jochim, and Jennifer Wohl—deserve special mention, as does another clinician and friend, Eileen Van Koppen. I am grateful as well for the funded support of the University of California Interdisciplinary Psychoanalytic Consortium, whose meetings at the UCLA Lake Arrowhead Conference Center were a highlight of those early years of the project. Many very pleasant and productive conversations were had with the participants, too numerous to mention here individually, but all fondly remembered. Of these, Melvin R. Lansky deserves a special mention for his generosity in many very helpful conversations. I owe a special debt to two founders of the Consortium: Peter Loewenberg of the UCLA History Department and the Southern California Psychoanalytic Institute, now part of the New Center for Psychoanalysis, Los Angeles, California; and Ursula Mahlendorf, emerita colleague from UCSB and a partner on many long drives to and from the greater Los Angeles area, which were made richer by her perceptive observations and stimulating conversation. In addition, my analysands made important contributions to my understanding of dreams and their power in psychic life, and I am most grateful to each one for being willing to take the risk to share their struggles and their joys with me.

As the project took its shape as a full-blown history of dream beliefs and practices, many colleagues from history, the humanities, and the social sciences offered support and assistance. I am grateful for a 2007 Mellon Research Fellowship at the Henry E. Huntington Library, where much of the primary research took place, and I am particularly indebted to Emeritus Director of Research Robert C. (Roy) Ritchie for his help during my time there. A presentation to the joint USC-Huntington American Origins series in fall 2009 helped solidify some of my thinking, and comments by Peter C. Mancall, Susannah Shaw Romney, and others were much appreciated. Funding during these formative years came from the Interdisciplinary Humanities Center at the University of California, Santa Barbara (Faculty Teaching Release Award), and travel grants from the Academic Senate of the University of California, Santa Barbara, and the Phillips Fund of the American Philosophical Society.

A period of residency as the Erikson Scholar of the Erikson Institute at the Austen Riggs Center in Stockbridge, Massachusetts, offered wonderful access to New England repositories when I was not engaged in the hum of activity at this longtime psychiatric hospital. Edward R. Shapiro, James L. Sacksteder, Eric M. Plakun, M. Gerard (Jerry) Fromm, Jane G. Tillman, Jennifer L. Stevens, E. Virginia Demos, John P. Muller, S. Daltrey Turner, Mika Awanohara, Lee Damsky, Spencer Biel, and Christina Biedermann, and the many other wonderful folks on the staff, as well as returning Erikson scholars Jean-Max Gaudillière and Françoise Davoine, provided thoughtful responses to working papers and graciously allowed me to join case conferences and nearly all other aspects of community life. Many offered the most precious gift of all: a warm and loving camaraderie despite a sometimes bracing professional pace. Thomas A.

Kohut and other members of the Williams College–Erikson Institute reading group in Culture and Psychoanalysis offered thoughtful comments about an early version of Chapter 3, even as snow came down ever more rapidly through the evening's session, threatening that we might actually be there all night discussing Samuel Sewall's strange climb to heaven.

Other friends and colleagues in New England and beyond have contributed to this project in innumerable ways, large and small, over its long gestation. Cornelia Hughes (Nina) Dayton, John Demos, Robert A. Gross, Katherine A. Hermés, Susan Juster, John Kemp, Kevin McBride, Martha McNamara, Alice Nash, Mary Beth Norton, Neal Salisbury, Nancy Shoemaker, Mechal Sobel, and Walter W. Woodward know all the ways that they have been of help over the years. Fellow Brandeis alumni Richard Cullen Rath and Richard Godbeer deserve very special appreciation here as well. Donald Larson was kind enough to share his work in progress on Thomas Minor, and I have much enjoyed our conversations and email exchanges. I am grateful as well to Drew Lopenzina, whose own work on dream reporting in the *Jesuit Relations* was particularly eye-opening for me. I appreciate his permission to cite his forthcoming work, and look forward to more exchanges over dreams in the future.

Old friends Therese Henderson, Dana Salisbury, and Irene Woodward opened their homes to me on several occasions, making long-distance research more financially feasible and vastly more pleasant. Very special thanks go to Joanne Pope Melish and H. Jefferson Melish, with hopes of future visits and stimulating conversation in both the Narragansett country and the mountains around Greenfield. Former colleague Cynthia J. Koepp of Wells College has been a trusted friend and confidante throughout, and I am grateful to her and her husband John D. Place for their hospitality.

I have benefited from the expertise of the staffs at several repositories in the region: the American Antiquarian Society, the Massachusetts Historical Society, the archives of Pilgrim Hall, Plimoth Plantation (and William Rudder Jr.), the Rhode Island Historical Society, the Newport Historical Society (and Bertram Lippincott III), and the Redwood Library. Outside the region, the Frank G. Speck Collection at the American Philosophical Society and the Henry G. Huntington Library were consulted as well. All quotations from manuscript collections appear by permission of the respective repository. Parts of Chapter 3 appeared as "Indian and English Dreams: Colonial Hierarchy, and Manly Restraint in Seventeenth-Century New England," in *New Men: Manliness in Early America*, ed. Thomas A. Foster (New York: NYU Press, 2011), 31–50, and

Chapter 6 appeared originally as "Falling 'Into a Dreame': Native Americans, Colonization, and Consciousness in Early New England," in *Reinterpreting New England Indians and the Colonial Experience*, ed. Colin G. Calloway and Neal Salisbury (Boston: Colonial Society of Massachusetts, 2003), 84–105. I am grateful to be able to use extensively revised, and updated versions of each of these here, by permission of their respective publishers.

In addition, I am deeply grateful for the assistance of those scholars with special ties to the living Native American cultures of the region who were willing to share their thoughts with me, especially Stephanie Fielding, Paula Jennings, and Trudie Lamb Richmond. I profited from visits to Plimoth Plantation (Plymouth, Massachusetts), the Mashantucket Pequot Museum and Research Center (Ledyard, Connecticut), the Tomaquag Indian Memorial Museum (Exeter, Rhode Island), and the Tantaquidgeon Indian Museum (Uncasville, Connecticut). Lisa Brooks of Amherst College provided crucial advice at the eleventh hour.

I am grateful for the support and suggestions of many West Coast colleagues, including Susan D. Amussen, Sharon Block, James F. Brooks, Patricia Cline Cohen, Eve Darian-Smith, Jane Sherron Dehart, Matthew Dennis, Susan Derwin, Edward D. English, Sharon A. Farmer, L. O. Aranye Fradenburg, Mary E. Hancock, Melody Knutson, J. Sears McGee, Mark A. Peterson, Erika Rappaport, Elizabeth Reis, James Spady, John E. Talbott, Ann Taves, Stefania Tutino, William Beatty Warner, and Mary Watkins, many of whom have listened to me talk at length about the project at various stages, as well as for the support of my dean at UCSB, David Marshall. UCSB students Jonathan Forbes and Anna Cristina Curzi provided excellent research assistance, and the members of several graduate seminars offered invaluable first reactions to early chapter drafts. H. A. (Hal) Drake and Kathleen Drake were helpful with translations from Latin, and John W. I. Lee gave great guidance about allusions to ancient history. Trevor Burnard—who, at the University of Melbourne, is very far west indeed—remains a trusted, if often irreverent, sounding board, and I am most grateful for his insightful reading of the manuscript.

I am also incredibly indebted to all the scholars who participated in the anthology on dreaming in the Atlantic World (*Dreams, Dreamers, and Visions: The Early Modern Atlantic World* [Philadelphia: University of Pennsylvania Press, 2013]) that I coedited. My deepest thanks go to Leslie Tuttle, a very perceptive coeditor, who righted our little ship many times, and to Peter C. Mancall, Michael W. Zuckerman, and one anonymous reviewer for the project who each tried to sharpen our thinking in innumerable ways. As well, I would like to thank Mary Baine Campbell, Carla Gerona, Maria V. Jordán, and Janine Rivière. Dr. Rivière took time away from her own dissertation revisions to send extremely thoughtful comments on the entire manuscript, just the latest of many acts of generosity on her part, and I am grateful.

This book is doubtless the better for the comments of many who heard it presented over the years in a host of venues. In particular, I wish to acknowledge the contributions of those who heard it first at annual conferences of the American Historical Association, the Organization of American Historians, the Omohundro Institute for Early American History and Culture (and co-panelists, in 2008, Brian D. Carroll and R. Todd Romero), and the British Group in Early American History (special thanks to co-panelist Sarah M. S. Pearsall), and in presentations to audiences at Brandeis University, the Colonial Society of Massachusetts, Cornell University, the Los Angeles Psychoanalytic Society, Holy Cross College, the California American Studies Association, the European Conference in Early American and Atlantic History, the Early Modern Studies Center (UCSB), the Austen Riggs Center, the Humanities Institute of the University of Connecticut, the University at Albany, Wells College, the McNeil Center for Early American Studies, the Literature and Mind Research Focus Group (UCSB), and the University of California at Merced. Particular mention goes to Raymond D. Fogelson, who, in a memorable discussion together with Shepard Krech III, challenged my thinking on midcentury psychoanalytic anthropology. This education continued in several discussions with Anthony F. C. Wallace. I was fortunate to be able to visit Dr. Wallace at his home in upstate New York and to be able to work together with him on a project that developed from my research in the Speck Papers at the American Philosophical Society. His fluid grasp of history, culture, and psychoanalysis had long been an inspiration to me, and it was real magic to share an afternoon together.

A special note of thanks goes to the team at the University of Pennsylvania Press. Robert B. St. George and the two anonymous readers provided many extremely helpful comments; the editorial, production, and marketing staff has been unstintingly helpful, with special thanks to Noreen O'Connor-Abel and Rachel Taube; and Robert Lockhart's genial presence has been much appreciated through the years. But my deepest thanks go to Peter Agree, my editor through three volumes now, whose steadfast and unswerving loyalty helped me get through the difficult times. He remains all that an editor ought to be. To add icing to the cake, he always seems to know the best local restaurant, no matter the city. I am fortunate to have enjoyed many great meals and much good conversation with Peter and his wife, Kathy Peiss.

I am especially indebted to David D. Hall for his generosity over the course of my career. With regard to the present project, I thank him for sharing his own work in progress on the sixteenth-century "hot" Protestants, and also for reading advance versions of Chapters 1, 3, and 5 and providing thoughtful edits and comment. He guided my first paper in graduate school, and it is a particular honor to have his help with this manuscript, which owes so much to his pathbreaking work in the field.

Two friends remain to be mentioned. To Terri L. Snyder, my "ideal reader," I could not have gotten through the penultimate draft without the knowledge that you would read the whole. Thank you for embodying all that epitomizes collegiality. Your incisive comments meant more to me than you can know. To Carol Lansing, thank you for, well, for everything over these last eighteen years. It is too much to put into words here, but we both know what you have given.

This book began when my children, Daniel Weinraub and Sarah Weinraub East, were still children. They patiently endured countless trips to Los Angeles by a mother who decided to get a second advanced degree, and each is now launched into adulthood; my stepchildren—Mitchel, Cecilia, and Isabella Polichetti—have ensured that my household remains busy, filled with life, and full of dreams. To my husband, Richard B. Polichetti, I am so grateful that we found each other, and I look forward to sharing many more dreams together. My in-laws, Helen and Richard S. Polichetti, provided important support at the eleventh hour. My godmother, Mary Ann Coghill, would have loved to read this book, and my grandmother, Altha Margaret Warren Plane, would have loved to know that it was finally done (she always asked). I am grateful for the love of my brothers and sisters, David A. Plane (and Katherine L. Jacobs), Martha Lu Plane, and Jennifer Moore Plane. When tragedy struck our family (again), we somehow weathered the storm and emerged on the other side, more or less together. Who knew that this project would have to develop in the cradle of so much unwelcome experience?

Finally, I dedicate this book to my parents, Robert A. Plane and Mary Moore Plane, who are the very definition of optimism, persistence, and hope. For their constant support and confident encouragement I am ever grateful.